# Who
# Will
# Believe
# You?

KIM CHOWN

# Who Will Believe You?

A true story of survival,
courage and hope

JB

First published in the UK by John Blake Publishing
An imprint of Bonnier Books UK
80–81 Wimpole Street, London, W1G 9RE
Owned by Bonnier Books
Sveavägen 56, Stockholm, Sweden

www.facebook.com/johnblakebooks 🅕
twitter.com/jblakebooks 🅧

First published in paperback in 2021

Paperback ISBN: 978-1-78946-222-7
Ebook ISBN: 978-1-78946-223-4
Audiobook ISBN: 978-1-78946-447-4

British Library Cataloguing-in-Publication Data:
A catalogue record for this book is available from the British Library.

Design by www.envydesign.co.uk

Printed and bound in Great Britain by Clays Ltd, Elcograf S.p.A.

1 3 5 7 9 10 8 6 4 2

Text copyright © Kim Chown 2021

The right of Kim Chown to be identified as the author of this work has been
asserted by her in accordance with the Copyright, Designs and Patents Act 1988.

Although this book is based on a true story, some names, dates and places
have been changed to protect the identity and privacy of those who form
part of the narrative.

John Blake Publishing is an imprint of Bonnier Books UK
www.bonnierbooks.co.uk

*This book is dedicated to a number of people …*

*To current victims and all fellow survivors of this dreadful, ongoing and largely hidden scourge on our society, whether or not you have had the strength, support or means (or all three) to confront the evil that you have suffered, I want you to draw comfort from knowing just sometimes the perpetrators do get found out and have to face the consequences, often ending their lives in the shame and humiliation they deserve. I hope you can find strength in knowing this book is not only my voice, but yours too.*

*To Jonathan, my wonderful husband: you believed I was worth fighting for. Without knowing it at the time, 'You were the wind beneath my wings'. Thank you, my darling, for your devotion and perseverance and thank you for always being there. Thanks to you, we can now look forward to the later chapters in our lives together.*

*To our loving children, Harry and Clara: you two are my world. I tried to shield you from my pain, but it was too much, even for me. Children should never be exposed to the pain and suffering you have both experienced in watching your mother struggle with her past.*

*And finally, to dear Mum, who always lit up a room.*

# Contents

# Prologue

*June 1996, Yorkshire*

'Right, let's get started.'

I roll up my sleeves, pull the vacuum from under the stairs and flick on the radio. Beats from the classic Abba song 'Dancing Queen' burst into the living room.

I love this one. I turn the volume up, swaying my hips. It's Friday so I wonder if we could treat ourselves to a takeaway tonight. Chinese? Pizza, maybe? I hoover under the sofa, plump up the cushions, then brush a cobweb off a picture frame.

I hum along happily. Our children – six-year-old Harry and Clara, aged five – will need picking up from school in an hour. There's just enough time to squeeze in chores. Fitting my nurse training course around the kids means life is hectic but I like to keep busy.

I grab a can of polish and dust our wedding photo frame. Five years have flown by. We've had a few ups and downs but I'm so proud of the little family we've created. I push the duster across the mantelpiece then stop mid-movement.

The opening bars of the next tune turn my stomach into a hard ball as I watch the silvery dust plume fall to the floor in the sunlight.

The bass of 'Telephone Man' by Meri Wilson is unmistakable.

I hear a crashing sound. The spray has fallen from my hand as the song lyrics, filled with double entendres about doing 'it' in the hallway and bedroom, transport me back to the late seventies.

And I'm back there. In the house in Kenya. In the heat. I feel his hot breath against my cheek. His clean-shaven face against mine. I smell his familiar soapy scent that turns my stomach. One of his favourite songs – 'Telephone Man' by Meri Wilson – is on the record player.

Every part of my body is screaming 'no' as he pins me to the wall, just like the song suggests. I go limp like a rag doll as I know all resistance is futile. Long ago I'd learned the more I struggled, the more he'd hurt me.

'Stop it, Dad.'

I am begging but it comes out as a faint whisper. Because there's no point. My mother is 4,000 miles away. There is nobody else to hear me. And like he's told me so many times before …

*Who will believe you?*

'I am a university lecturer and you are a stupid little girl,' he says.

I also know what he'll do if I ever speak up. In his lab at work, he has access to sulphuric acid and he's told me there would be nothing but teeth left behind if he dumped me in a bath filled with it.

I squeeze my eyes shut and feel for the carpet beneath my feet to remind myself where I am. Who I am. A wife. A mother. A trainee nurse, safe in her family home. Not a little girl silently screaming as her father rapes her over and over again. I run to the radio and switch it off and there's silence.

Except for an uncontrollable sob that I realise is coming from me. Only then do I realise tears are dripping from my chin.

'Kim, you are going mad,' I say out loud. 'What's wrong with you?'

Impatiently, I take a deep breath to steady my heart rate. Once again, the memories recede like the tide.

Until next time.

I need to get a grip.

# Chapter 1

*Lagos, Nigeria, 1968*

*S wallow it.*

I ground my teeth as hard as I could, but the chewy, gristly piece of steak didn't get any smaller.

'I said, "Swallow it",' Dad repeated.

A fat tear plopped onto my plate. I tried, but the meat still wouldn't go down.

'It's too hard,' I said.

How I wished I was small enough not to eat grown-up food, but now, at three years old, I had to eat what Mummy and Daddy did. I was alone with my father as our nanny was looking after my younger siblings, Lucy and Sean, and I'm not sure where my older sister Susan was.

I chewed and chewed as the clock ticked on the wall. Dad always made us sit there until we'd finished, however much we hated our dinners. He was strict, he said, because we needed to be taught good manners and must always clear our plates.

About an hour and a half later, the sun was going down

outside, the air had cooled and there was no food left on my plate. Thankfully, dinner was over for another night.

Aside from the stress at mealtimes, most of the time we loved living in the sunshine of Africa. Among my first memories are walking from our house with whitewashed walls along a tree-lined avenue to nursery following our monkey we named Monica. The cheeky little creature would run ahead up the tall trees, chattering away to herself as she waited for us to catch up with her. Holding Mum's hand, I'd giggle as Monica slid down to run up the next tree as we caught up. After dropping me off at nursery, Mum went home. She didn't work and although I didn't quite understand what Dad did, I knew he had a big important job at a university, teaching people things about science.

Before the end of the year, life changed. When my dad was out at work, Mum would occasionally take me to her friend Grant's bungalow, where I was made to wait on a chair in the hallway outside his bedroom.

'You sit there, wait and don't move,' she warned as she disappeared into a room with Grant. It was very boring waiting for Mum, so I swung my legs on the chair, singing away to myself for what seemed like ages, hoping they'd come out soon.

I believe Grant was part of the expat circle of friends my parents mixed in. He had a pilot's licence and flew light aircraft. They probably met him socially at one of the many clubs they were members of.

Around this time civil war broke out in Nigeria so one afternoon before all the blockades were put in place, Dad and Mum came to pick me up from nursery and drove us all somewhere safe while flights were arranged back to England. My parents' marriage had broken up and Dad was sending us away. I think he knew about Mum's affairs (apparently there were a few of them), although he was no saint either. Dad stayed on in Nigeria while Mum and us four children travelled back to the UK without him. Before I knew it, we were in a colder country, in a place called Horsforth in Leeds, West Yorkshire, where Mum said they used to live.

To begin with, we stayed with my grandad. He lived on his own as Grandma (Mum's mum) had died in 1965. After a few months we moved into a council house just down the road on King Edward Avenue. Swapping a beautiful house with a garden in Lagos for a three-bedroom damp council house with a tiny garden in 1970 meant life became greyer and harder. Mum didn't have much money, so we'd often have jam and bread for tea. After she had children, she never worked again. Prior to meeting Dad, she had worked as a tailoress in a big warehouse in Leeds. Now she spent her days sunbathing when it was hot, drinking sherry and Martini, and keeping the house tidy.

We lived hand to mouth, but Mum always made sure we had everything we needed. On our first day at our new school, St Margaret's C of E Primary in Horsforth, she beamed with pride as she made sure me and my sisters' white, knee-high socks were even, our shiny hair neatly tied with ribbons. Being the only boy, Sean was her pride and joy. He was well turned out in new trousers and shiny shoes.

'Just look at you all,' she said, smiling fondly at us as she waved goodbye at the school gates. From that day onwards, our neighbours always commented on how beautifully turned out we were. Mum looked beautiful herself too. A naturally petite woman, she never needed to wear much make-up, but still turned heads with her big, doe-like eyes and her life-like wigs.

Mum's wigs were of various styles and a mix of blonde and brunette. Most of them were 'up-dos' or 'bouffant-style', where the hair was backcombed and pouffed up. The finished look was covered in a cloud of hairspray. In the early seventies, I hardly saw her real hair apart from when she added a hair extension to it. These extensions were often placed on the crown to create height or to make her hair look long. Sometimes she had a flicked-up bob.

Mum saw Grant a few times when he called in from his home down south somewhere. He didn't like me, possibly because she had told him that I'd told Dad about them meeting in secret at his bungalow when we lived in Nigeria. When nobody was looking, he'd hit me round the head with my dolls.

After we settled back into school, we heard our dad had returned to the UK from Nigeria and had found a new girlfriend, Janet. I overheard Mum saying Janet's parents didn't like Dad because he was thirty-three and she was only seventeen. They were married and had a daughter together in 1971, called Lisa. But tragedy struck and Janet apparently found their daughter dead in bed when she was just eighteen months old – Dad was away in Kenya, working in his new job. In 1973, Dad left for Kenya again, returning long enough for Janet to become pregnant with Robert, who was born in 1974. He then left them for good, and as far as I know, never saw them again. He and Janet were in effect separated from when Robert was born and I believe he allowed her new partner to adopt his son.

Dad's new job was at a polytechnic in Nairobi in Kenya to teach histology and histopathology. The two subjects go hand in hand. I don't think Mum had a clue what he did – she used to say he worked at the poly lecturing students. Histology is the study of body tissues and their structure/function, while histopathology is the microscopic examination of tissue and mainly diseased tissue. I only know this due to seeing his work when I lived with him later on. I remember seeing him place specimens of tissue on glass slides before staining them pink (or other colours) and looking at them through a microscope.

We hardly ever saw him and I assume he must have sent money for our care. A couple of times a year, he'd pop into our house unannounced, bringing us presents we'd open excitedly. Once he brought me a colourful dress in traditional batik style, which came down above the knee. Lucy had the same and our elder sister Susan had a rather garish mustard and black top that she tucked in her jeans. Sean was given a blue multicoloured batik top, which hung loose over his jeans. It surprises me how Dad managed to get the right sizes. Mum dressed us up and made us pose in the garden, wearing these strange and colourful clothes. Dad took the photos. Afterwards, Mum enveloped us all in a big hug – she always gave the best cuddles.

Sometimes Mum and Dad still had a kiss and cuddle when they saw each other – this had been going on even before he split with Janet.

While we settled into our new lives, making new friends and playing out all weekend, Mum found it less easy. Before her life in Nigeria, she had worked as a seamstress but after the extravagant expat lifestyle she'd enjoyed in the Sudan and Nigeria, she struggled to adjust to life on a council estate in Horsforth. She made good friends with her neighbour Patricia, who, like her, was a housewife. During that first summer the pair of them started to spend afternoons sunbathing together. I often looked at her and thought how beautiful and brown she was – I longed to look like her one day.

Mum started to struggle to get up in the mornings and sometimes she never got up at all, so my older sister, Susan, had to get us ready for school. I avoided Mum when she woke up late. Sometimes she'd chase us up the stairs, smacking the backs of our legs with a belt. By the time I was six or seven, she never bothered tying our hair up with ribbons or worried about our socks being straight.

About two or three years after we returned to England, Mum met a new man called Barry, who had his own garage. He would always come home in overalls covered in oil and grease and more often than not, she would have a hot meal prepared for him. As Mum's drinking progressed, she'd be too drunk to cook for him and he'd come home to a cold house, with her snoring on the settee. In summer, she'd still be in the garden with her neighbour Patricia, lapping up the remainder of the sun's rays, drink in one hand, cigarette in the other. Often, we'd come home from school to find Mum in her bikini, the straps down her shoulders to avoid tan lines, Martini in hand.

'What's for tea, Mum?' Susan would ask before being told

to help herself in the kitchen. Before too long, she stopped asking and just made tea for all of us kids. More often than not, it was just jam and bread. Once we returned home to the most amazing smell coming from the kitchen. Unfortunately, the food giving off this delightful aroma was not for us: it was a meal for Mum and Barry. Instead Mum pointed to four small plates at the dining-room table.

'You're having kippers,' she announced.

I'd never had kippers before and the four of us sat huddled around the tiny table in the cold, damp dining room. I looked distastefully at the fish on my plate – the one eye still intact in the fish's head appeared to be staring at me.

'Eat up,' said Mum as she brushed past with what looked like a delicious stew on her plate. She disappeared into the lounge and plonked herself down in front of the warm electric fire. The familiar signature tune of *Coronation Street* filled the house. Suddenly, the lights went out.

'I'm scared, I can't see!' yelled Lucy.

This was an all-too-familiar situation for us: the electric meter had run out of coins again. Mum must have raided the pot so she could buy her usual bottle of sherry or Martini. A clattering came from the lounge as she ran past us towards the meter before a clunk and a zap when the lights came back on. She and Barry always ate their meals on a cushion or newspaper on their laps in front of the fire in the lounge while watching TV. Meanwhile, back in the tiny dining area, us kids looked down at the cold fish on our plates and I giggled, pointing at Lucy's plate.

'Look, Lucy's eaten its eyes. Its eyes have gone … Ugh, it'll be looking around now inside your tummy!' I joked.

Lucy immediately started sobbing and only stopped when I convinced her that I was just kidding.

Barry's dad and step-mum, Donald and Elaine, lived nearby and welcomed us to their home with open arms. Their house was considerably warmer than ours, with electric or paraffin heaters dotted about, soft carpets and something delicious-smelling always baking in the oven. It was a world away from ours.

The arrival of Barry in our lives not only meant there was more money for our household but for a brief time, Mum had better days too. Every so often she would brush and tie ribbons in mine and my sisters' hair before school.

Outside home, life was more fun. In school, I had loads of friends to play French skipping, hopscotch, Tig and hide-and-seek. I was known as 'The Marble Queen' as I was so good at winning games. During the holidays, Mum often sent us out of the house in the mornings and we were warned not to come home until teatime. There was a big orchard nearby and for hours we'd play in there, eating the under-ripe apples for lunch or we'd excitedly call in at June's, a little sweet shop with dozens upon dozens of jars filled to the brim with different sweets. I'd look at the 2p clutched in my hand and then up at the sweets in the jars. I could only ever afford the rainbow sherbets unless I saved up all my 2p pieces for a week and then I'd choose the liquorice torpedoes.

I grew into a mischievous little girl. Despite my playfulness, I sometimes wet the bed and I was so scared I'd get in trouble or be hit with the belt again. I shared a bed with Lucy so I'd pull the wet side across to make it look as though my sister had wet it. Lucy never got a telling-off, maybe because she was the youngest.

Life was certainly better now Barry was living with us. The house seemed warmer and a little more stable. Mum seemed happier at times. Other times she'd revert back to her old habits and stay in bed, sending Susan out for cigarettes.

One day, I stumbled over one of Mum's full Martini bottles outside the back door. I later found out that she used to get her neighbour Patricia to collect a bottle on a daily basis and put it outside the door for her once she knew Barry had gone to work and the coast was clear. I didn't understand why she was hiding the amount of booze she was drinking from him.

Often Mum and Barry went to the local, the Stanhope Arms, for nights out, leaving Susan in charge. For an eleven-year-old, this was a huge responsibility but she loved being boss and didn't hesitate to tell on us when we'd done something wrong.

Once I was so hungry, I waited until Mum and Barry had gone before slipping downstairs to pinch an extra piece of bread from the kitchen.

Susan immediately caught me and said she was telling.

'I thought you were a burglar, Kim. You scared me half to death,' she told me.

I said sorry and promised I'd never do it again, but hours later woke to hear Mum's voice screaming for me. I crept downstairs and into the lounge to find Susan, Mum and Barry standing in front of the fire.

'Come here, in front of me!' yelled Barry.

Before I had the chance to react, he grabbed my wrist.

'This is for coming downstairs and frightening Susan!' he yelled. He pulled me towards him and hit me so hard on my backside that I fell over on the little rug in front of the chair, where Mum was now sitting. Sobbing, I stood up and then realised I'd wet myself. My long, thin nightie was soaked and there was a puddle on the rug. Mum demanded I clean up the mess and go straight to bed.

I was shocked at what had happened and even more upset that Mum had just watched Barry do that to me.

We looked forward to visits from Dad as Mum seemed to make more of an effort and would clean up. Often, Dad would appear unannounced and usually when Barry was at work. When he came home, it was like the biggest treat as we crowded around him in excitement. Around five foot seven or five eight, he appeared taller than he was because of his tan, dark hair and slim physique. Always immaculately groomed, he looked and spoke differently to the other men in our lives. I only knew it as 'posh' then, but he spoke with a clipped Queen's English, carefully pronouncing every word. He'd smile and joke with us, making us feel so special; he was kind too, giving us gifts and taking us out for fish and chips.

He told us all about his important job and said one day we might even be allowed to visit him. I couldn't remember much about our old lives in Africa, but loved the idea of going back.

In 1976, a week or so before our long school holidays began, Dad appeared for another visit with news.

'Kim, I'm taking you and Sean to Kenya for a holiday.' He beamed at me. 'How would you like that? You can enjoy the sun and we'll go on safari too.'

I was gobsmacked.

'Wow!' I cried. 'That would be amazing!'

He told us when Susan and Lucy were out of earshot so I wondered how jealous they would be. Although I'd been looking forward to spending the summer holidays playing with friends before we started secondary school that September, all of that could wait – I had a big African adventure to enjoy first and couldn't wait to tell everyone.

Mum seemed happy with the plan so I felt comfortable too. Then Dad had another surprise for us.

'You and your brother are far too white,' he said. 'I'd be embarrassed if my friends saw you like this so you need a few sessions on a sunbed.'

Dad took us to a place called Tinshill Mount in Cookridge, Leeds. He had a friend there who had his own sunbed, which seemed terribly exciting to us. I wasn't sure what a sunbed was, but Dad said I'd look nice and brown like him and Mum – I couldn't wait.

Arriving at the house, we were ushered into a room where a long box lay. It had a lid and looked a bit like some pictures I'd seen of coffins.

'Right, you two,' he said. 'Strip off. This is the sunbed you need to use.'

I exchanged glances with Sean. By then, I was eleven and stripping off in front of people felt uncomfortable. But Dad was looking at me impatiently so I slowly pulled off my T-shirt and vest. I left my pants on as he pulled out some baby lotion. Roughly, he rubbed it over my body.

He ordered me to put on some funny-looking glasses that he called goggles and told me to get in the box. My thin frame hardly touched the sides and my feet were a long way from reaching the end.

'Right, I'm closing the lid now,' he said. 'Stay there until I tell you to come out.'

'Okay, Dad,' I agreed.

Dad pulled the lid shut over me and I squeezed my eyes shut as the lamps fizzed near my skin. Once I'd heated up almost to the point I couldn't bear it, he opened the lid and I was allowed out. Quickly, I got dressed while Sean climbed in.

'It's not too bad,' I whispered to reassure him. 'Doesn't take long.'

I assumed every kid had to do this before such a big trip to a place as exotic as Africa.

As Sean lay inside the box, sizzling like I did, Dad spoke excitedly about where he lived.

'My house is huge compared to your mum's.' He grinned. 'I have a dog called Mickey, who can be your pet, and a servant called Johnny, who cooks and cleans for me.'

Dad's home sounded like a palace compared to our damp council house.

I smiled with pride at this father I didn't really know. Maybe life was changing for the better if we could go and stay with Dad more often?

A few days later, I hugged my friends goodbye, but assured them I'd be back before school started.

'I'm not going forever,' I said. 'I'll soon be back to beat you all at marbles.'

# Chapter 2

As I clicked the seatbelt around my waist, I giggled with pure excitement. Peering through the plane window as we prepared to take off for Nairobi, I could hardly believe this was happening. This was the stuff of dreams. Most people we knew had never even been on an aeroplane, let alone gone on holiday to somewhere hot for six weeks.

I'd been sad to say goodbye to everyone but Mum reassured me it was a big adventure and Susan said I should think myself lucky. She couldn't understand why Dad had chosen me over her, the eldest. Mum said it was his choice so we just accepted it as that. There was the promise Susan could come out for a holiday herself soon though, something she said she'd definitely be up for.

I turned to smile at Dad as the plane took off; I looked forward to us spending more time together. We had few memories of him growing up and we'd never even met any of his family. I knew he was one of four brothers but Mum said they'd had a falling-out. Once I overheard one of them had gone to prison and committed suicide. But we never asked questions about it. Dad seemed like the cleverest and most successful of them all and now we had him all to ourselves for over a month.

By the time we landed in Nairobi, we were exhausted. The smell of the hot, dusty air filled our nostrils as we emerged off the plane and into Arrivals. Already it felt so different here – the darkness outside was inky black and I could only just make out the landscape of hills against the horizon. As Dad ushered us through Passport Control into a waiting taxi, I could barely keep my eyes open.

'It's a long journey to my house,' he said, 'but you'll love it when we're there.'

Sean and I fell asleep on the way so he woke us up when we arrived.

'Wake up, sleepyheads,' he laughed, 'we're here!'

I'll never forget hearing the incredible, overwhelming sound of insects chirping as I opened the car door and stepped out into the warm air and the darkness of Africa – there were no street lights and no traffic. Even though I was tired, it was completely magical and new to me.

'Can you hear the crickets?' Dad asked. 'That's what they're called.'

I laughed – I'd only ever come across Jiminy Cricket in *Pinocchio* before.

Out of the darkness, a dark-skinned man in his thirties met us. He had a kind, open face.

'Meet Johnny,' Dad said. 'Our house boy.'

Johnny gave Sean and I the biggest, beaming smile I'd ever seen. He was a man rather than a boy, but things were described differently here.

'*Jambo* [Hello],' he said with a strong accent.

I giggled as he picked up our bags. It seemed unreal my dad had a real-life servant in the house – I felt like royalty.

Johnny led us into the house in Jamhuri Crescent. It was a cool, large detached bungalow, with clean white exposed brick walls in Kabarnet Gardens on the border of Parklands and Westlands in the suburbs of Nairobi. As we looked around, a large dog bounded in. His long tongue wet my outstretched hand.

'Aww, who's this?' I asked, bending down and rubbing my nose in the sandy coloured dog's head.

'This is Mickey,' Dad replied, 'he's a Rhodesian Ridgeback crossed with a Great Dane. Puss Puss will be around somewhere too.'

My eyes darted around the sparse-looking lounge with wooden floors and spotted a fluffy black cat.

After seeing Johnny, the house and the pets, I knew I was going to love it here.

'It's so clean and tidy!' I whispered excitedly to Sean.

Johnny noticed my stifled yawn and bent down to pick up our small cases.

Although I didn't understand a word he said, we followed him down the hall towards more rooms. It felt more like a hotel than a house. I'd never had my own bedroom before – wow! My room was at the very end of the narrow corridor. The first room on the left was Sean's, nearly opposite the bathroom, then Dad's (also on the left) and mine was at the end straight ahead, very near Dad's. The corridor was usual for a bungalow, but to us it seemed strange not having stairs as we had in England. Although we'd lived in bungalows in Nigeria and the Sudan, I couldn't recall them very well.

'Goodnight,' Dad called down the corridor. 'Just you wait and see the garden in the morning!'

I woke from a deep sleep to a different world. I heard unusual sounds of birds singing and smelled the most amazing smell. It was the scent of heavy overnight rain on dry grass and soil. Instead of shivering, I pulled off the blankets and jumped out of bed, eager to explore. After getting dressed, I wandered down the corridor, into the open-plan dining and living room, where Johnny was laying out breakfast.

'Welcome to Jamhuri Crescent, Kim,' said Dad, who was already sitting at the table. 'Have a cup of Kenyan coffee.'

We didn't drink coffee at our house – it was a bitter grown-up drink and I didn't really like it. But Dad insisted I should try it, so I did to please him.

Sean was up too, so we wandered into the back garden with Mickey the dog. Lush green foliage surrounded the edges of a large lawn, with a pond and a little bridge over the top. Dad told us he'd made the bridge. I was in awe: *Dad had made that bridge, how clever!* Purple flowers that Dad said were called bougainvillea clambered over the walls of the garden and exotic flowers and plants I'd never seen before emerged from the borders of the lawn. I was even more mesmerised when I saw a lizard dart out from the foliage and scurry up the white walls of our house. It felt as if we'd stepped into the pages of a fairy-tale book.

'This garden is about four times bigger than ours back home,' said Sean excitedly. 'Brilliant for hide-and-seek!'

I tapped him on the shoulder and shouted 'Tig!' so he chased after me with Mickey.

Already this was the best holiday ever.


Later, after we had explored the heavenly garden, Johnny made us lunch. He brought through salads and homemade chapatis – a delicious feast that was a world away from the jam and bread we usually had for tea. It was strange sitting at a table with a grown-up; this never happened back in England as Mum and Barry always sat on their own in the lounge to eat. The plates and cutlery were laid out in an unfamiliar way and we all had an extra knife. I wondered quietly what the extra knife was for, but didn't ask for fear of sounding stupid.

As we ate, chatting away happily, Dad looked over at us and frowned.

'You two sound very common,' he said seriously as he ripped a piece of chapati in two. 'That terrible West Yorkshire accent is quite *dread-fell*.'

Dad pronounced his words very clearly, like he always did. My friends always told me he sounded dead posh, which I suppose he must have.

'I'd be too embarrassed to introduce you to my friends until you stop speaking like that. Both of you need to be taught how to enunciate correctly using the Queen's English. I won't have anything less,' he added. 'In fact, Kim, I'll start right here with you now. I've been listening to you say "*brekfast*". It's not pronounced like that, you need to say "*break farst*", okay? Now say it back to me.'

I repeated it back, my voice sounding odd.

'The reason it's said like this is because you're breaking your fast after a long night. Don't let me hear either of you say "*brekfast*" ever again. Do you both hear me?' he said.

The chapati suddenly felt dry in my mouth. Dad had never criticised us like this before. I didn't like it, but perhaps he was right? We were common kids from a council estate and needed to try and fit in when staying somewhere as posh as our father's house. The last thing I wanted him to feel was embarrassed by us – Dad had an important job at the university, his friends would all be educated folk.

'Okay, Dad,' I said, suddenly feeling self-conscious about the way my vowels sounded.

For the next few days, Dad went to work in the mornings while we stayed at home with Johnny and played in the garden with Mickey. Johnny was great fun, telling us all about his wife and children and how he belonged to a tribe – something I'd only read about in books before. He lived in the servants' quarters on the premises, just outside the kitchen, and made all the food and kept the house in order so Dad could focus on his important work, he said.

Dad came home for lunch and was always keen to correct our grammar and enunciation. Within a few days, we started talking as if we had plums in our mouths as we mimicked him, but this seemed to please him as he stopped moaning. And, after all, maybe he was right: we *were* a bit common when it came to the expat life in Kenya.

One afternoon, Dad took us to meet Pam, a woman he knew (I think it was a mutually beneficial arrangement). She had children our age, a girl and a boy, and lived a short drive away. Her house was quite different again to ours. It was hidden away in a lovely garden.

'This is like paradise,' I whispered to Sean.

Pam greeted us warmly as Dad made excuses for our awful accents and pale skin. He whispered something to her, but she ignored him. Brushing past him, she grabbed our hands.

'Come and meet Penny, she's drinking lemonade around the back. Do you like lemonade?' she asked.

Nodding eagerly, we followed her around the house, where vibrant bougainvillea flowers covered the whitewashed stone walls of her bungalow. Its beauty took my breath away. In the garden was a slight, barefooted blonde girl sipping a drink.

She stood up to greet us, towering over me. I peered up at her: Penny was Pam's daughter and only a year older than me.

'See what I mean, Pam,' Dad said from behind me. 'Their growth is stunted. I have a lot of work to do with them.'

We spent a nice afternoon with them and I wondered at the end when we might see them again. However, I quickly realised my father wasn't serious about Pam. We only saw her again when we went to the Woodley Club, where Dad ran the disco on a Friday night.

Going to the Woodley became part of our routine. One night a week, Dad dressed up in a patterned shirt and flamboyant tie to spin tunes from his large vinyl collection. On the first night, we watched in awe as the dance floor quickly filled up as he picked the songs. I knew Dad liked music, he often had tunes playing on the record player at home, but watching how he enticed people onto the dance floor was incredible. He played modern hits like 'I Love to Boogie' and 'Ride a White Swan' by T. Rex and other classics like 'Save All Your Kisses for Me' by Brotherhood of Man and 'Leaving on a Jet Plane' by Peter, Paul and Mary.

We bopped around, watching people cheer at Dad as he chose another floor-filler. I noticed lots of pretty young women circling his DJ booth, and how he bent over so they could whisper requests in his ear. I couldn't help but feel proud of our popular father.

While I loved Mum to bits, she was more often than not passed out on the couch, drunk after school whereas our dad was like a mini-celebrity who made everyone's faces light up.

During those first weeks, my brother Sean and I grew closer. At home we usually played with our own circle of friends, but here we had only each other. Together, we explored outside the house gates, meeting local kids while Dad was at work. As *Mzungus* (a Bantu term referring to white-skinned people), our pale skin and unusual blue eyes attracted a lot of attention, so we soon found a crowd around us to play Tig with.

We didn't know where our new friends lived – we didn't see their houses as they lived in some of the tin shacks by the *duka* (Swahili for shop). In order to get their attention, we'd run up and down the dusty murum bike tracks and shout words Johnny had taught us, *kuja hapa pasi pasi* (which means 'Come here quickly, quickly'). We'd know they'd heard us as we'd hear them saying among themselves '*Mzungu, mzungu*' (white man).

I was surprised to see that our new friends didn't wear shoes. One or two had grubby old flip-flops, but mostly they played in bare feet. They wore the same clothes each time we saw them. We never told Dad about them though as we knew he would disapprove as they were not white-skinned. He'd already warned us about the Africans here in Kenya, saying they'd rob us if we turned our backs on them. We'd never seen any evidence of this, but decided to keep them a secret from him. When we told Johnny about them, he shook his head, looking scared for us as he said, 'No, *Bwana* angry, *kali sana.*' Which I understood to mean Dad would be really angry.

One evening, Dad came home from work with a cage for us.

'Come and meet your new pets, some Siberian hamsters.' He beamed. 'They'll help make you feel more at home.'

We peered through the bars to see a gorgeous pair of grey-coloured hamsters gazing up at us, their noses pushed against the cage.

'They're surplus to our stock at work,' he explained. 'I thought you might want them.'

'Wow, thanks, Dad!' I cried.

Sean was just as excited as we tried to catch them. The hamsters were clearly unused to being handled. They were making distressed, screeching sounds I'd never heard before. My golden-coloured pet hamster Nibbles in England never made that noise.

'Ouch!' I exclaimed, pulling back my hand. 'One's bitten me.'

I glanced up at Dad and noticed his mood had changed.

'You stupid girl! You shouldn't put your hand in like that, they're frightened. Put the lid back on and put them away in the kitchen,' he snapped.

I looked down at the drop of blood at the end of my finger, picked up the cage and fled to deposit it in the kitchen.

Running my finger under the cold tap, I could feel tears welling up in my eyes. I wondered why Dad would bring us vicious pets and then get angry with me – they weren't like Nibbles, back in England.

Dad followed me into the kitchen, his mood normal again.

'I got them from the polytechnic,' he said calmly. 'They were animals used for experiments but I saved them to breed. This will teach you about the facts of life.'

Sean wasn't within earshot of this and I didn't have a clue what Dad was talking about. Back in England, we'd not been taught anything like this at school although we'd once come across some pictures of rude women in a magazine under the spare bed. I'd assumed one of my uncles who'd been staying in that room had left it behind.

Dad explained it was our job to clean out the cages. We tried to tame the hamsters but they kept biting us. I wondered whether we'd have to take them home to England with us in a few weeks, but decided to ask him later. I pretended to like them, so I didn't hurt his feelings.

That evening, I wrote Mum my first letter home.

*Dear Mum and Barry,*

   *We're having a great time in Kenya. It's so hot and sunny. The house and garden are beautiful. Today, Dad even bought us hamsters! Miss you, Susan and Lucy.*

   *Love Kim, Mickey and Puss Puss x*

I carefully put the letter in an envelope and gave it to Dad. He said he would post it himself that day and that all replies would be sent to his work as he had a PO Box there. I grabbed my letter back and wrote on the back: Please reply to Miss Kim Beaumont, Kenya Polytechnic, PO Box 52428.

Pocketing the letter, Dad told us all about a safari we would be going on.

'There will be lions, leopards and hyenas,' he said, excitedly.

I wasn't too sure about the idea of hyenas but Dad had been living here for ages so he would surely know what to do if we saw one, I told myself.

About four weeks after we'd arrived, Dad's face dropped when he sat down to join us for dinner with a serious expression on his face. We'd been asking several times when our flight home would be, but he never gave us a straight answer. Suddenly he had one.

'Your mum doesn't want you back, I'm afraid,' he announced bluntly. 'You're going to live with me now and go to school here.'

Sean stopped chewing and glanced anxiously at me.

'Erm, what do you mean, Dad?' I asked. I didn't need to be so careful with my vowels as my new accent was coming to me more naturally now, but I still made an extra effort when he was around.

'Your mum doesn't want you, and especially not you, Kim,' he said rather sharply. He put down his knife and fork carefully to look us in the eye. 'She's a drunk, she can't cope with you. That's why you're here. You're better off with me.'

Hearing him use the word 'drunk' to describe our mother made me shift in my seat. Even if she wasn't the best mum in the world, she was still our mum. I couldn't understand what he meant about her not wanting me either. I'd never heard anyone say anything as nasty as this before. However, I knew some parents fell out when they got divorced so I guessed perhaps they'd had a row.

'You can stay here, Kim. Get a proper education. You'll learn nothing in that school in Horsforth. You came here unable to eat or speak properly, no? Here, you will be cared for properly, not by a mother who can't even manage to feed or clothe you.'

I opened my mouth to speak, but he carried on.

'Why do you think she let you come over here and not the others?' he continued. 'She told me you were too much trouble for her, too demanding and naughty. She doesn't even like you, let alone love you.'

He ordered Johnny to clear up, then poured himself a whisky and ginger ale. As I hung my head, tears dropped onto my bare legs. I felt a pain like my heart was broken.

*My own mother didn't even like me, let alone love me. Was this true?*

I knew I could be naughty when I stole the odd slice of bread or told on my siblings, but that was all. Mum had never said I was naughty and if I knew she was going to send me away for good, I'd have stopped.

'We can't stay here forever,' Sean whispered, out of Dad's earshot. 'I don't like what Dad said about Mum.'

I nodded in agreement, trying not to let him see my tears.

'But Mum will want us home, won't she? I'm sure she'll just tell Dad that and we'll be on a flight in no time.'

I tried to reassure him, but inside I felt nothing but confusion. I couldn't believe Mum would just hand us over without even telling us her plans. The only thing to do was to ask her in a letter.

The next day, I asked Dad to send Mum another letter for me.

He looked at me with a strange expression I couldn't read on his face, but agreed. Before I put my letter in the envelope, I read the words one more time, hoping my mother would pay attention to me.

*Dear Mum and Barry,*

*Dad says we're going to go to school here too and I wondered why. Did I do something naughty in England? If I did, I'm very sorry and I won't do it again.*

*When can we see you? I thought we were only coming here for six weeks. We don't want to stay here because we miss everyone. Hope to see you all soon. Tell Susan and Lucy we miss them.*

*Love Kim, Mickey and Puss Puss x*

I began to wonder why Mum hadn't written to us since we'd arrived. Why she'd never called either. For the first time I wondered if maybe it was true, Mum *didn't* like me. The thought was too horrible to bear, but what else was I supposed to think?

Later that evening, Dad explained that he was going to start home-schooling us.

'There aren't any spaces left in the good school I want you to go to,' he told us. 'And I don't think they'd even accept you at the moment with your level of education. I'll have to teach you some of the syllabus and hope you catch up.'

The idea of home-schooling wasn't appealing. I was keen to make new friends as I missed mine from home. Right now, all my friends would be getting their new uniforms to start secondary school in September. Just thinking about it made me feel homesick.

Dad stared at me, as if he could see right into me and read my mind. He came over to me, his eyes narrowing as he plonked a whisky glass down in front of me. The vapour made my eyes water. It smelled horrible, far worse than the Martini Mum drank.

'Kim,' he said, 'it's more important for girls to get an education than boys. Do you want babies? Do you want to be tied to a house and stove all day, looking after screaming brats? Well, that's what will happen if we don't get you educated. You're to stay away from boys. They're nothing but trouble, do you hear me?'

I didn't know what this lecture meant and I didn't like to ask – I always played with boys around our way back home and they seemed harmless enough to me. But I nodded. Hopefully, Mum would write back soon and we'd be home before too long.

# Chapter 3

Next morning, Dad was waiting for us with a set of textbooks laid out on the breakfast table. He hurried Johnny, snapping at him to get things cleared away after we ate our toast so he could get started.

Often he spoke sharply to Johnny, especially after he'd been drinking whisky or his home-brewed beer, but I assumed that was just what happened when you had a servant. I could tell Johnny was always trying his best, rushing to tidy up or bring us our food, but for Dad, it was never quite good enough.

'Yes, *Bwana*,' Johnny replied, running around the table to clear the plates as fast as he could.

What made me feel even more uncomfortable was the things Dad said about anyone who wasn't white. He called them nasty names I'd never heard of, like *bloody monkeys*.

'Here's the syllabus,' Dad said, stabbing at the words with a biro. 'I will leave this with you to learn from the books while I'm at work. First off, it's algebra.'

I managed to stop myself from wrinkling my nose. Maths wasn't my favourite subject. I much preferred sports, especially netball and cross-country running, but eager to please, I pretended to look interested.

'Okay, Dad,' I said.

Dad went off to work as we settled ourselves down with the books. Within about half an hour, Sean was yawning and I was struggling to carry on. There were too many distractions. The table was positioned alongside a huge window overlooking the beautiful garden where our pets hung out – far more interesting than the boring books in front of us.

'I can't do this,' I told Sean. 'I'm playing outside. Dad can help me when he comes back.'

We jumped down from our chairs and ran outside into the warm African sunshine. I stood still, screwing up my eyes as I gazed up into the blue sky: there wasn't a cloud in sight. Life was so different here from Leeds.

When we heard Dad's car pull up at lunchtime we rushed outside and told him excitedly about the big birds we'd seen flying above and the massive mouse that the cat had caught, but the look on his face told me he wasn't interested.

'What are you doing down from the table?' he demanded.

He frogmarched us back to the table where our books lay, shouting for Johnny.

'Yes, *Bwana*,' Johnny said.

'Don't *Bwana* me, you daft fool!' Dad yelled. 'I told you not to let the children down from the table at all. Do you want this job? Now, get out of my sight!'

Although Johnny didn't speak a great deal of English, he understood far more than he let on and hurried away.

I was so sad that we'd got him in trouble – I didn't want him to lose his job and go away. I liked Johnny, he felt like a friend.

Dad banged his fist down right in front of my nose.

'Are you trying to annoy me?' he yelled. His face was inches from mine, his breath stank of whisky and cigarettes. Puss Puss jumped on his lap as if to calm him down, but he grabbed him by the scruff of his neck and threw him onto the floor. Then he turned back to me.

'You thick twit!' Dad spat. 'I really do believe you're going to be no use to anyone when you're older but to have babies.'

He let Sean down from the table, saying he was younger and that I should know better.

'Stop crying and get all of this done. It'd better be done properly by the time I get back from work later this evening,' he ordered.

By now, I was crying so much, I could hardly read the algebra formulae in front of me.

When Dad got annoyed, it was almost as if he was annoyed with himself for getting annoyed. It was like he couldn't control his temper, no matter how much he tried.


That evening, I went to bed in tears, more homesick than ever. I had no idea what to expect the next day but braced myself for the worse. And like I feared, it was a repeat of the previous one, except this time we tried our hardest to get things right.

Although Dad had lost his temper many times over our schoolwork, I hoped nothing else would make him angry. I imagined things would be better once we'd started school, but gradually mealtimes became more stressful too.

Dad always liked to see us eat. Ever since we arrived, he told us we were far too skinny and encouraged big portions. To begin with this was wonderful as Mum had never bothered cooking much. Here in Nairobi, there was always plenty to eat. We'd generally have tomato soup with homemade chapatis at lunchtime or sneak into Johnny's little annexe once Dad had gone to work and taste his traditional dish of posho (a type of maize flour mixed with water and cooked) and beans. By itself, it was pretty tasteless and reminded me of a solid lump of mashed potato, but it was lovely with the sauce Johnny made.

As growing children, we were often ravenous but quickly Dad made it a rule we had to finish everything on our plates, even when we were full up.

'Make the most of it now while you're young,' he said. 'I wish I could eat all of that without putting on weight.'

One day, Dad called me into the kitchen. He was holding a tall bottle of what looked like a pale golden oil.

'This is cod liver oil,' he explained as he poured the golden liquid onto a dessertspoon. 'This will help fill you out as you're far too thin.'

I didn't have time to object as the spoonful of oil was pushed straight into my open mouth – it tasted vile.

'Swallow it all,' Dad said. 'You're to have this daily.'

One evening, before Dad went out for the night with friends, he called me as usual into the kitchen to give me my cod liver oil.

'I don't have any cod liver oil so you're to have this for now,' he said.

I glanced at the tin of Kimbo, a white vegetable fat, sold cheaply in Kenya. Dad was melting it in a saucepan. He forced a spoonful of hot oil into my mouth. Physically unable to swallow it, I started to gag.

'For God's sake, hurry up and swallow it!' he said impatiently. Suddenly, he leant forward and pinched my nostrils together so I couldn't breathe.

'Now swallow it!' he bellowed.

I opened my mouth to breathe, spraying oil all over his suit. He looked at me in fury, before rushing off to change. Already late, he had no time to tell me off, but I didn't doubt I'd be for it when he got home.


Sean and I gradually grew to dread mealtimes because often we couldn't finish the mounds of food on our plates. On one occasion Dad had prepared fishcakes and chips with mushy peas. He used very large potatoes, sliced them thickly and placed a slither of fish between the two, while Johnny fried them. Instead of preparing one fishcake each, he gave us three or four. Johnny put the plates down in front of us with pity in his eyes – he knew we'd never manage to eat it all.

I stole a glance at Sean, noticing the dismay on his little face.

'Right,' said Dad, 'I want those plates cleaned.'

We tried our best, but fifteen minutes later, our tummies were fit to burst. The longer we took, the more drunk Dad became, and the worse his mood grew. The dry batter felt claggy in my mouth. I asked for water, but he refused.

'You're both so ungrateful!' he yelled. 'This is all your mum's fault. I should save Susan and Lucy from her too.'

In desperation, I sprinkled pepper over my fishcake, hoping it would make it more palatable. I sneezed as the pepper reached my nose and it made Sean and I giggle.

'What the hell was that, Kim?' Dad yelled.

'I sneezed,' I spluttered, trying to stop the giggle.

He looked at me strangely as if a memory occurred to him.

'You're just like your thick mother; she used to find sneezing funny too.' He jabbed me hard in the back. 'She's obviously told you I used to get annoyed with her for putting too much pepper on her food,' he continued. 'Here …'

He picked up the pepper pot and emptied the entire contents onto the remaining fishcakes. 'See if you find eating that funny.'

Miserably, I tried to eat with him eyeballing me from across the room while he poured a glass of homebrew. When he finally nodded off into a drunken stupor, Johnny stepped in to quietly remove my pepper-splattered fishcake, hiding it in the bin.

Over the next few days and weeks, we learned to wait for Dad to pour himself a drink before trying to get rid of our piled-high plates of dinner. We'd either throw them on the floor for Mickey or spit into a napkin.

'You're to sit here until it's all finished,' he snapped.

Each meal would frequently end in torturous mouthfuls and us in tears while Dad raged about how ungrateful we were.

Often after dinner before bed, I'd write another letter to Mum.

*Dear Mum, Barry*
  *Please can we come home? We don't like it here*
*anymore. We don't want to go to school. Dad isn't very*

*nice to us. I miss you all so much. Please can you*
*write back.*

    *Love Kim, Mickey and Puss Puss x*

The next day, Dad took the envelope when I asked him to. Over time, I began to suspect him of not sending the letters, or at least opening them, so I became more careful about what I wrote just in case he was reading my letters. Often, after I'd given him a letter to send to Mum and if I'd hinted in my letter about not liking it in Kenya, it seemed coincidental how that evening, when he returned from work, he was always off with me. He'd make more of a point about how Mum didn't like me, which would make me feel even worse.

We had no other way of contacting Mum either. We couldn't use Dad's phone without his permission and I couldn't travel to the Post Office by myself to post a letter – we lived too far away. As the weeks dragged on, we knew we were stuck. There was no way we could buy flights home; there was no other way of sending a message home either. Now we were trapped on a never-ending 'holiday' with a dad who didn't seem to like us.

One day, Dad told us we were going on a safari to Mtito Andei in Tsavo West National Park. We'd clung to the promise of this exciting trip, a treat he had promised us before we left Leeds.

*Perhaps he might lighten up a bit,* I thought, *and get less angry during a proper holiday?*

But I couldn't contain my excitement and even Dad's face broke into a huge smile after hearing my infectious laughter. I chatted about what I'd do if I saw a lion, what I'd be wearing, and how I'd tell Mum and the others all about it. Sean joined in, causing Dad to turn up the volume on his record player to drown us out. He settled back into a chair, ignoring us, while he topped up his beer from a keg of homebrew – he made it in the traditional way with hops brought back from visits to England. His suitcase was always full of hops! They smelled so strong, everything else in the case would smell of them too.

On the day we left, loading up the car felt like a big adventure. Dad made sure he had all of his camera equipment too. He often walked around with a camera or video recorder around his neck – it was one of his favourite hobbies.

I whispered to Sean as Dad loaded the last bits into the boot.

'Look at his funny hat,' I giggled.

With his khaki safari clothes on, Dad looked like a character from a film set in a jungle. Despite his bad moods, at times like this we couldn't help but feel proud of him.

'What do you want to see the most, you two?' he asked as he settled into the driving seat.

'Elephants!' I grinned.

'Hyenas!' laughed Sean.

I giggled, jabbing Sean in the ribs. 'Wonder if they laugh like you do?' I teased.

We rolled off down the roads dimpled with potholes. As our house disappeared in the rear-view mirror, I thought about how we were going to miss Johnny, but I couldn't wait to see Africa in the wild. Best of all, Dad seemed to be more relaxed in our company again.

The journey seemed to take forever, but eventually in the late afternoon we pulled up at some large gates. They were in the shape of a rhino and made from black metal. A huge animal skull, apparently of a buffalo, sat below a huge sign which scared me.

*Stay in your car at all times*, it read.

Dad exchanged some words with a local, who was taking money near the rhino gates. I couldn't quite catch what he was saying, but I did make out the words: *Lions and elephants*. As the huge gates opened to let us through, I questioned him, eager to know what the man had said.

'Oh, it's nothing much,' Dad replied. 'He said for us to be careful as a family were trampled at our site by elephants last week.'

'Are they okay now?' I asked.

'Of course they're not okay, Kim! They're all dead,' Dad said casually. 'They were trampled in their tent as they slept and the man said hyenas and lions ate some of them.'

I suddenly felt sick, Sean started to cry.

'I don't want to stay here,' I said, trembling. 'Can we go and stay in a hotel?'

Dad ignored me with a smirk on his face.

*We're being driven to our deaths*, I thought, terrified. A wave of homesickness washed over me. How I longed to be back in Leeds, where no lions roamed freely.

Being on the equator, it got dark at roughly the same time each evening, about 7pm. At 5.30pm, we still had a bit of time to set up camp before darkness fell.

Mtito Andei Tsavo West campsite was just outside the main gates, no more than 200 yards away. From there, you couldn't see the gates or the main road because of the dense trees and bushland. Dad pulled up. There was a large grubby building that he identified only as the toilet and shower block, but nothing else.

The campsite was deserted – in fact, there were no fences or lighting or anything.

'Where is everyone else?' I asked.

Dad shrugged. 'Maybe the incident last week has put tourists off coming.'

Then he went on to tell us the story of a pair of man-eating male lions that were responsible for the deaths of many construction workers on the Kenya–Uganda railway between March and December 1898. He told us menacingly that the workers had had a number of campsites spread over an eight-mile area and that one of the camps was in Tsavo. Lions had stalked the campsites, dragging the men one by one from their tents at night and devouring them whole. He told us excitedly there was a book published called *The Man-Eaters of Tsavo*.

Sean and I were rather anxious but assumed it must be safe as lots of Western tourists went on safari, but by the time Dad had finished talking about the stories in the book, we could barely move with fear.

'C'mon,' said Dad impatiently, 'everyone out of the car! We need to get the tent up and collect firewood before it's dark.'

We followed his instructions. First, we had to erect the tent. Being a perfectionist, Dad made such a meal out of this. Every guy rope had to be the right tension (when it rained, we were not allowed to touch the roof canvas from inside as he said this caused it to leak). We hated doing anything like this with him as he always shouted at us, and this time he made us hold the tent poles for ages in a certain position. If we moved, he yelled at us.

'Careful!' he shouted as we disappeared off to find firewood. 'There are loads of scorpions hiding in dead wood. If they sting you, you'll die a slow, horrible death.'

After wondering why our father had sent his children off to do a job so dangerous, I grabbed a long, hard stick, hitting at dead wood and using it to overturn stones to ensure no insects or deadly creatures lurked underneath.

'Watch out in that long grass for snakes too,' Dad added. 'We'd never get you to a hospital in time all the way out here.'

Hurriedly, we grabbed the first pieces of wood we could find and returned. Dad expertly started a fire and finally I thought I could relax beside the crackling flames. However, he even made sitting around the fire frightening as he played music from a cassette player running off batteries. It was placed on the dusty ground and we weren't allowed to move it. He instructed us not to sit with our feet on the ground as the vibrations from the cassette player would attract scorpions. I often wondered afterwards why he would want to attract such deadly creatures to our feet.

While sitting around the fire, he gave us a geography lesson, pointing out Mount Kilimanjaro in the distance. He told us it was the highest mountain in Africa and the highest freestanding mountain in the world. It once belonged to Kenya but then in colonial times, Queen Victoria had presented it to her grandson, who governed what would become Tanzania. As Dad said, it was a rather lavish birthday present! From where we were, it could be seen on a clear day, and in the late afternoon we could make out snow on the peaks.

Hours later, we went to bed, looking forward to the morning.

The next morning, we woke bright and early for our first game drive. We unloaded our things under the canvas before we set off. Over the next couple of hours, we saw such incredible sights and I wished I had a camera like Dad's. Spotting rhinos, buffalo, lions, elephants and countless zebra, giraffes and gazelle in the wild was like a dream come true.

We came across a massive herd of elephants. Some had tremendous tusks and there was a baby among them. Dad told us he was keeping his distance as elephants were very protective over their young, their behaviour was unpredictable and they could charge our vehicle. I kept my eye on them at all times.

'Okay, we've seen them now,' I said, sensing the mother elephant's nervousness. 'Can we go?'

As we drove away from the herd, Dad spoke about how awful poaching was around there before adding: 'Those elephants are headed in our direction, they'll be at our camp by nightfall or later.'

I secretly hoped he'd be wrong, but feared Dad knew so much, he would be right.

Back at the camp, Dad lit a fire to heat up a stew he'd brought with us. I watched as the big African sun started to disappear on the horizon and the moon lit up the area where we were sitting, around the fire.

I used to love looking up at the African sky and the bright, twinkling stars and planets. At least that was until Dad decided to educate us about the names and location of the planets. He pointed out the Seven Sisters constellation, telling us they were really called the Pleiades and how they were the 'seven daughters of Atlas, a Titan'. I quickly lost interest and clung to the idea of the Seven Sisters, but Dad would always question me about this and lose his temper if I couldn't remember everything he had told me. I soon learned to recite the names of the Pleiades parrot-style so as not to annoy him.

'Let's see who finds a shooting star first,' I whispered to Sean. As frightened as we had been earlier, this place also seemed magical.

Suddenly we heard a loud snapping sound from across the camp, near the toilet block.

'Shhhh, did you hear that?' Dad jumped up and shone his torch across the camp. In the dark, dense bush, we could see the outline of the herd of elephants we'd seen earlier. It was hard to tell from a distance but it looked as though they might be stripping bark from the trees, peeling it back as effortlessly as if peeling a banana.

I sat frozen to the spot as we heard other sounds besides the elephants. In the distance, not too far away, we heard a strange cackling.

'That's the sound of a hyena,' said Dad, getting up. He shone the torch at the bush behind us, where what looked like hundreds of eyes were reflected back at us.

'What are they?' screamed Sean, grabbing Dad's hand for protection. But he shook off his hand and began legging it to the car.

'I don't know exactly but I'm not waiting to find out,' he yelled as he ran off. He jumped into the car, locking the door, while we stood helplessly outside.

Dad wound his window down.

'Remember, hyenas have most powerful jaws, they'll bite

through to the bone and strip your flesh. Best get over to the car while you can,' he called.

But Sean and I were rooted to the spot by the fire with fear. We begged him to come and get us, but he just laughed.

'I'm not getting out of the car for anyone,' he said.

He wound up the window, turned off his headlights and then the only light we had was the light of the moon and from the dying embers of the fire. Terrified, I grabbed Sean's hand and said we should make a run for it. We raced over to bang on Dad's window and plead for him to let us in. After what seemed ages, he opened the door and ordered us to lie in the back.

I spent a sleepless night being bitten by mosquitoes. By the time the sun rose, I was smothered in painful bites.

'They go for bad blood,' Dad sneered when he saw them. 'Make sure you take your malaria pills otherwise you'll be very ill or worse still, you'll die from malaria.'

Far from being a treat, the holiday was a complete nightmare. On tedious days out in Dad's car, on safari for what seemed like hours, we would see the occasional open-top van filled to the brim, mostly with German tourists. On the side of the van would be the name of the hotel where they were staying. I was so envious, wishing I could stay at one of the lodges, sleep in a proper bed, not get bitten by mosquitoes or have to search for firewood with the threat of scorpions lurking beneath it. We would often call in at these lodges for a drink and to use the facilities. Dad would always scoff at the tourists, saying they were fat and lazy and that's what happens if you stay in an expensive lodge, eating high-calorie food. I stopped asking if we could stay in one of those lodges once I realised that he grew increasingly irritable, the more I asked.

By the final day, neither Sean nor I could have been happier to get back to civilisation even if it meant more home-schooling.

While taking a shower at the very basic shower block, I was stung on the foot by a huge insect. It was agony! Dad told me it must have been a hornet and that it was all my fault as I was the one who trod on it.

'You've always been clumsy, Kim, and never looked where you're going,' he said dismissively as he walked away, leaving me to writhe in pain.

Once, I admitted to him how scared I was after dashing to the shower block and back. I was always afraid a baboon or monkey, or worse still, a wild animal would creep in under the huge gap below the door or jump over the top of it and get me.

'See, Kim,' he said. 'That's what happens when you leave my side. You must stay close by at all times.'

# Chapter 4

Soon after the safari, I was back home, lying in bed, trying to sleep, when I heard a strange sound. I suspected it might be the wardrobe creaking, but it sounded like footsteps just outside my bedroom door. I mentioned this to Dad in the morning.

'Oh yes,' he said, not looking up from his newspaper. 'Did I not say? I think this house may be haunted. I've heard funny noises since I've been here. Mickey often growls and stares down the corridor outside your room, Kim.'

I put down my toast, feeling my heart beat faster.

'Have you ever seen anything?' I asked.

Dad smirked at me. 'Finish your toast,' he snapped. 'I don't want any food wasted!'

That night, as I lay in bed, I pulled the covers over my head as every little sound played tricks with my mind. All the shadows on the walls seemed to move and every sound of rustling in the garden seemed louder. Then, all of a sudden, a tune began to play, an eerie tune with frightening lyrics. It was the song 'Brain Damage' by Pink Floyd. My dad loved the *Dark Side of the Moon* album and this song spoke of a lunatic being in the hallway. And now the words were playing out loud, down our hallway.

I tightened the covers around my head as I listened to these creepy lyrics, imagining a ghost drawing closer as the words grew louder and louder and hardly daring to breathe in case it came into my room. The music seemed to get louder as the band sang about a lunatic being in the hall, being in the singer's head who was not him.

Awful, sinister laughter followed. It seemed to come from right down the hallway outside of my bedroom. Terrified, I screamed as I jumped out of bed and flung open my bedroom door.

'Dad!' I yelled, running out into the hallway.

My father stood a few feet away, smirking. I had no idea if I was dreaming or what had happened.

'You look terrified, Kim,' he said. 'What's wrong?'

Tear-stricken, I told him about the noise outside my room and the laughter in the hall.

*Am I going mad?* I thought to myself. *Was it the song or was it really a ghost?*

As if reading my mind, Dad simply said, 'It'll be the ghost. Probably annoyed because you've taken its bedroom. Come on, you can sleep in my room tonight.'

Somehow, he managed to convince me he had heard sinister laughter down the hallway and outside my bedroom window from the garden. He had come to investigate, he said, and that's why he was standing outside my door.

Blinking in the light of his bedroom, I slid into Dad's bed, curling myself into a small ball. The room was bathed in a glow from the red bulbs inside the bedside lamps and seventies-style orange curtains. It was a strange light that made me feel as if I was going to get a headache so I closed my eyes. Dad got in the other side of the bed and turned to face me.

'At least you're away from the ghost now,' he whispered. 'I've seen a ghost at the bottom of my bed too. It spoke to me. But cuddle up and go to sleep, it's not there at the moment.'

I fell asleep with his arms around me. Hours later, I woke to a peculiar sound coming from Dad – he was grunting and shaking the bed. In the darkness I couldn't make out what he was doing, so I soon fell asleep again. Then I woke to him running his hands across my chest. I didn't have any breasts yet and wondered what he was doing. I moved a bit further away, but he moved closer again so he could reach. There was no room left to get away so I lay there very still, hoping he'd stop. I guessed it would make him angry if I said anything.

When I woke up again, Sean was lying on the other side of the bed – he must have been scared in the night too. Dad was getting ready for work so I got dressed.

Recently, Dad had suggested I shouldn't wear trousers as much, even though I loved playing outside in jeans.

'I've bought you some skirts, Kim,' he said, handing me a selection. 'You're growing up now so you need to look like a lady, not a boy.'

I didn't want to wear a skirt, but didn't want Dad to get annoyed so I reluctantly put one on. Later, when my father was at work, I took the skirt off and pulled my jeans on as we wanted to play outside.

That afternoon, when I came in and flopped onto the sofa, Dad told me off.

'You're sitting with your legs apart, Kim,' he scolded. 'It's not polite. Put them together.'

I was only wearing jeans. It wasn't like anyone could see my knickers, but I folded one knee over the other anyway.

*Maybe Dad was right, I needed to look more grown-up.*

Soon afterwards, he told me I was *only* allowed to wear skirts around him so I got changed whenever he asked. The last thing I wanted to do was to make him angry. His moods were confusing: one minute he was being horrible, the next he seemed very kind.

*Maybe that's what grown-ups were like – confusing and stressed out a lot.*

Another confusing thing was the number of hamsters Dad continued to bring home for us. Although we loved pets, we didn't need any more.

Sundays were already a nightmare without having to spend hours cleaning cage upon cage of dirty hamsters. Then he bought some guinea pigs too and made some little hutches on stilts in the garden outside of the kitchen.

Just a week later, Dad purchased some long-haired golden hamsters from the UK.

'These are more docile,' he explained. 'We'll breed these, Kim, and sell them to the pet shop. You're in charge. Don't let them die, they're expensive.'

Terrified of upsetting him, I looked after them as best I

could. Weeks later, I walked into the kitchen to find Dad with a face like thunder. He marched me over to the hamster cage, where, by now, about twenty hamsters lived.

'Look in there and tell me what you see!' he snapped.

I gazed into the cage and felt physically sick. The female long-haired hamster had a small baby in her paws; she peered up and bit off its little head then chewed and swallowed it right in front of me before going on to the next baby. Already there were a few headless babies strewn around the cage, only a couple of living bald, blind pink ones were left in the nest.

'Oh my God, why is she eating them?' I cried.

'It's all your fault because you disturbed them!' Dad shouted. 'The mother will eat the others and I want you to watch, then you can clean out the cage.'

So I watched, tears rolling down my face as the mother picked up the next baby and then the next, biting off their tiny heads and chewing them up as if they were peanuts.

Next, Dad ordered me to clean out the blood-splattered cage.

'I have also deducted your pocket money to pay for them,' he said.

Despite him blaming me, I knew it wasn't my fault and my cheeks burned with the injustice of this. The hamster cage had been placed in the kitchen where everyone, including Johnny, walked past frequently. It seemed the mother had become distressed by this.

Days later, Dad also got us a new cat – a Siamese called Bandit. One morning, I was sitting in a wrought-iron framed chair with bright orange cushions in the living room, with Bandit on my lap, when Dad walked in. She jumped off and wandered away as he came over with his camera.

'What are you going to do today?' Dad asked.

'I don't know. Maybe play outside with Sean in the garden?' I replied.

He sat opposite me in the chair, fiddling with his camera. Then he raised it to his eye, focusing the lens on me.

'Kim,' he said sternly, 'sit up.'

I did as I was told, wondering if maybe he might take a photo of me that I could send to Mum. She still hadn't replied to any of my letters.

'Right, now open your legs a bit wider,' he instructed.

I smiled in embarrassment, fidgeting with my skirt. It was too short to cover my knees. If I sat with my legs open, he'd see my knickers.

*I was confused. Hadn't he just told me that sitting with my legs apart was impolite?*

The camera shutter clicked as I smoothed the skirt over my legs.

'Wider,' Dad said simply.

Reluctantly, I moved my legs apart a little as he trained the camera onto my knees. Bandit walked past so I grabbed her to sit her on my lap, to give me some dignity.

'Get that stupid animal off your knee!' he snapped.

I brushed Bandit away and Dad took a couple of shots. The cat wandered back. Afraid he might throw her across the room like he'd once done with Puss Puss before, I shooed her away gently.

'I want you to just sit there alone,' he spat.

I didn't like this – I couldn't understand why he was taking such photos. But fearing his reaction if I refused, I just looked at the camera and hoped it would be over soon.

From then on, when Sean wasn't around, Dad would sometimes ask to take a few shots of me, always in my skirt. He made me wear ankle socks with some red-heeled sandals he'd bought me. Always, he used an additional lens attached to the main camera – he never showed me the photos he'd taken either.

By now, eight weeks had gone by and we knew we were not going back home to Mum. I really missed her. I'd often look at the stars or the moon outside and think, *Mum can see that same moon, she's not far away. I wonder if she's thinking of me.*

I didn't care about her drinking or us having jam and bread for tea, I loved my mum more than anything in the world and I missed her terribly. Before bed, I'd kneel and pray: *Dear God, please look after my mum and dad, especially my mum. I hope I can see her soon. I know I've been naughty in the past but I promise I'll be good from now. Amen.*

I made this my ritual every night or whenever I could as I felt that something awful might happen to Mum or I would never see her again if I didn't do this.

By then, Dad had more news for us: he'd got Sean and me into a private school called Braeburn. By this time, we had missed a full term. We'd have to work hard to keep up with the other students – at least that meant we'd get out of the house for the weekdays.

Behind closed doors, our father resembled a Jekyll and Hyde character. It was like treading on eggshells, I never knew when he was going to snap. To the outside world he was a respectable, charismatic and intelligent university lecturer who had got a bad deal in taking on his unruly children from a previous marriage – he'd had no choice in the matter because their mother was a drunk.

One night, while doing his DJing at the Woodley Club, a respectable couple came up to me as I was standing by the records, carefully placing them back in their protective sleeves as instructed by my father. They first spoke to Dad and I had to stifle a giggle as I heard one of them say, 'Oh, Bernie, how on earth do you cope with two youngsters on your own?' I'd never before heard him called Bernie, and to me it sounded so funny. The man then addressed me, while he turned and looked at Dad. 'Isn't your father amazing, taking on two children your age just like that? Most men wouldn't do it,' he said.

I nodded, wondering if anyone would ever know the truth.

Occasionally, Dad would tell people how difficult I was, as if to make himself look good.

'Oh, I have the patience of a saint! Kim can be so difficult at times, can't you, Kim? She's lazy too. Demands lots of pets but is reluctant to clean up after them.' He said this with a smile, knowing I had little choice but to go along with the façade. I knew that I had to just smile and pretend what he was saying was all true as this would make him happy. If I defied him, he'd certainly let me know.

*Only Sean and I knew the truth.*

Dad always found a way to make himself look good in front of other people. He'd invite friends and colleagues back to our house for drinks. He loved dinner parties too, being the centre of attention. He'd tell Johnny what to cook and he poured everyone's drinks.

All the expats had plums in their mouths; they all sounded

so fake. Sean and I would laugh behind their backs. We'd imitate their Queen's English and, out of sight of Dad, roll on the floor, squealing in fits of laughter.

'Oh, *Bernie!*' we'd laugh, imitating them. 'You are simply amazing for doing what you're doing. It can't be easy.'

Johnny had Sundays off so he didn't always see what was happening in our household on this day. I grew to loathe Sundays with a passion. Those were the days when I had to do absolutely everything, which included making a full roast dinner.

The first time Dad asked me, I admitted I didn't know how.

'I'll teach you,' he said.

Standing in the kitchen with a whisky in his hand, he began pulling out pots and pans. He wanted me to cook a chicken, peel the potatoes and then boil the other vegetables.

He pulled out a huge bag of spuds, far too many for us three to eat.

'I want every single one peeled,' he said, handing me the peeler.

The peeler felt tricky in my small hands as I tried to use it as fast as I could. Fearing his criticism, my hands were jittery so the slippery spuds dropped onto the floor.

'Pick them up!' Dad roared.

As I began trembling, it made peeling them even harder. Then I scraped the outside knuckle of my thumb.

'Ouch!' I said, automatically clutching the wound.

'Don't infect the potatoes, you stupid girl! Go get a plaster quickly,' Dad barked.

I dropped the peeler in the sink and rummaged through a drawer. All the while my father was shouting at me for being useless.

*Dad cares more about blood on the potatoes than he does about my finger*, I thought.

He picked the potatoes up, rinsed them under the tap, then ordered me to continue. As I carried on, he pulled out some jam jars. It was difficult doing the rest of the potatoes with the plaster in place so Dad made me wear a rubber glove. It was far too big, but I didn't dare complain.

'While you're doing this, I want you to make me some jam,' he said.

Quickly, he rattled through instructions about sterilising the glass jars with water, making sure the water was hot enough to kill germs but not so hot that they would crack. I was to put sugar and fruit into a saucepan and then stir it continuously. If it burned even slightly, he told me I'd have to throw it away as the entire batch would be tainted.

I stared in panic as he clattered the utensils in front of me. There were so many jars. And potatoes. And now fruit. And I still had the meat to cook. He stood, drink in hand, barking order after order, rushing me on as dinner had to be on the table for 3pm.

For the next four hours I dashed from potatoes to boiling the kettle, to filling up the jars, to mixing fruit, until my head was spinning. He demanded I clean the chicken properly, removing the giblets and stuffing the cavity with a dried mix made up according to his instructions. Johnny had once left the giblets in a chicken and poured dried stuffing mix into the cavity, he told me, berating him for being so thick. This didn't go down too well as it was a meal for some friends Dad had invited over.

As I placed the chicken in the oven, I was pleased with myself.

'Don't look so smug yet,' said Dad. 'You've got to keep stirring the jam otherwise it'll stick to the bottom of the pan.'

Immediately, I diverted my attention to the bubbling pan of jam, turning it down to simmer. I stirred like I'd never stirred anything before, my hand and elbow aching within minutes. Then I heard the familiar sound of a needle on vinyl and sure enough, the music began: Rod Stewart's 'Sailing' filled the house.

It was so loud, I could barely think, but within minutes I checked and Dad was in a drunken doze on the sofa. By the time the food was ready, he had woken up, tipsy and unsteady on his feet.

Finally, by 6pm, dinner was on the table. By then, Sean had come back from playing by himself outside. Too exhausted to even consider eating, I knew better than to try and excuse myself so I sat down and did my best to eat.

The next Sundays followed the same pattern: Dad got drunk while standing over me like a bullying head chef ordering his kitchen porter around. Once I accidentally poured water that was too hot into one of the jars so it cracked into pieces. Another time, when Dad tasted the jam, he went berserk because it tasted slightly burned. I had to start again from scratch, preparing all the fruit, measuring out the sugar, etc. while he barked orders at me and played his music. He always bought too much fruit so there was more than enough for another batch.

One week, I was so exhausted from spending hours making the dinner, I started to nod off at the table. Dad yelled so loudly I sat straight up, wondering if someone had broken in.

There was no peace at night-time either. Dad continued to

play the Pink Floyd track 'Brain Damage', which would send me running terrified into his bedroom. One evening, as I tried to settle in my bed, the mattress even lifted up. It felt as though it was being pushed from under the bed, where my feet were. About five minutes earlier, I'd heard tapping on my window. I pulled the blankets over my head, trying to control my breathing. After bracing myself, I leaped out of bed, my heart racing so hard, I thought it would burst out of my chest. I couldn't see Dad anywhere so I jumped in his bed and pulled the covers over my face as I heard him creep into the room after me.

'Th-the mattress moved ...' I stammered.

'Ah, I told you,' he sighed. 'It must be the time of year for the ghost to feel spooked and to want to make his presence known.'

Only much later did I realise it was Dad who had hidden under my bed to move the mattress just to frighten me.

One night, my father lay next to me in bed and put his hands over my breasts again. As usual, I froze, wondering why he was doing this. I felt sick as he started to push his fingers into my pants while he started making the grunting sound I'd heard before.

'Rub it,' he said, taking my hand and forcing it into his pants.

I felt this was wrong. I didn't like it at all – I couldn't understand why he was doing this, especially after all his warnings about boys. But when I tried to pull away, he grabbed my arm.

'Rub,' he repeated menacingly.

I didn't know what I was doing so I rubbed until my hand ached. Suddenly my hand was wet and sticky and he pushed me away.

'Go wash your hands now. Don't get it on the sheets, hurry!'

As I fled towards the door, he called me back: 'This is our secret and ours only,' he said.

Confused as to what just happened, I cleaned my hands in the bathroom, closed the toilet lid, sat down upon it and sobbed quietly.

Too scared to go back to my own room, I didn't want to go back into Dad's room either. Instead, I waited until he was asleep before climbing back into bed.

The next night he waited patiently until Sean went to bed. I too stood up to say goodnight as I didn't want to be alone with him. Dad muttered under his breath as my brother left to go to his room.

'Stay there, Kim, I've got things planned for you,' he said, eyeing me up and down.

He gestured for me to follow him into his bedroom. He'd been drinking a mixture of whisky and homebrew so I began trembling, anticipating the worst.

'Take your nightdress off,' he ordered.

So, I did as I was told, shivering.

'You're very small-breasted and you've got one bigger than the other,' he sneered. 'I can help.'

He pulled me roughly towards him and began sucking so hard on the one that he said was smaller, it brought tears to my eyes.

'I'll have to do this every day on this one otherwise it'll stay smaller than the other one and you'll look ridiculous,' he explained. I really didn't know if what he was saying was true, but I didn't dare argue. He continued to tell me how much he was helping me.

'You don't want to be lopsided,' he said.

He then made me rub him through his pants again, removing them completely and insisting I carry on despite me complaining that my hand was hurting.

'Remember,' he said, 'this is our secret. This is what all dads do to their little girls. Did you know that?'

I shook my head.

'Exactly! The reason why nobody has told you is because nobody talks about it – it's a secret for *everyone*.'

I swallowed hard, eager to go and clean him off me, but he grabbed my arm and dug his fingers into it.

'Besides, who will believe you?' he continued, clipping his words in his best Queen's English. 'Nobody! Nobody will ever believe you, a stupid child, over someone like me, a university lecturer.'

He let me go, so I could turn away finally. Soon he nodded off, but I lay there for hours as hot tears soaked my pillow. I felt confused, dirty and trapped.

*Why was my daddy doing this?*

The next day was a Saturday morning. Dad was at the breakfast table, reading a book, and barely looked up as I arrived. Exhausted through lack of sleep, my mind was whirling with confusion.

My head was spinning, but I was much too scared to say anything.

He half-smiled, poured me a coffee and asked about my plans for the day as if nothing had happened. So, I sat on my chair and pretended nothing had happened either.

# Chapter 5

As an eleven-year-old girl, my life had been turned completely upside down within a matter of weeks. I had lost my home, most of my family and now I had to live with a man who took pleasure in abusing me. In order to survive, I told myself it wouldn't last forever. I counted down the days until school was going to start and didn't give up hope that Mum might reply to a letter. I fantasised about going home. I imagined Mum coming to get us or sending us plane tickets home. Even if, as the days rolled by, it seemed less likely.

Meanwhile, Dad's girlfriend Pam announced that she was leaving Kenya to return to England. He said he was sick of women ruling his life and they weren't worth the hassle. However, this didn't ring true because shortly afterwards a woman called Jane Morris came to stay for six weeks.

He hadn't met her before so I don't know how he found her all the way from Kenya to England. I didn't think to ask as I was secretly excited, hoping if he had a new girlfriend, he'd leave me alone.

At first, Dad was on his best behaviour, offering to pour Jane coffee in the mornings or take her out for lunch, but his attitude towards her soon changed. One evening, they were going out to the Woodley Club and Jane spent ages in her room getting ready. During this time Dad had been drinking and I could see his mood worsening as he waited.

By the time Jane emerged looking beautiful, with make-up and a dress on, Dad was in a foul temper.

'You've taken absolutely ages getting ready and don't look any better than you did before you started!' he snapped.

I couldn't believe he could be so unkind. I didn't want to sit there listening to this, seeing how he was treating this lovely lady.

Jane's eyes filled with tears and she ran back into Dad's room. We could hear her sobbing, but Dad simply turned up the music on his record player to drown her out. His nastiness was breathtaking. Even as a little girl watching this, a terrible realisation formed in my mind: my own dad hated women.

Jane stayed until she could get her ticket back to the UK changed. She hardly spoke and kept herself to herself. When she left in the late afternoon, Dad took her to the airport. Secretly, I wished I could hide away in her suitcase and travel back with her.

I still wonder where this lovely lady is – I want to tell her how sorry I am that she met up with such a monster and how I knew how badly he was treating her and how I wished I could have helped her, but I was only a child and being abused by him myself at the time.

Even while Jane had been staying with us, Dad refused to leave me alone, making me rub him inappropriately whenever he wanted or touching my private parts when nobody else was looking. He confided in me that he found Jane extremely boring and she took too long to get 'in the mood', something I barely understood as an eleven-year-old but assumed wasn't very nice.

After Jane left, I dreaded what was in store for me. As soon as Mickey jumped up, wagging his tail and running to the door, I knew my father was back. I felt sick and quickly disappeared down the corridor to my room, almost barricading myself in as I knew what the evening likely held for me.

Dad let himself in and like clockwork, put the record player on and poured himself a drink. After Sean had gone to bed, Dad whispered across to me. I had to come out of my room to see what he wanted.

'Come in, Kim, and close the door behind you,' he said from his room.

Nervously, I opened the door to find him sitting in the orange glow of his room in his underpants. Reaching over to the chest of drawers, he pulled out a packet and a box. He placed the box on the floor with such care I wondered what was inside. Then he very gently pulled out something from the packet – they looked a bit like the tights Mum wore.

'They're stockings,' he explained impatiently. 'They're more hygienic than tights. Put them on, very carefully.'

I slid them over my legs while he wrapped a suspender belt around my waist. He kept adjusting the seams on my small, thin legs, obsessively trying to get the line straight. Then he ordered me to put on some ladies' underwear. Shyly, I pulled off my pants and replaced them with black silky ones. He looked pleased with himself, then finally asked me to put on a pair of shiny red high-heeled shoes. Now I was feeling ridiculous, like a trussed-up chicken. He ordered me to walk back and forth. I stumbled, much to his annoyance.

'Right, Kim, stop,' he said suddenly. 'With your back to me, bend over.'

So I did as he said, hearing him grunting from behind. I squeezed my eyes shut while the blood rushed to my head. How I hated this.

Just when I thought he'd finished, he opened the box, his face lighting up.

'Do you know what this is?' he asked, pulling out a black plastic object.

'No,' I said, peering from the sides of my legs as he hadn't told me I could stand up yet.

He told me it was Jane's toy. Inside the box were lots of other things. I was too young to know what they were, but I was sure I was going to find out.

'Come here and lie on the bed,' he told me. 'I'm going to be nice and use this on you,' he added, waving the black object. 'It would be better if I did it myself, but I have morals and you're a little too young yet. Plus, I don't want blood all over me.'

I didn't know what he was talking about.

He pulled off my pants and rammed the black object into me. The pain was excruciating and I wanted to scream, but he placed his free hand over my mouth.

'Shut up or you'll wake Sean,' he hissed.

I straightened my legs to try and stop him so he ordered

me to lift them up. He struggled to get the black object inside of me, so he reached for a tall white candle on the dressing table and rammed this in instead.

'Stop struggling,' he spat as I writhed in pain.

To my horror, he switched between objects, trying to ram each one harder inside of me while I was screaming with pain. Eventually he gave up, looking at my tear-stained face with disappointment.

He made me rub him and rammed my head down so that I was forced to take his penis in my mouth. Towards the end, I gagged and was almost sick as he forced me to swallow, telling me his semen was full of vitamins and good for my pale complexion.

Sobbing, I closed my eyes and did as I was told, until finally he began to fall asleep. While he nodded off, I looked down in horror to see blood seeping from in between my legs.

*I am dying*, I thought.

Too scared to move, I was also petrified as I didn't want to get blood on his bedding. Eventually, I went and sat in his bathroom, salty tears streaming down my face. I was terrified that I was bleeding internally and dying. Within an hour, Dad woke from his drunken doze.

'I am hurt,' I sobbed, showing him the blood.

He scoffed and told me to wash the candle and black object, but first I had to carefully remove the stockings to avoid soiling them. Dad very carefully returned them to the packet as if they were the most precious thing.

'Clean everything else,' he barked. 'I don't want Johnny asking questions tomorrow.'

I spent ages scrubbing at the sink, my tears dripping into

the blood. By the time I had finished, I could hear the birds starting to chirp. Their cheerful song made me want to cry.

*After all, what was there to be so happy for?*

After falling asleep for what seemed like only minutes, Dad called for me to get up. I was exhausted and in pain. Sean was already at the breakfast table and teased me for being a 'Lazy Bones'.

Dad had the record player on as usual. 'Puppet on a String' was blaring out and that's what I felt like.

'This is by Sandie Shaw,' he said. 'She's an amazing woman, she always sang in bare feet.'

I couldn't believe that he was acting as if nothing had happened the night before. If I didn't know any better and if I hadn't just hidden a blood-stained sheet in my wardrobe, I'd have thought I'd had the worst nightmare ever.

Despite Dad telling me he had morals and wouldn't have sex with me himself until I was older, he decided after all not to wait any longer. The night after the black object incident, which I later learned was a vibrator, he climbed onto me and raped me for the first time.

All through the day he had worked up to it, eyeing me up as if I was a piece of meat. He'd made me wear a skirt and told Sean to go out and play while he was helping me in the kitchen, making lunch. As I was preparing the vegetables, he groped me under my skirt. I'd try and hop out of his way but he'd drag me back.

He drank his whisky or homebrew constantly. His music was always blasting out too. Often, I used this to my advantage, making it a conversation we could engage in, taking his mind off raping me for as long as possible. One song he played was 'Ben' by Michael Jackson. Dad told me excitedly that the song was about a pet rat – I don't think he interpreted the song as I did, he just went on to say that Ben got killed and how sad it was. However, the song reminded me of myself and to this day, it still takes me back to that little girl all alone in Africa with her daddy, who made her feel rejected, very, very sad and confused. I too was running away from fear and longed for a friend like Ben in the song.

The night of the rape, I had no idea what he was going to do. He made no excuses and no apologies afterwards. Without saying anything else, he ran a bath and ordered me to step in and wash myself first internally with soap. He didn't only rape me the once but over again. I was like his new toy, one with which he was so infatuated, he couldn't leave me alone. If my life was bad before, it was a whole lot worse now.

Eventually when he'd finished, I lay there in silence, tears pouring down my cheeks, running into my hair. He didn't have to say anything but I could tell Dad felt like this was an achievement – he'd got what he wanted.

'Remember,' he growled afterwards, leaning across his bedside table to take a swig of whisky and light up a cigarette, 'this is what every daddy does to their daughter. It's just nobody talks about it. If a boy had done this to you, he wouldn't be as caring as me.'

I didn't even know what 'this' was, I just knew this was deeply wrong and made me feel disgusting. *Was it really something every father did?* I found it hard to believe, but then who was going to believe it happened to me either? I lay there quietly crying, but not wanting him to see me cry as it would only make him angrier. Then I turned my head away and lay for what seemed like hours but was only minutes, confused about what my father had just done and longing to be back home in England. After that, rather than spend any longer with Dad, I went through to my own bed and cried myself to sleep.

From that night on, Dad raped me most nights, but not every night. Somehow this made it worse because I never knew exactly when it was going to happen. I'd always be on my guard, expecting to hear my bedroom door open at night-times, only to wake up the next morning and find he'd left me alone. The worst thing was I didn't benefit from knowing I'd be safe from him that night, instead, I dreaded every bed-time. Even throughout the day, he'd make me sit on his knee or grope me when Sean wasn't looking. Once, he turned up the volume on the record player to drown out any sound ('December, 1963 (Oh, What a Night)' by Frankie Valli & The Four Seasons) before forcing me onto his lap to rape me while Johnny was in the kitchen. When he'd finished, he screamed at me to get a cloth, pretending I'd spilled drink down his shorts.

My life had become unbearable – I didn't know where or when he'd demand to rape me or ask me to rub him. It was worse when Sean wasn't there as he'd make lewd remarks all day so I'd know he was building up to one of his lengthy ordeals.

One Sunday, when Johnny was away and Sean was at a friend's house, I was in the garden in an area that was not visible. If someone had pulled in the drive or come through the garden gate, they wouldn't have been able to see us. Dad called me over like I was an obedient dog and I went to him, thinking he wanted to show me some flowers or something like that. Instead, he ordered me to take my pants off and touch my toes.

I thought this was strange but did as he asked. Suddenly I felt the most excruciating pain: he rammed himself so deep into me that I nearly fell right over. He grabbed the hair at the back of my head while pushing back and forth. I tried to keep my balance and bit my lip so hard, it bled. Eventually it was over and he went off to light a cigarette and came back with a tumbler of whisky with a pink elephant cooler in it, as he always did.

He loved to rape me with any objects – the vibrator, candle, bottles – anything he could lay his hands on. He'd marvel at the female anatomy, as if it was a sick challenge to see how much of an object he could get to disappear inside of me despite my screaming out in pain.

Not only did Dad swear me to secrecy, he made sure I was too scared even to contemplate telling anyone. He never actually said the words, 'I will kill you,' because he didn't need to.

A few weeks after the first rape, once he'd finished, he whipped out a plastic bag and in one swift movement, pulled it over my head. He twisted the bottom of it tighter and tighter as I grappled with him to stop, but he held firm, saying nothing. Almost immediately I was unable to catch my breath, panting for air, as panic overcame me. In vain I tried to push him off as I felt myself fading.

*I am going to die. I am going to die …*

I opened and opened my mouth, wanting to find my voice,

but nothing emerged. I began to feel myself going, just as he whipped the bag off again.

Gasping for air, I clutched at my throat as I turned my head away from him. With whisky-soured breath, he spoke into my ear.

'You know what I do for a living?' he spat. 'I work in a lab. I can dissolve bodies with sulphuric acid. Nobody would ever know. The only part I can't dissolve is teeth. So how do you think I'd get rid of teeth, Kim?'

'I don't know,' I sobbed.

'Pretty easily when we go on another safari. I could just throw them in the *bundu* [Swahili for 'bush'] and pretend the lions have eaten you,' he whispered.

As I trembled with fear, he took my hand and forced me to touch him over and over again. I closed my eyes, willing it to be over. I decided then it would be easier if I just allowed him to do whatever he wanted. The plastic bag was always kept under his pillow as a reminder of what might happen if I even contemplated resisting.

Thankfully, just before our first Christmas in Kenya in 1976, we finally started our new school. It would have been normal to feel nervous about being the new girl, but I was so eager to escape from Dad for the day that I embraced school life with excitement.

Quickly, I made friends: other girls from expat families, who also welcomed me into their groups. One was a bubbly Canadian called Claire Harrison and another was Bridget Tooley. Although Dad had changed my life forever, he hadn't destroyed my personality completely. I still liked to laugh with friends and play the joker whenever I could. My way of surviving was to make the most of every second of school. Nobody knew what was happening at home so it was my chance to feel 'normal' again.

We all bonded over our dislike of Alison Long, the posh owner of the school we attended, who was known to be a rather wealthy woman. We laughed at the slow way she spoke to Africans in Swahili. A somewhat forbidding-looking woman, with a hard face, none of us dared cross her. She had two daughters, Kirsty and Claudia. Kirsty was the eldest and Dad always told me she had learning difficulties.

I was often invited around to my friends' houses, but Dad hardly ever allowed me to go. Only once did Bridget come over after school. We were chatting when she told me how much fun it was to be a lesbian.

'What's that?' I asked.

'Girls who kiss girls,' she laughed.

I was still learning about sexuality, so I just changed the subject, not understanding what she was on about. Later, I repeated the conversation to Dad at dinner time. He often quizzed me closely on my day and I always told him everything. During those conversations, he would show a keen interest in me in a way Mum never had done. Part of me felt relieved by this ordinary fatherly attention, despite what he did at night.

He looked shocked when I told him what had been said.

'You're not to have Bridget round again,' he told me.

'Why?' I asked.

'Because we don't want lesbians in this house. They're not normal and should be put down at birth!' he snapped.

This upset me, as I liked Bridget, but as Dad had made her

out to be such a weirdo, I didn't want anything to do with her after this episode.

A few weeks later, because Dad was out for the night, I was allowed to stay over at Claire Harrison's house. When I woke in the night and needed the loo, I spotted her mum and dad walking around the house stark naked, so I asked Claire about it.

'Oh, they're naturists.' She shrugged. 'Means they don't always wear clothes.'

Later, when Dad quizzed me about my stay, I told him what I'd seen.

'Being a naturist means you don't like wearing clothes,' I explained.

'What?' he yelled. 'That's disgusting! They're weirdos and paedophiles. You're not going anywhere near that house again.'

I didn't have a clue what the word 'paedophile' meant, but because of his menacing tone, I decided not to repeat it to Claire.

Around March 1977, Dad bought me a bushbaby for my twelfth birthday. This tiny primate with the most adorable large eyes and ears peered out at me from a cage. I fell in love instantly and decided if it was a boy, I would name him Ben after the song I loved – my friend Ben.

I took the cage with me everywhere, patting this timid creature so he could get used to me. One day, my friend Kathryn was dropped off after school by her parents so we could go through some schoolwork together, a rare occurrence. Unbeknown to me, the cage wasn't fastened properly on Ben's cage and Kathryn's dog, who she had brought along with her, stuck his head in the cage, dragged my beloved pet out and ripped him to pieces on the wooden floor. With both of us sobbing hysterically and me doing my best to comfort my friend, Dad came in to see what all the commotion was. He went berserk and demanded I leave Kathryn alone and clean up the mess. Kathryn went home and after I had cleaned poor Ben up, I went to my room and sobbed.

The quality of teaching at school was of a higher standard than back in Horsforth, Leeds, and the teachers really encouraged pupils to follow their talents. Here, I discovered that I excelled in sports. I was very good at the high jump, long jump and sprinting and also made the hockey and netball teams. My PE teachers recognised I was talented and even wanted to put me forward for further training, with a view I might even make an Olympic team eventually.

I couldn't wait to tell Dad. Part of me sought his approval, probably because I had no one else to seek approval from. I didn't have any other adults to speak to either – he was my only sounding board, something he used to his advantage. I viewed him as being the clever one in his family, but also part of me hoped he might stop hurting me if he could see how hard I tried at school. But if I expected him to be pleased, he wasn't: Dad immediately said no when I mentioned the prospect of training in sports.

'Sports is not a career, Kim,' he said casually. 'What are they teaching you at that school? You couldn't ever win a thing, so get that out of your head! Plus, I don't want you wearing shorts and showing your legs off.'

I felt totally crushed. I never pursued the idea of a sporting career again although I played an active role in the netball and hockey teams and won Overall Best in everything on sports day.

At lunchtimes, I often used to wander around the huge school grounds and one day I spotted a dishevelled-looking thin guard dog, sitting with an Askari (native security guard). I worked out from what he said that the dog was called Usiku, Swahili for 'night'. The next day, I saw Usiku by himself, tied up with a large chain in a shady area where no children ventured. Despite his frightening look, there was a loneliness I recognised in him and I felt strangely drawn.

The dog took a lot of coaxing before he learned to trust me but eventually, he backed down. As I moved towards him cautiously, he snarled as I approached. As I held my hand out so he could sniff me, he flattened his ears. I sat down next to him.

After that, I visited him whenever I could, sneaking him some of my lunch until I knew he trusted me. The dog would eagerly scoff the food and lick my hand, looking for more. He wasn't always there, but soon learned to trust me and would lift his tail from between his legs and give it a wag. He whined a little, his ears tightly laid back against his head, which suggested to me that he was fearful and timid. Despite this, I could tell he loved the attention and the fact that someone was being nice to him. He soon backed off and would hide if anyone else approached. Sensing I could trust him, in a world where I felt I could trust nobody, I started to confide in him about my awful dad and I'd tell him how I'd escape one day.

'He attacks me every night,' I confessed, allowing a tear to roll down my cheek. 'He makes me touch him. I hate it. He makes me feel sick, the look of him, the smell of him. He hurts me so badly. Nobody can know. But I can tell you, can't I?'

Usiku cocked his head as if listening to me with sympathy. He had beautiful eyes.

One day, I went to visit him and he wasn't there. I went the day after and the day after that, but I never saw him again. I was so upset.

Back home, Dad continued to confuse Sean and me with his mood swings. On the one hand, he could behave like a 'normal' father, buying us bikes and a huge Scalextric set for my brother, but then his generosity flipped into him losing his temper with frightening speed.

One night, Dad went out, leaving Sean and me in with Johnny watching us. I went to bed in my own room but was woken by the commotion taking place at around midnight when Dad returned. Johnny had already retired to his servant quarters and Dad made his way to his own bedroom, where he found Sean in his bed. Dad yelled for me and, half-asleep, I ran to his bedroom. There was a massive half-eaten bag of black licorice toffees on the floor. Most had been unwrapped and were stuck in the sheets and blankets. Sean had a black gooey mess all over his face and on the pillowcase where he'd been sleeping. He'd obviously fallen asleep while eating the sweets!

I'd have laughed as it all looked so funny but I didn't dare. I was glad Dad's bed was a sticky mess. Sean began to stir, obviously wondering what all the noise was about.

Dad dragged him out of bed, demanding he get cleaned up. I got the blame as my brother was much younger and could have choked. Dad screamed at me to remove the sheets and replace them but the next morning, he too was laughing about it. Because Dad was laughing, Sean and I were able to laugh too.

One Saturday, Dad bought a huge play set of figurines for us to paint. At first it seemed like a fun thing to do, but he soon turned what should have been an enjoyable activity into drudgery. Using tiny paintbrushes, we had to sit and paint for hours, something Sean found boring. But Dad didn't care – he ordered us to finish a certain number a day or we'd face a punishment of some sort.

Sometimes, if Sean wandered off, I'd quickly paint his models for him. I hated seeing him get into trouble with Dad. Often, he hit or spanked my brother for the slightest thing. Sean started to spend a lot of time around his friends' houses to escape. This suited Dad, especially at weekends or nights. It meant he had more opportunities to rape me for as long or short a time as he wanted, and it was something he found hard to resist. I never knew if Sean heard anything when he was around. He certainly didn't say anything or try to see what was happening – I suspect he was too frightened to do anything.

Dad was careful to make sure Johnny was never around either when the attacks took place. I always dreaded the moment he was dismissed for the day in the evenings. He'd return to his separate living quarters just outside the kitchen. They were not attached to the main house so I knew nothing could be heard. At weekends, he'd go home to his family. He knew Dad hit me and I could see him eye my bruises sometimes. With his warm and gentle nature, I knew he was full of sympathy for me, but what could he do? He relied on this job to feed his family. Even when from the outside it looked as if we were a normal family, I guess he knew we were not.

Even a simple board game could make Dad lose his temper. He forced us to play games like Risk, a tedious activity where players moved troops around a battlefield. Of course, Dad liked to play the enemy. Sean and I would try to find something to laugh about while we played, but Dad never found the funny side and my brother was always unaware of Dad kicking me under the table. He'd upturn the board, making pieces fly everywhere and then he'd yell at us both. Frightened, we would sit there with straight faces, not knowing what to do and sometimes we'd run off.

Our most dreaded day of the week, Sunday, continued to get worse.

One week, Dad bought a bottle of Lea & Perrins Worcestershire sauce. As it was imported from England, it must have been very expensive. He only bought it to get the exact same ingredients and compare the taste with homemade. He demanded I make him a sauce that tasted exactly the same. After giving me the ingredients – proper molasses, anchovies, the right amount of vinegar, etc. – he stood over me, whisky in hand, as he watched me in tears, trying over and over again to get it right. There was no recipe so it was purely trial and error to start off and took ages to make. Each time he tasted the sauce he said it wasn't right so I'd have to start all over again while he barked orders at me. Eventually, on the umpteenth go, he nodded.

'That tastes exactly the same,' he said, pleased.

He called the sauce 'Beaumont's Worcester Sauce' (after his surname), designed his own label and got me to decant it into bottles. Over the next few weeks we had to make ketchup and mushroom sauce to sell in a local shop. Sean was roped in to help. Often, we would scald our hands as we tried to sterilise the glass bottles without breaking them. My brother and I also had to stick all the labels on the bottles once they had cooled.

When the season for string beans came in, we were ordered to prepare them for the Sunday dinner. Dad showed us how to pull the whole string off in one movement. If it snapped, he would also snap, yelling at us to do better. He was obsessed with getting the string off completely. If he ate a cooked bean at the table and it hadn't been stringed properly, he would go berserk at me. Mealtimes became highly stressful as I dreaded him finding a missed bean. He was always reminding me I was like Mum and it was my fault I was like her.

Sean earned a slap as often as me this time. But it was Yorkshire puddings we dreaded making the most. Dad was obsessed to the point of OCD that they should be made with what he saw as the perfect level of crispness and height. The baking tins had to have the right amount of lard in them and be piping hot. The oven must be the hottest it would go and the wire rack placed high up in the oven. I'd have to time the fat for about five minutes, quickly open the oven door without letting any heat out and pour the batter into the hot fat at lightning speed, then get the tray back in the oven even faster without spilling anything whatsoever. The batter had to be a particular level to ensure the right height too.

I prayed the puddings would rise properly otherwise I would be in trouble. Often, I burned my hands through holding the tins with a thin tea towel but I didn't dare complain or Dad would have yelled that the fat was going cold. The gravy had to be made properly too. We weren't allowed Bisto (we couldn't get it in Kenya anyway) and so it had to be made from scratch. If the puddings and the gravy were not right, the mood and atmosphere at the table throughout the entire meal would be terrible.

By the time it was dinner time, I'd be at the table, exhausted and needing my bed. Sean and I would be made to feel extremely uncomfortable and Dad's rants when the food wasn't right would be just so awful. I tried hard to get everything perfect, but it was my first attempts at cooking as a young girl and it just wasn't possible.

The punches and kicks at the table became so common, I was constantly bracing myself. He'd slyly kick my shins underneath the table so no one could see. I tried my hardest not to cry. Dad often made out to others that there was something wrong with me.

'Kim is such a cry baby! There's always tears for no reason,' he would say, tutting to Johnny or Sean or a neighbour who'd popped round.

Soon, I stopped crying. Dad didn't care if I cried or not. Nobody did, so there seemed little point – it almost felt as if my tears had dried up.

At weekends, we'd often have to have wine with our meals. Sean always hated it, holding his nose and sipping slowly. At first, I did too, but the drink made it easier to switch off and pretend my body didn't belong to me later on when I was lying in bed with Dad on top of me.

# Chapter 6

Life hadn't been perfect at home with our mother back in the UK, but at least we knew she loved us. She liked to give us hugs and called us 'love'. Even though we were smacked sometimes, the memories of her when I was younger, doing mine and my sisters' hair in ribbons, dressing Sean in smart trousers and a lovely jumper and taking photos of us, were something I clung to. We three girls would have matching coats and Sean had a green Parka. He'd pull the hood up, exposing the fur trim.

The longer we spent away from Mum and the greater the abuse I was forced to endure, the more desperate I was to go home. Mum never had much of a bad word to say against Dad. However, he didn't hesitate to slag her off whenever he could. After downing his whisky at night, he told us stories we'd never heard before. He blamed her for having to leave his job in Nigeria and for having to leave Sudan, where Sean was born.

'She would flirt with my colleagues because she was such a tart,' he told us one night. 'She's nothing but a common drunk. The bottom of a bottle is more important to her than any of you were.'

Whatever he said about our mother, it didn't stop me missing her. I would go to sleep thinking of her, hoping she was thinking of us. It might seem strange but I can't remember Sean saying anything about this. I don't think he had it as tough as me – he could go out and stay over with friends so I think he was happy to go with the flow and not make a fuss.

About six months after we'd arrived, Dad finally said we were allowed a phone call home to Leeds.

'I have her number and you can call from the house phone,' he said, carefully watching for our reaction.

Sean and I were so excited. We couldn't quite believe we'd finally get to speak to Mum after all this time. I was smiling, though deep down, I had reservations too. After all, I'd written to her a few times now and not once had she written back. I'd told her we didn't like it here, although it never crossed my mind to explain what Dad was doing to me – I still believed he'd kill me if I did.

Dad explained he was the one who had to call Mum as she couldn't afford to ring us, then she had to give permission to accept a call from Nairobi. Before he picked up the receiver, he gave us a look which told me we didn't have long.

I swallowed down a rising feeling of wanting to cry. I wanted my mum. I wanted to talk to her properly and honestly so she could come and take us home. I also missed my sisters Susan and Lucy too. Playing outside in the orchards all day long seemed like a lifetime ago now.

I wouldn't ever complain about the cold in her house or feeling hungry again because anything, *anything*, was better than this. All these thoughts went through my mind while Dad glared at us.

Finally, the call was put through and as we heard the beeps, he whispered one final warning: 'Remember, I'm listening to every word,' he hissed.

Mum's voice emerged faint and crackling at first, but clearly it was her.

'Hello, Kim love, how are you doing? Oh, it's lovely to hear your voice!' she said. 'It's been ages, hasn't it? Are you okay?'

There was a slight lag on the system so we had to wait a few split seconds before we could answer. I bit my lip so hard, it almost bled. Just hearing the sound of Mum's voice made me want to sob into the receiver. But Dad was standing so close to me, I could smell his whisky breath.

'Yes, Mum,' I said loudly as he leaned in to try and listen. 'How are you doing?'

After around thirty seconds of stilted chat about the weather and our pets and asking after Susan and Lucy, Dad started to lose patience. He pushed Sean into my side to indicate it was his turn.

'Mum, I have to go,' I said, cutting her off as she asked more questions. 'Sorry, bye!'

Dad snatched the phone and passed it to Sean. After about thirty seconds more, he hissed in our ears: 'This call is so expensive, say goodbye!'

Sean tried to say goodbye but his voice dissolved into tears. I knew he'd face a slap for crying after he put down the phone to Mum.

When it was over, Dad yelled at us to go and start painting our quota of model figurines for the day. These all had to be placed in Sean's Hornby railway set. There were scenes like pubs and train stations and each figure had to be recreated as if it were real. Dad said he wanted the entire thing finished by the end of the week.

The model railway, something our father appeared to buy for our pleasure, had turned into something we'd grown to resent. Back in our rooms, we sat in silence, lost in our own sense of misery. We both missed home in Leeds so badly and we wanted Mum more than ever.

As I brushed paint onto each model's face, I thought how it reminded me of my own. I was trapped like one of these little statues, unable to move, unable to say anything.

*At the mercy of Dad, as his plaything.*

By now I was living a double life. On the outside, I was Kim Beaumont, a sporty girl who had plenty of friends and loved animals. On the inside, behind closed doors at Jamhuri Crescent, I was an anxious, withdrawn, frightened little girl, living with a father who raped her sometimes up to four times daily.

While I struggled with the turmoil inside, Dad's confidence about what he was doing grew. He even began to make innuendoes in front of people at the Woodley Club about what would happen to me when we got home.

There was a catchy new song called 'Telephone Man' by Meri Wilson and Dad would play it on a Friday night at the club, then sing it to me in front of laughing expat guests. To them, it was just a joke between father and daughter. To me, it was terrifying but I had no choice but to laugh along. Inside, however, I was trembling, knowing what awaited me when we got home.

Later, Dad would sing the lyrics while raping me. He'd tell me the woman in the song was a slag and obviously gagging for it.

The terrible toll of missing sleep every night worsened. Each morning, I was utterly exhausted, but had to drag myself up to go to school. After a long day of lessons, I'd find myself dozing on the sofa, desperate for sleep by 10pm. Dad liked me to nod off just before Sean went to bed because then he knew he'd got me alone and I hadn't made things harder for him by jumping up to go to bed at the same time as my brother. As soon as he knew Sean was in his room for the night, he would prod me painfully in the ribs.

'Don't think you're escaping that easily,' he'd spit.

The abuse continued, escalating if that were possible. I'd have to wear the awful stockings and suspender belt around the house when Sean and Johnny were not there. Dad would leer at glimpses of the suspender belt below my skirt and pull me towards him.

'You're so sexy,' he'd say. 'You're all mine.'

It made me feel sick. I'd try to talk about something else or make an excuse that I'd forgotten something and dash off. I'd even pretend I hadn't heard him say anything at all. I'd try not to dress in things that he might find attractive – I'd wear baggy clothes to hide my shape but being so thin, I had no shape anyway. I wasn't allowed a bra: my breasts had started to develop and were visible under my T-shirts and clearly a turn-on for him in retrospect. Anyway, how does a girl in her early teens ask her dad to buy her a bra?

I was still so small and skinny, the stockings barely fitted me and I'd pull them over my knees. Looking down at my legs, they appeared as if they belonged to someone else. I felt like a piece of meat, as if my body belonged to someone else in a bizarre play. Except the audience was my dad and his own sick pleasure. My stomach twisted in knots as I knew what was coming next.

One evening, when Sean was out, Dad pulled a peculiar-looking object out from behind the fish tank, in which he had exotic fish called Guppies, with fanlike, spotty tails. He pulled off his underwear and demanded I use the pump on him to make his penis bigger.

'I'm aware I'm not that big,' he smirked. 'I want to be bigger for you. We don't want you looking elsewhere, do we, Kim?'

I didn't have a clue what he meant, but he showed me how to use the pump.

I don't know what was supposed to happen but all it seemed to do was make him want more and more sex. It was horrific. I tried to focus on the little fish swimming behind the glass in their exotic home, thinking I'd prefer to be one of those fishes right now than me.

Often Dad got so worked up, lust overtook wanting to finish up cooking in the kitchen. He'd forget what he'd been doing, the half-made bottles of sauce and other things were often thrown away as he fell asleep, tired and drunk.

Most nights, he would be snoring in the middle of it all. I lay there, blinking away hot tears as usual.

*At least it's over now, Kim*, I told myself one night, hugging myself to try and reassure myself. I rolled over to try and sleep, but just as I started dropping off, Dad pressed himself into my back, clawing at my body again. This attack went on and on until 4am.

I woke again at 7am as the alarm went off for school.

'Get up or you'll be late,' he growled.

Dad made me a coffee, humming to himself as he got ready for work. He must have been tired too, but I knew he'd go into the university late or have a nap at lunchtime to make up for it. For me, there was no chance of catching up on sleep.

The knock-on effect of the sleep deprivation inevitably affected my schoolwork. My grades began to slip, something I knew would anger Dad. My teachers were forever talking about my school report. They'd pull my father in to discuss it, but he'd just say I wasn't naturally gifted and that I needed to work hard as I lacked intelligence. I remember one teacher looking distinctly uncomfortable when he said something like, 'Kim will never amount to anything. She's backward, like her uncle.' This was in reference to my Uncle Jake, mum's older brother, who was born with learning difficulties. 'Obviously in that side of the family as her mother is thick too,' he added. However, he did offer to supervise my homework, which made me more fearful as I knew what that meant.

If only my teachers had known the truth. In his Queen's English, clean shirt and collar and newly dry-cleaned jacket, Dad was so convincing – the epitome of the perfect father.

By then, I still hadn't started puberty. Dad continued forcing me to drink cod liver oil or melted Kimbo to fatten me up. He also continued to suck hard on my breasts, telling me he was 'encouraging' my development. At the same time, he seemed relieved I'd not started my periods because he said he didn't need to worry about pregnancy.

Even then, I still had no idea how I could get pregnant. Or what sex was, although I had an idea it was what Dad was doing to me. There was no sex education at school, nobody talked about it. As my body slowly began to develop into a womanly shape, I hated it. Putting on weight on my tummy and boobs, my hips widening, made me feel even more self-conscious.

Whenever I could, I chose to wear shapeless baggy jumpers or bottoms. I didn't want anyone to look at me; I didn't want to look nice. I definitely didn't want any boys to find me attractive. Ideally, I would have faded into the background and disappeared if I could.

One evening, after yet another attack, Dad smeared my face with his semen. He masturbated on my face and made me leave the semen there. Instinctively, I'd gone to wipe it off, but I was forced to sit there with it on my face, bits dripping down into my eyes and mouth and onto my lap and the floor. Sometimes I had to sit with it until it started to dry on my face, then I'd go and scrub away at it with a facecloth.

'Sit with that on your face and don't touch it,' he smirked the first time he did this. 'You've got spots. It's good for your skin, it'll help clear them up.'

His face was full of concern, like he genuinely cared about me, however briefly.

I sat up in bed, blinking in the half-light of the moon through the curtains, feeling sick to my stomach as the stuff dripped off my chin. Although desperate to run into the bathroom and scrub my face clean, I knew better than to defy my father so I sat there feeling like a ghost and stared outside, willing time to go by.

*Wishing my life away. Wishing I was anywhere but here. Wondering if it was possible to wish yourself dead.*

# Chapter 7

One afternoon, at the end of the school day, Alison Long – the owner of the school – approached Sean and I in the playground.

'Today, I am taking you back to my house,' she said. 'And your dad will pick you up later.'

I looked at my brother in confusion. *What was she on about?* Before we had chance to ask, she walked towards the car park and her orange Toyota Corolla like we were expected to follow her.

As she opened the car door for us to slide onto the back seats, I looked over my shoulder. I wondered what was happening and what my friends would think if they saw me.

As we set off, I spotted the leftover school dinners in big shallow silver trays in the footwell of the car. As Alison turned the corners sharply, the contents slopped over the edge. I wrinkled my nose at Sean. Everyone hated the dinners at school – the stews, the casseroles, the pasta dishes all seemed to have the same sloppy, salty consistency.

We arrived at Alison's house, a large colonial-style white

mansion. Still not saying anything, she nodded for us to go inside, where her daughters, Kirsty and Claudia, were watching TV. Alison told us to sit on the sofa as she went to reheat the slop on the tray. She served the leftovers on two plates for our dinner and then told us our dad was coming.

We sat in silence as Alison's children stared at us as we poked at the mess on our plates. Kirsty stared at us in a particularly strange way. I remembered how Dad had said she had learning difficulties, but she looked normal to me. After a while, we gave up trying to eat the revolting dinner and watched TV instead. I just wanted to go home and see my pets – the one thing I had to look forward to every day.

Hours later, Dad finally turned up. There was something in the way that they looked at each other that made me think that they were together. They seemed such an odd couple. Alison was in her fifties and Dad was in his early forties. Without any explanation it was clear they were now an item. Even then, I suspected Dad only wanted to be with her for the money. He said nothing about it as he drove us home – we were to simply accept this new relationship and that was that.

Later that evening, as he started pawing at me in bed, he told me what an old cow Alison was. How I was young and sexy in comparison. I felt sick. As always, I moved as far as I could to the other side of the bed to get away from him. I knew he'd get me anyway, but it was a natural physical response.

'What's wrong with you?' he growled. 'Kirsty likes it when I do it to her.'

Another wave of nausea swept over me as I thought of poor Kirsty. Was my dad raping Alison's daughter too?

The new relationship between Dad and Alison meant a new routine for us. Alison would take us home from school and then give us the school leftovers for dinner in a separate room while her daughters watched TV. Then Dad came over to have dinner with her later on. She had her maid prepare steak and other lavish food for her and Dad, but on rare occasions we would eat together and we would have their leftovers. Mostly, we were kept away from the pair of them until it was time to go home. Alison didn't even pretend she wanted us around – we were told to keep quiet and out of their way.

If I had hoped Dad would leave me alone now he had a new girlfriend, I was wrong. None of this stopped him raping me each night because bizarrely, he never spent a single night with Alison (we never stayed over with him either) and she never came to our house in Jamhuri Crescent. Later, he lied in court and said he lived with Alison, but he never did. It was a strange set-up, but we accepted the new normal as we had no other choice.

Months later, Dad told us he'd married Alison. She still didn't live with us and didn't have any plans to. It made me even more suspicious he was after her cash.

Shortly afterwards, Alison said me and her daughter Claudia were to leave our school and attend the Loreto Convent Msongari, an all-girls school in Nairobi's Lavington area in Kenya, while Sean was still at Braeburn. Neither of us had any say in the matter. It was a Catholic school run by nuns. I wasn't even Roman Catholic – Dad had lied to the school, telling them I was.

Days later, I cried as I was handed a new uniform. It was a scarlet, long-sleeved jumper with a white blouse to go underneath, navy, calf-length baggy skirt and white ankle socks. I was very scared. I'd barely had time to even say goodbye to my friends and each day I'd have to come home to Dad. Starting again was the last thing I wanted, but more upheaval was to come.

I hadn't been at my new school for very long when Dad had more news for us: Alison had told him she wanted me and Sean to be sent away to boarding school. Claudia and I had soon grown to hate the convent, which was run by strict nuns and having told Dad on a daily basis how awful it was, I was ecstatic at the news.

'I agree with her, it could be good for you,' he said.

After my last experience of a new school I felt a rising sense of anxiety. The last thing I wanted was to endure another Catholic school, but it was clear I had no choice and we were not welcome in Alison's life.

'Where will we go?' I asked.

'You have a place at Hunmanby Hall,' said Dad. 'In Yorkshire.'

My mouth fell open. We had been in Kenya now for almost two years. Would we really finally be returning to the UK? Sean was also going to boarding school, Woodhouse Grove Boys' School, just twenty minutes away from Mum's house. I was careful not to smile; I knew Dad would hate the idea of me escaping his control. If I looked too happy, he might cancel it. But as the date loomed for us to leave, I started to have doubts again: I didn't want to leave Johnny and my friends, they were the only thing that kept me going. Yes, I'd be free from Dad's attacks, but the idea of starting over again didn't appeal. The school was also about an hour and a half away from Mum's house so I knew she'd not be able to visit easily without a car. Of course, for Dad that's what appealed about the school's location – the last thing he wanted was for me to be seeing my family regularly.

As the time for me to leave grew nearer, his chats about keeping everything a secret intensified. He'd tell me I'd regret it if I told anyone about us and he'd know if I'd had sex with a boy (not something I wanted to do) – I'd definitely catch a disease and die. Soon, I decided any life was better than this.

If I dared imagine we'd just fly to the UK and Dad would say goodbye, I was to be sadly mistaken: he travelled over with Sean and me to stay over at Mum's in Leeds. Instead of going straight there, he arranged a stop-off in a London hotel for a couple of nights. All we wanted was to see Mum but he made it a long, drawn-out process. We had to traipse around London, bored stiff, seeing the sights.

As always, he made me dress up in a mini skirt and high heels and took me up to the room on his arm as if I were his wife. I was so embarrassed, I didn't look at the other people there, but I'm sure we must have got some odd glances. As soon as the door was shut, he attacked me, as always.

Dad hired a car in London so we could drive to Mum's. During the long journey up North, he complained bitterly about being tied to a woman he never wanted to see. He told us it was like having a noose around his neck.

'I got divorced for a reason,' he said. 'I never wanted anything to do with that headcase of a mother of yours ever again and because you want to see her, for reasons I'll never understand, it means I have to see her too.'

I closed my eyes, trying to block him out as he went on.

'She doesn't even like you,' he said. 'She doesn't care where you are or what you do.'

I ignored him. In my head I counted down the hours, minutes then seconds until I'd see our wonderful mother.

It was August 1978 and I hadn't seen Mum for nearly two years. That is such a long time for a child not to see a parent, especially a mother. I didn't really know it at the time but Dad had stolen so many important years from Sean and me and our mother – years we'd never get back, years spent apart.

Our three-bed council house looked the same from the outside as spots of rain pattered at the window. The streets seemed so small and grey here, but my tummy was in knots as suddenly I had such a longing to see my mother, I couldn't bear to wait a second longer.

As we saw her shadow at the door, a wave of unexpected shyness overwhelmed me until Mum's face broke into the biggest smile and I stepped into her outstretched arms. The smell of the cigarette smoke on her cardigan was so familiar. When we cuddled, she cried just as I did.

'Aw, love,' she said, kissing me. 'I've missed you!' She stepped back to glance at me. 'All tanned and grown-up.' She smiled, her eyes shining. 'You're looking so well.'

I bit my lip to stop my tears. I'd been forced to grow up in a way she'd never have imagined. A strange sense of sadness overcame me. I'd been through so much and Mum didn't have a clue about it. And ultimately, she hadn't been there for me. I realised then that the bond between us would never be the same.

Mum beckoned me in. As I followed her down the hallway, I noticed how skinny her legs looked compared to her bloated and fat face. Still in her late-thirties, there was a tiredness about her that hadn't been there before.

She ushered me inside. Susan was at boarding school, so only Lucy was there, looking so much older than I remembered her. We shyly said hello, and I wanted to sob again – we were sisters but felt like strangers. The days of us roaming the local orchards stealing apples or playing marbles seemed a million years ago.

Mum fussed around Sean and me, saying we could have something to eat. Dad followed her out to the kitchen and came running back to say the food was drab and her fridge was so filthy, he wouldn't eat anything from it.

'I'll go to the shop, Joan,' he told her.

He gave me a look. I knew it wouldn't be long before he started criticising Mum again. With him gone, I longed for her to tell us we didn't ever have to go back to Kenya, but instead her eyes were searching for the last fags in her packet as she made chit-chat about the neighbours. Then she poured herself a glass of Martini and sank into the settee.

'I know it's early, but it's a little celebration about you being home,' she giggled.

I wanted to believe her but I knew it was any excuse for a drink.

'So, tell me all about Kenya.' She grinned.

Like parrots, we recited all the nice bits – the safaris, the house, our pets, our friends. We just left out the beatings, the terror, the rapes.

Dad was back minutes later with snacks from the corner

shop. He made me eat them quickly, telling Mum we needed an early night before tomorrow when we were staying in Hunmanby village so we could buy my uniform.

'See you soon, love,' she said, giving me a big hug as we said goodbye.

Sean was allowed to stay at Mum's but I wasn't and it took every ounce of willpower to stop myself from screaming. It was so unfair. I longed to be able to sleep for one whole night without being disturbed but Dad insisted I go with him.

I wanted desperately for Mum to hug me and ask if I was all right. I wanted to tell her about what my own father was doing to me. Also, I wanted to tell her how I was dying inside, but I knew it wasn't worth the risk. Already I knew what Dad was capable of, and as he had menacingly told me many times: 'Who will believe you?' So, I forced myself to smile, gave Mum one last hug and climbed back in the car with Dad. He had booked us into the White Swan hotel in Hunmanby village.

When we arrived, Dad seemed delighted when the hotel receptionist mistook us for a couple – he'd made me change into adult clothes in the car. I didn't have a clue where he'd got them from. He waved me through, holding the doors open to me courteously and thanking everyone who helped us with our bags. Once again, I knew to the outside world he looked and sounded like a middle-class, educated gentleman.

The hotel was very old, with sloping floors, and our bedroom was dark and dingy. I wondered if the place was haunted, shuddering at the thought. The shared toilet was down a corridor – I hoped I didn't have to use it at night.

We had some sandwiches in our room and I think I may have had a glass of wine. I don't recall drinking lots myself – Dad had bought lots of barley wine and beer for himself. That night, my father raped me as usual, forcing himself on me for hours and hours, in between nodding off in a drunken stupor.

The next morning, Dad took me to the school uniform shop in the village, looking every inch the doting father to the outside world.

I had to try on a camel coat and uniform. As I stood in the changing room, trying on the shirt, skirt and woollen blazer for size, I wanted to weep. The clothing felt stiff and scratchy and swamped my tiny frame. I didn't want to be the new girl yet again. Dad paid for the lot, then bought me a bright red trunk with my name on. Afterwards we went back to the hotel and he booked us in to the downstairs restaurant for dinner.

Beforehand, we got ready upstairs. He laid out an outfit he wanted me to wear, including a short skirt, suspenders and heels. Like a robot, I put it on. Then he told me to sit on the bed and close my eyes. I flinched slightly as I sensed him move around me. He made me put my hair up and put on some make-up too. He twisted my shoulders around so I could see myself in the mirror opposite the bed.

*The girl who gazed back at me looked about five years older.*

'There,' he said, satisfied. 'Now we're ready for dinner downstairs.'

As I trotted down the stairs in my heels, I felt ridiculous and overdressed. I could sense the other diners glancing up. A waiter came over to ask what we'd like to order.

We had some sandwiches and a drink as Dad chatted about how brilliantly he was doing at his university, but how stupid the students were. They didn't realise how lucky they were to have a teacher like him, didn't I know? I nodded in all the right places, wondering how long he'd rape me for that night. Bone-tired, I was dreading my first day at school.

Once again, that night I was raped into the early hours.

By the time he'd finished I was desperate to escape, wishing we were back home in our house so at least I could go to my room. Here, I was scared of even using the toilet down the corridor so I lay awake until exhaustion overcame me. All I could think of was the safety of Mum's house in Leeds just a few miles distant but it might as well have been light years away.

# Chapter 8

Hunmanby Hall girls boarding school in East Yorkshire was a giant, forbidding brick building at the end of a long driveway and looked like the setting for a film where terrible things happened. Despite its appearance, it was one of the leading boarding schools in the country and on the way in the car, Dad lectured me about how lucky I was to be going there. I kept quiet, worrying I might be homesick despite all that had happened. Not for Dad, of course, but for my old friends and my pets.

After we parked up, the bursar came across the crunchy gravel drive to greet us. Dad gave his usual firm handshake before introducing me with what sounded like fatherly pride. Despite myself, I felt a pang of hope. For a few short minutes my dad seemed like a normal dad, with a normal relationship with his daughter – something I longed for so badly. I couldn't help wanting his love and approval, even though I got the exact opposite. He might have been an abusive monster, but he was the only parent I had, really

– I relied on him for everything and couldn't help but seek validation from him.

The teacher rattled through the school rules and we were shown around briskly. Pupils weren't allowed out any further than Filey town, three miles away. We had weekends off, but Dad had already said I wasn't to go anywhere without his permission. I knew that meant no popping back to Mum's. As usual, he was friendly, caring and kind to me in front of people, fussing about whether I had everything I needed and asking how often I could call home. He even pecked me on the cheek like an ordinary father as he said goodbye. The teacher smiled at him, obviously thinking what a loving relationship we had.

I was to be a full-time boarder, so I had to share a dorm with other girls. We had our own cubicles within these dormitories. I had mixed emotions – I felt excited at the prospect of being able to sleep uninterrupted but I also felt alone and terribly homesick. It was then that it dawned on me – despite the abuse, I depended on Dad for absolutely everything. He would tell me what to cook, what to eat, how to dress and what I could watch on TV. Not having my routine dictated to me suddenly felt very frightening.

I locked myself away in the cubicle, sobbing into my unmade bed. Soon, I fell asleep and woke to an exceptionally loud bell early the next morning.

The school was a vast labyrinth of corridors. Already I felt jealous of the day boarders who lived close to home as I watched them come in happily. My mum was an hour and a half away, so she lived too far away for that. I wished I could have gone to a school nearer her, as my brother had done. She might not be the best mother in the world, but I didn't doubt she loved me. She would give me a hug, and how I longed for a parent to do that, without wanting anything.

It took weeks to settle in but eventually, I made some good friends. My best friend was a girl called Lizzie. Her dad was a top barrister involved in some high-profile cases at the courthouses in York and Leeds. I remember she and I stayed with her parents in Weeton, just outside Harrogate, one weekend. Her dad was in court that day and we were playing roly-poly down the steep bank outside the court in York. Afterwards, we bought a custard slice each and sat at the back of her father's court eating them and kicking our feet against the wooden benches until we got some dirty looks and decided to leave! My other friends too were from middle-class backgrounds – we were all similar, being mischievous.

At school, we were allowed pocket money so Mum would send me £5 in the letters she'd write and slowly, day by day, I embraced my new freedom and ability to make decisions. I'd either buy sweets from the tuckshop or new jeans with my friends on a shopping trip. We'd choose really tight ones and then sit in the bath to shrink them even more. To be allowed to decide what to wear was wonderful. And to be able to sleep at night for the first time in years without being abused felt amazing. As a result, I could concentrate better in class and my grades improved.

Within a month, I found myself feeling more at home. All in all, life was good. At weekends, we'd roly-poly down the big grassy banks near the courthouse, buy vanilla slices and hang around the town like normal teenagers. Sometimes we even went to the White Swan to try and buy a drink, but with my friends I'd get chased out for being underage. Thankfully, the bar staff didn't recognise me.

Dad would write to me regularly. He spoke about getting a new dog for me when I got home. There was general chit-chat about Kenya, a place I didn't miss.

That first half-term, Dad allowed me to go and stay with Mum after all during the holiday and at weekends. I couldn't wait. We always had to travel in our school uniform, looking smart in public so we didn't bring the reputation of the school down, but as soon as the carriage doors closed with our teachers left behind on the platforms, we stripped off our uncomfortable uniforms and changed into jeans. I even threw my socks out the window while laughing with my friends. For the first time in what seemed forever, I felt completely free.

Despite her drinking, I was thrilled to be back home with Mum and Lucy (Susan was away at Queen Ethelburga's boarding school in North Yorkshire). Mum still couldn't cook very well and we were often hungry, but to hang out with my siblings like the old days was lovely. Not to be raped every night and to be allowed to sleep was heavenly.

Sometimes we stayed at Mum's friends' house, Eric and Debbie, who owned a B&B in Bridlington, only nine miles away from school. I loved Friday nights, knowing a whole weekend stretched ahead of me, but equally, I got terrible Sunday night blues, knowing I'd have to leave Mum again.

While eating dinner, we'd listen to *Top of the Pops* on Radio 1 so I could record a tape of the songs to listen to during the week. As the DJ counted down from 40, by the time they reached 10, my heart would sink as they got closer to revealing the number one record. By the time the last record was on, it was our cue to leave for the bus stop to start the journey back to school. I'd go really quiet, not wanting to leave Mum's side. After giving her a long hug goodbye, I'd cry all the way back to my dorm. It was always unsettling as I had to adapt to school life again. Having to adhere to the different bells, which meant different things, only being out as far as Filey (three miles max) on our own, often having to do classes on a Saturday morning, chapel every Sunday. Also, having to sleep in a dorm, although there were cubicles but these were separated by wooden panels. Some of the girls were loud at night, which made it difficult to sleep. No wonder it took a few days to settle in again.

After the first holidays with Mum, Dad started to come over to the UK himself to visit very occasionally for weekends but rarely during the school holidays as Sean and I were ordered over to Kenya three times a year. He sometimes travelled back with us to see us into school again, but not often. We often stayed in the White Swan. As usual, he'd dress me up to the nines and take me downstairs for a pub meal.

He always complained about how common everyone was and how awful the food was. Then he'd rape me in the bedroom. The rapes went on for hours and hours. He was so drunk, he'd fall asleep while doing things then I'd try to fall asleep too but he'd soon wake me up to start over again. This continued until the early hours. I never resisted as there was no point – I didn't want to alert other guests to what was happening, as I feared what Dad would do to me if anyone suspected anything.

After several months, Dad made it more difficult for me to visit Mum at the weekends by telling her I wasn't allowed to come or arranging for school holidays to be spent with him in Kenya. Mum never argued with him because she was intimidated by him. He always talked over her and often because she'd been boozing, she didn't have the willpower or strength to fight back.

Landing back in Nairobi felt like stepping back into a hellish existence I'd escaped from. Sure enough, I knew what would happen most nights. The only consolation was to see Johnny again. He was always so happy to spend time with me and wanted to know all about my new life.

During this trip, Dad took us regularly to a place called Hunter's Lodge, set in a beautiful location in Kiboko on the Mombasa Road, a good ninety-minute car journey from Nairobi. Despite the abuse I endured there, having first visited when I was twelve years old, I still loved the surroundings. It was an adventure for us kids because during the day we could run wild and free. There was a massive lake where you could fish for tilapia. We caught them in a big bucket and took them home to keep in our garden pond. There was a boating lake, so we could row out as far as we could go.

Once, I saw my first Monitor lizard there. Over a metre in length, it was so huge it looked like a dinosaur. We also spotted gazelle, monkeys and rock hyrax, incredible creatures that look like guinea pigs. Often, I went off on my own to explore. I loved catching fruit spiders, scooping them up in jars and bringing them back to show off to Sean. We'd sometimes come across them in Tsavo in our shoes – Dad always warned us not to leave our footwear out.

During one school holiday, my sister Susan was flown over.

I loved being reunited and Sean and I were thrilled to show off Kenya to her. Not once was I tempted to tell her about the abuse – I was still convinced nobody would believe me. Also, I didn't fear Dad would do the same to her. Susan had a very different relationship with our father to me – they'd clash and she would stand up to him.

*I doubted he would ever try to rape her.*

One evening when we were on holiday at Twiga Lodge in Mombasa, near the coast, I sat and listened to the warm wind's familiar swishing sound blowing through the palm trees off the sea. I wished I could sit there all night, drinking in the view and the sounds without knowing within hours it would all be spoilt by the inevitable abuse. It was the backdrop to everything in my life. I could never look forward to something so simple as an uninterrupted evening and night, something most people happily take for granted.

What bliss that must be, but for this girl, it was only a dream.

Dad was very sly about when and where he chose to abuse me too. During our trips to Mtito Andei on safari, he'd slip in the shower to quickly rape me before anyone else came in. He also insisted I'd sleep in the car with him, while Susan and Sean had the tent. How I sobbed, asking to stay with them despite being scared of the wildlife, but they thought I was lucky being allowed to sleep in the car. And anyway, Dad told them there was no room for them in the car. Back at home, he would wait until my siblings had gone to bed before sneaking into my room.

Nobody questioned why Dad made me sleep with him,

either in his car on safari or in his room at home. It was just accepted as the norm and nobody dared ask.

One day, while on holiday from Hunmanby Hall, I was sitting by a swimming pool near Hunter's Lodge in my school costume when Dad came over. The costume was blue and white with horizontal stripes and made me look chubbier than I was.

Instinctively whenever he was around, I flinched, folding my arms across my chest as he leered over my body.

'I can see your breasts,' he said. 'So, you're finally developing.'

I turned my head, pretending I hadn't heard him.

'Hope you don't wear the swimming costume elsewhere,' he continued. 'Your body is just for me to see.'

I shuffled over as he sat down next to me.

'You're putting on weight too,' he said, wrinkling his nose. You have childbearing hips, urgh! That costume doesn't suit you. I'm going to put you on a diet when we get home.'

True to his word, that afternoon he told me I wasn't allowed any bread or potatoes.

A few days later, back home he decided I should go on a 'liquid diet', which meant drinking only whisky or his homebrewed wine (he'd make banana or paw-paw wine, bringing 100 per cent alcohol home from work to add to the mix). It was beyond potent stuff. Just one sniff made me feel queasy, but he didn't take no for an answer. I'd be made to sit and finish a glass. By the end of the evening, I'd be so drunk I'd vomit in the bathroom, with a headache and dehydration.

Thankfully the school holidays always ended and I was

free to return to school. But before I did, Dad bought two more dogs, Rhodesian Ridgebacks called Digby and Bunty. As always, I instantly fell in love.

'You have to come home now,' he said, watching me make a fuss of him. 'Digby needs you.'

It was obvious Dad bought pets to try and tempt me back and often it worked, as I loved them so much. Not that I had much choice anyway.

I returned to school covered in bruises on the tops of my arms and my inner thighs. As I had them all the time, I barely noticed them but I knew better than to allow anyone else to either – the last thing I wanted was friends asking questions. During PE lessons, I always changed cautiously so nobody noticed, carefully pulling on my sports top underneath my school shirt.

Back at school, I received some news from Dad. He had moved house to a bungalow in a new, upmarket expat community called Loresho Grove and he'd sacked our beloved Johnny. He'd accused him of stealing from him, something I knew was a lie. I suspect this may have been because Johnny might have seen too much of the abuse. Perhaps he even said something to Dad; who knows? I cried when I found out. He was the one person at home I felt cared about us.

I never got to say goodbye and never saw him again.

Whenever I could, I still snatched visits to Mum's. On one rare weekend when I was fourteen years old, she took me out to a local pub, The Old King's Arms in Horsforth. Her drinking was constant by now, her favourite tipple still being Martini. Sometimes, when she visited me at school, she'd even share it with my friends, who all thought she was hilarious.

While drunk, she'd giggle with them, cracking silly jokes and telling me to lighten up. She'd pull me into a cuddle, calling me 'love', and sometimes I pretended she was just a happy soul, rather than a drunken one.

One Saturday evening, as we started drinking at the bar, a rather handsome chap with thick, curly hair came up to us. Mum knew him as the local butcher's assistant Will Myers and invited him to sit down with us to chat.

Seven years older than me, aged twenty-one, he had no idea of my real age as we got chatting. He had the most amazing smile and a shock of thick permed hair.

During our conversation Will made me feel at ease, especially as he winked across the table at me. By now I was suspicious of all men, thanks to Dad, but there was something very friendly and safe about this young man. By the end of the evening he hailed us a taxi to make sure we got home safely.

'I'd like to see you again, Kim,' he said. 'Here's my phone number.' He passed it to me through the cab window, giving me another wink that made me smile as widely as he did.

As I settled back in my seat, Mum looked pleased.

'Ooh, he's a nice man to have as your first boyfriend,' she said. 'You could do a lot worse than Squirrel.'

A boyfriend was the last thing on my mind as I knew Dad would go berserk if he ever found out, but on a whim I called Will the next day and we met up again.

Over the next few weekends, Will often took me out to the pub – The Old King's Arms where we'd met or The Old Ball. He would hold my hand but never tried to kiss me or do anything else. It felt like we had a lovely warm friendship, which was all I could handle anyway. When he started calling me his 'girlfriend', I didn't mind – he didn't seem interested in sex or anything like that, thank goodness.

One evening when we met up, he mouthed the lyrics to a new song to me over his pint.

'When You're in Love With a Beautiful Woman' by Dr Hook was the latest release and he knew all the words. Watching him sing to me, I blushed, but inside I was thrilled. For years, Dad had told me I was stupid, fat or ugly and here was a lovely man telling me the exact opposite. I was mesmerised by him in that moment. Maybe it was love, I couldn't say.

For more than a whole year Will and I secretly dated, always making each other laugh and feel cared for. Whenever I saw him after meeting Dad, I was careful to hide my bruises, but we never got intimate so I didn't need to worry about undressing in front of him. Being around a man who didn't want anything sexually from me made me feel safe.

I told Mum not to tell Dad about Will and she didn't until she got so drunk it slipped out, which she admitted on the phone one day when I was in school.

'Why did you tell him?' I cried.

'Sorry, love, it was an accident,' she said.

I dreaded the next letter or phone call from Dad, but strangely he never said anything. I let myself imagine, perhaps, he was even okay with it. But a few weeks later, as I turned up for class, I had a call from a teacher: I was to go to the head teacher's office immediately.

'I am afraid, Kim, we have to ask you to leave, on your father's request,' she said, looking genuinely upset.

'Why, what's happened?' I asked, immediately fearing for Mum or my siblings.

'Nothing to worry about, although your father is claiming the school isn't good for you. I must say I'm confused as I've checked your report and you're doing very well. Your grades have shot up. But your father is your legal guardian and it's his wish so there is nothing we can do, I'm afraid.'

I was told to collect my belongings and a cab would be waiting the following morning. I had been at Hunmanby School for about a year and a half by now and just like that, on Dad's whim, it was over.

Just before I returned to my dormitory to pack, I had to take a call in the office: it was my father.

'Have you heard the news?' he asked.

The sound of my hoarse voice from crying told him I had.

'Good. I have plane tickets to Kenya ready at the airport for you to collect.'

'But why, Dad?' I sobbed. 'What have I done?'

'The school isn't any good,' he spat. But deep down, I knew this wasn't the only reason, even if I daren't mention it.

'I like it here. Please. Please can I stay?' I begged.

His tone darkened. 'Do you want to end up like your mum? A drunk? Living in a council house? Because that's what'll happen. I won't be giving you any money, so you'll be penniless and she doesn't want you living with her anyway. You're coming home. And if you don't, you won't ever see those pets of yours again,' he snapped.

At this, I began sobbing. I knew he meant it. Also, it was true: I feared having a life like Mum's – booze had taken over her life. What choice did I have but to return to him?

As I packed up my bedside cabinet in my dormitory, I began to shake with fear. I felt trapped between the devil and the deep blue sea.

Dad had paid for the flight he'd booked from Leeds to Heathrow, then Heathrow to Kenya. I had to travel alone but I knew full well what would be waiting for me in that Arrivals lounge. Through my tears, I folded up my belongings, including my jeans, which I wondered if I'd ever be allowed to wear again.

Saying goodbye to my friends hurt, but little did they know when I cried that it was because I was petrified of what would be waiting for me when I arrived back in Kenya. I didn't even have the chance to say goodbye to Will. In a conversation with him many years later, he told me that he was devastated.

On the flight home, all I could picture was Dad's face full of fury. I squirmed in my seat at the very thought of what he'd have in store for me. By the time I landed on the runway, I wished I could run away into town and find help. But I had no money and I didn't know anyone; it wouldn't have even been safe. So, I closed my eyes and fantasised about staying on the plane for its return to the UK.

One day, I promised myself, I would be on that flight.

# Chapter 9

I walked alongside other ordinary passengers – visiting families, business people, tourists – to collect my bags.

*None of them are about to face what I'm going to*, I thought as I pulled my suitcase off the carousel. I would have swapped their lives with mine in an instant.

With knees like jelly, I walked through the Arrivals lounge, not even needing to look out for Dad's face in the crowd. He was standing directly opposite the door, his eyes scanning passengers like a predator waiting for its prey. Within milliseconds, his pupils landed on me, locking onto my face with a look that made me want to faint. He reached down and grabbed my bag, silently. I walked as fast as I could, not wanting to further anger him. When we got to the car, he opened the door and shoved me inside.

*He still hadn't said a single word.*

I sat as quietly as I could on the passenger seat as he slid into the driver's side.

We travelled in silence. With every beat of my heart, I anticipated the moment he'd explode.

A few miles in, he began speaking.

'I am so disappointed in you,' he spat. 'This is all your mum's fault. She wanted you to meet a boy so you'd stay and live with her and pay her rent. Hmm? Is that what you wanted?'

He jabbed me very hard with the knuckle of his left hand.

'Owww!' I moaned, clutching the top of my arm.

He did it again and again as he pulled onto the highway. All the way home he ranted at me:

*'You've probably got a disease.'*

*'How dare you think you could get away with it? You're so stupid!'*

With each insult came a small thump on my chest, my arms, the top of my thigh nearest him. I squashed myself up against the door, wishing I could open it and jump out. At traffic lights, Dad reached over for another hard thump before the lights changed.

By the time we arrived in Loresho, after a forty-five-minute journey, I felt black and blue. Tired and aching, I slowly got out of the car. I would have done anything not to have to walk into that house, but there was no escape. If I'd run off, he'd just run after me. I couldn't tell anyone – I had no one to tell and no one would believe me. I had no money anyway.

*There was no escape, this was my life.*

Dad opened the door. He made me walk past him so I flinched, anticipating what he'd do to me. We had a new houseboy called Joseph, who was there, wide-eyed, pleased to meet me, but his smile soon faded as he spotted the look on my father's face.

'Take the rest of the day off,' said Dad, waving his hand dismissively. Both me and probably the houseboy knew he wasn't being generous – Dad wanted time alone to punish me without a witness. In that moment, I missed Johnny more than ever. I was desperate to see a friendly face and someone who cared about me.

Once the houseboy had disappeared, Dad poured himself a whisky while he went berserk. His face turned the colour of a beetroot as he screamed into mine, 'If I catch VD from you, I'll be furious. I hope you haven't told anyone about us either!' Then he leered at me and went on and on, telling me what a useless person I was. How I was never going to get away with it. After putting the song 'Matchstalk Men and Matchstalk Cats and Dogs' on the record player loudly, he poured himself another whisky. He sat down to drink it, eyeing me up and down.

I stood, not knowing what to do; I didn't dare to sit down.

Suddenly, he marched me to the bathroom, grabbed a bar of soap and forced me to wash myself internally until I was in pain.

'That'll teach you,' he said. 'A dirty girl needs a good wash!'

Once I had dried myself, I sat sobbing on the bathroom floor, waiting for his next move. If I'd hoped he would at least let me sleep for a few hours to recover from the jet lag, I was wrong. That night, he had me up all night long and raped me over and over again. Often, he'd drop off to sleep midway then wake up and start all over again.

Just as I thought it was impossible for him to become more depraved, he did. He pulled out a video camera and filmed himself raping me, then watched it back, forcing me to sit next to him. I tried not to look, but as I saw him heaving himself on top of me, tears poured down my cheeks. I felt so ashamed, embarrassed and helpless. Watching it back was like watching someone else: my own body didn't belong to me.

The next evening, when no one was around, the family dog, Digby, got into the room. Dad started to touch the animal so he got it excited then encouraged him to lick me in private places and mount me. I twisted my head to the side as my father shouted at the confused animal, who whimpered, not knowing what to do but trying to lick what he could. Then he started a new game, getting me to rub the dog off while he'd film it. He'd then rub himself while watching the dog trying to do things to me. I closed my eyes, unable to believe what was happening to me.

*This was a whole new level of horror, including one of vile humiliation.*

The next morning, Dad got up early for work and left me to drink coffee alone. Aching all over, I sat and stared at the wall – I was so heartbroken to be back here. I listened in silence to the clock ticking on the wall.

Before I knew it, there was the sound of Dad's tyres screeching on the driveway later was enough to make me want to vomit as I knew what was coming. The only way I could cope was to become completely compliant. If I just let him do whatever he wanted to my body, it would be over faster.

The sessions of rape went on for several days until even Dad seemed to tire of the torture. It was then that he announced I had a new school place starting the following week: a private school called Hillcrest. Broken as I was, I could at least count down the days to escaping during the day.

On the first day of school, I felt like skipping out of the house. Ignoring the pain of my bruised body, I couldn't wait to go as it meant seven or eight whole hours away from the house and Dad. It meant meeting new friends too. It would have been normal for a young girl to feel anxious about starting all over yet again, but this time I embraced it.

*I could be myself again, even if it meant putting on a brave face.*

The school was several miles away. It meant Dad had to drive me to a bus stop and then it was a rough forty-five-minute ride. There was no suspension on the bus so we felt it turn every corner on two wheels, but I loved every second, watching the world rush by the window. The journey was heavenly as I could pretend I was free again.

Thankfully my new school lived up to expectations. The bus had been full of new faces too and that was exciting. Within a week or so, I'd made new friends, was losing myself in my beloved PE lessons again and revelling in the freedom. One new friend in particular, like me, also wasn't allowed to wear make-up, so we made a pact to dash to the loos to do our eyeliner before school began. We'd scrub it off on the bus on the way home. Even getting away with the tiniest act of rebellion made life worth living.

At Hunmanby, I'd started my periods. I'd already been very sore and bled occasionally after Dad attacked me, so the next time I had my period, I told him, hoping that he would keep off me.

This means I need to stop you from getting pregnant now, doesn't it?' he said.

That day, I faced the humiliation of waiting for my father

to buy me sanitary products for the first time. He chucked me a box of tampons, muttering that they were more hygienic.

All over again, I missed Mum. How I wished I had a female presence in my life to confide in – the thought of Dad monitoring my periods, which I guessed he would do, was too much to bear.

As I sat in the bathroom, feeling safe for once behind a locked door, I thought at least this must mean I was safe from his attacks that night. I even allowed myself to look forward to going to bed for a proper night's sleep. But as usual, Dad kept me awake until he was ready to go to bed. He nodded at his bedroom door, glaring at me as if daring me to say no. Meekly, I slid under the covers as usual, turning my back on him. I closed my eyes, pretending to sleep, as I heard him rummaging in his bedroom drawer.

'Get on all fours!' he barked.

Swallowing down a tremble in my throat, I did as I was told, like a robot. Dad pulled at my clothes before ramming something into me that made me scream in pain. I twisted around to see what he was doing, glancing between my legs to see a candlestick in his hand. He was forceful, but never yelled at me. Then again, he didn't need to – by now I was completely compliant in everything he wanted.

By the time he was finished, I was in agony. He then handed me the blood-soaked candle, which looked like a murder weapon.

'Go wash that,' he ordered, thrusting the candle into my hands.

Scrabbling to get my underwear back on, I grabbed the candle and took it into the bathroom. With the hand soap,

I clawed at the candle wax until it turned white again. As I watched my blood swirl down the plughole, I felt sick. How I wanted to disappear with it, scrub my whole body away and just vanish. Then I thought of Dad's threat of the acid and shuddered.

*Perhaps that really would be my fate in the end?*

The next day, I got home from school to find my father looking anxious to see me.

'Open your mouth,' he said.

Automatically I did as I was told as he punctured a piece of plastic in his hand with rows of tiny tablets. He pushed one onto my tongue and watched me swallow. Then he told me to open it again.

'Take another for good measure,' he said.

I swallowed again, not daring to ask for a glass of water to help.

'You need to take the contraceptive pill so you don't get pregnant,' he told me.

Over the next few weeks, my father made me take the tablets. I had no idea where he'd got them from as I hadn't seen a doctor myself. There was, of course, no question of him using a condom, and at the time, I wouldn't even have known what one was. Some days he forgot to give me any so he'd give me a few extra to make up for it. This quickly made me feel very nauseous. I started to vomit in the toilets at school and back at home before dinner. Soon I grew to hate the pills as I knew they would make me so unwell, but there was no way I'd dare refuse to swallow them.

Around this time Dad's divorce from Alison came through.

They had never lived as man and wife, and he clearly never received any money from her. Shortly afterwards she sold Braeburn and I never heard about her again. It was the end of another bizarre relationship. Increasingly, Dad seemed to talk to me as if he saw me as his wife instead. He wanted me to dress up and chatted to me over dinner as if we were a couple. He bought me presents, sometimes expensive clothes that made me look older than my years, other times, a new pet.

I viewed the pets as my friends. After all, they always listened to me. They never let me down, unlike the adults in my life. Dad also loved animals until he was angry. Then he'd kick or scream at them and I'd try and save them from him. Often, it was Bunty, my dog, he'd pick on. She got so excited that she'd wee on the floor and then he'd get very angry.

One night before bedtime, Dad put on the album *Surfer Girl* by The Beach Boys. I was in my room, when the song 'In My Room' was playing, and I clung on to the lyrics, tears streaming down my face. When they sang about a room they went to where they told their secrets to, it was as if they were talking about me.

*My dad was raping me and I was all alone in my room.*

By now it was 1980 and I had just celebrated my fifteenth birthday. Despite all of the abuse, all of his hatred, Dad could suddenly, when he wanted to, switch to being a loving father. Every birthday we had, he always made a fuss of me. In those moments I imagined again he might change. It was a fantasy I always clung to. There was no evidence he ever would, but I still longed for an ordinary loving dad who cared for me and, when he revealed these glimpses of himself, I hoped things might improve.

Once, he told me to invite a few friends over for my birthday. He rented a film (*The Rocky Horror Picture Show*) and all the reels and projector from the cinema. As he played the film, just like we were sitting in the cinema, he stood at the side drinking whisky, laughing at all the innuendoes and at the actors prancing about in stockings. Who knows what my friends thought.

Other times, Dad took me out at the weekends to the cinema, treating us to popcorn and sweets as we watched a film together. It was usually a boring film I wasn't keen on, like *The Empire Strikes Back*, but I was just happy to be out of the house. Very occasionally, he would also go for a whole week without attacking me. I had no idea why and never questioned it, just appreciated the peace.

When Sean was over for the holidays, Dad would take us to Hunter's Lodge for a weekend break, where all day long he'd be happy to explain the habitat of the local wildlife. During those times, my brother and I even kidded ourselves he might be mellowing. He'd speak with a quieter voice and appear genuinely paternal. Only it never lasted in the night-time for me, and it was never long before his aggressive side emerged again.

Sean only came home during the holidays and often not for long. He was happy to have escaped the house and stayed in his room whenever he could. I wondered if he suspected anything of what was happening. It was hard to believe he didn't know. But as a thirteen-year-old who was also scared of Dad, what could he do?

Once my periods started, Dad forced me to perform oral sex more often or even used a bottle on me. The pills he was force-feeding me still made me vomit but he religiously tracked my periods, logging when they were. He'd experiment with the pills, running them on sometimes so I wouldn't get a bleed at all, which suited him. Then one day he called me into the bathroom.

'You've not had a period,' he said, referring to a notepad, 'for, er, several months. I want you to do a pregnancy test. Please urinate into this cup.'

I swallowed hard, unable to believe this was happening. But I knew better than to argue, so I did as he asked. He looked at his watch while the stick changed colour. I didn't have a clue what it meant, but the look on his face warned me it was bad news.

'Oh my God, you're pregnant! Oh, how could you be?' he snapped.

I stood there, totally numb. It was as if I could hear his words but had a limited understanding of them.

*Pregnant? Me? With my own father's baby?*

It was an impossible series of events, even after years of rape and attacks. Something as innocent as a pregnancy didn't seem possible.

I stayed mute as Dad paced up and down, waving his hands around, occasionally shoving me backwards.

'Have you been spitting out your pills?' he spat in my face. 'You have really landed me in it!'

Abortion was illegal in Kenya. We'd have to go to a doctor. It could cost a fortune. All of this was my fault. I clutched my hands to my ears, waiting for him to stop.

'I could go to prison and so could you,' he continued.

Dad disappeared into the kitchen and then his bedroom. I guessed my pregnancy probably wouldn't stop him from attacking me but wondered what he was doing.

He came in with another packet of pills. Standing over me, he made me swallow them one after another with a whisky and ale. The sensation of swallowing so many at once made me retch. My body naturally wanted to reject them as they were like a foreign substance, poison that made me ill, yet I knew better than to argue. I swallowed as many as I could, bringing up foamy bile but forcing myself to re-swallow in-between Dad's yelling. When they'd all gone, I sweated with nausea and dizziness. I managed to hold them down for long enough for him to make himself another drink before projectile vomiting in the bathroom. By the time I'd finished, I sat on the floor completely exhausted.

The next morning, he made me repeat the pregnancy test. Then he called again, this time from the bedroom.

I walked in to find my father sat on the edge of his bed, untwisting a coat hanger with an electric torch by his feet.

'We're going to have to do something about your little problem,' he said.

# Chapter 10

My mouth went dry, as Dad ordered me to strip off my lower clothes.

'Hurry up!' he shouted. 'We haven't got all day!'

My whole body quivered as I wondered what he was going to do.

'Come here,' he said.

Tears dripping down my face, I did as he told me as he crouched down. He made me lie back on the bed with my legs in the air, then turned the torch on, using it to peer in between my legs.

'I estimate you may be twelve weeks gone,' he said.

As I squeezed my eyes closed, humiliation burned my face. Then I felt something cold and spiky as he shoved the coat hanger inside of me.

'Come on,' Dad muttered to himself as he jabbed it further and further into my body. 'I'm trying to reach the sac. Once that's punctured, the foetus will die and then come away.'

I winced as I felt a hideous scraping sensation internally.

Dad jabbed harder and harder as he grew more frustrated. The scraping soon turned into a stabbing sensation.

'We need to poke this thing out. I need to get up higher. Lie still. That's it, I need the angle to get a purchase,' he said, as if doing some DIY.

'Owww!' I yelled through gritted teeth. But I knew Dad wouldn't stop or try and be gentler. The humiliation turned into hot nausea; I gripped the bedsheets with white knuckles. The pain was horrendous. It was so deep inside, from beyond my belly button. I clenched my eyes shut as I tried to breathe. I felt so wobbly, I feared I might faint.

Dad finally sat down on his haunches, examining the end of the piece of wire.

'Only a bit of blood,' he mused. 'Right, let's try again.'

For the next fifteen minutes, my father used a coat hanger and torch to perform his DIY abortion. By the end of it, I was in agony, feeling parts of my body inside of me that I never knew existed before. By the time he'd given up, he was sweating with exertion. *And* anger.

'Why can't I get rid of it? Stubborn little thing, like you! Right, let's try something else,' he said.

He grabbed more boxes of pills. I had no idea where he'd got such a stockpile from. He started handing them to me one after another. I knew better than to argue, so I gulped them down, gagging after the first handful.

'Don't you dare chuck them back up!' he roared.

I carried on gulping, my head spinning. He handed me a glass of water so I could swallow the final few.

*How I hated those pills. How I hated him.*

My head spun with nausea. As I sat on the side of the bed,

I was trying desperately not to be sick as Dad disappeared. I waited for a minute, hoping he'd given up. But then he returned, a triumphant look on his face and a bicycle pump in his hands.

'Open your legs!' he snapped.

He fed the cold metal-tipped tube inside of me, then started pumping it as hard as he could.

'We. Need. To. Suck. This. Thing. Out,' he said, in between exerting himself on the pump. Meanwhile, I covered my face with the inside of my elbow, willing all of this to stop. This was painful, but thankfully not as bad as the wire coat hanger.

After a few minutes, Dad gave up again. It was clear the pump attachment wasn't long enough to reach high up enough inside of me.

That night, nothing would stop him from wanting to rape me and he was as vicious as ever with this assault. He told me that what he was doing might make the foetus spontaneously abort and even taunted me for being 'fat'. By the morning, he was worrying again about how to 'get rid of it'. This pregnancy was a problem that needed to be solved, as far as he was concerned. And quickly.

*The only problem was abortion was illegal in Kenya.*

My father might have been tracking my periods but due to him giving me so many packets of the pill, my cycle was completely messed up. He had no idea how far along the pregnancy was, so he booked an appointment to see our GP. On the way in the car, he gave me strict instructions on what to say.

'You cannot tell the doctor the truth. If you do that, you will be forced to have this baby and you will be locked up in jail. Nobody will ever come and see you and you'll be known as a slag. Is that what you want, Kim?' he warned.

At this, I shrank even further in the passenger seat.

'No, Dad,' I whispered.

'You'll have to say it's a one-night stand and you can't remember who the father is,' he added.

We sat in the waiting room in silence. I didn't look at anyone, I just stared at my hands in my lap, dreading what was to come next. It never even crossed my mind to try and tell the truth. Partly because of what Dad had said, but also because I knew how well he would come across. His clear, carefully enunciated voice and affable manner meant everyone always believed he was a nice intelligent man.

*No doctor would believe me over him, would they?*

When my name was called, we stood up and Dad gave me a tiny, sharp shove in the small of my back as we crossed the doctor's threshold. I knew what that meant.

*Say what I've told you or else.*

We sat side by side as the doctor looked up from his notes.

'So, how can I help you, Kim?' he asked, peering over half-moon glasses.

Before I could answer, Dad said, 'She's pregnant and only fifteen years old!'

I swallowed, unable to look the doctor in the eye. He paused, looking me up and down.

'Kim,' he asked softly, 'do you know who the baby's father is?'

'No, she doesn't,' Dad snapped, jumping in before I could even open my mouth to answer. 'She doesn't know because she sleeps around. She hasn't got a clue.'

I could feel both their pairs of eyes burning into the top of my lowered head. My life often felt like a nightmare but just when I thought things couldn't get any worse, they did.

'Do you want to keep the baby, Kim?' asked the doctor.

'No, she can't,' Dad replied for me. 'She needs an education so she needs an abortion.'

'What do you think, Kim?' the doctor persisted.

'Yes, I need an abortion,' I said, in a near whisper.

The doctor continued to look at us both for a beat longer than necessary before returning to his notes.

'Abortions are illegal in Kenya but something can, er, be arranged,' he said, clearing his throat. 'We would need a second signature from a gynaecologist. And, of course, there is a large payment involved.'

I felt Dad bristle at the prospect of it costing him money.

After making some notes, the doctor agreed to sort this out and we were to return in a few days' time.

The days passed in a blur. I still had to go to school as if nothing had happened. Dad continued to rape me most nights. I was in so much pain from the previous DIY abortion attempts, I often thought I'd pass out or be sick during those long, lonely, terrifying nights in his bed. I told no one at school. Instead I simply carried on, pretending I was fine – I just made sure I always wore a baggy jumper, however hot it was outside.

On the day of the abortion, I saw the gynaecologist – a Dr Jones – at the hospital. I knew him because his son Michael was friends with my brother Sean. My cheeks burned with shame as he went through the possible risks. All I could think about was the idea that everyone at school would find out and then tease me.

He told me coldly, factually, that I needed a general anaesthetic and might not ever wake up from it. The pregnancy had apparently gone beyond the stage where I could have a pill – I needed an operation.

'If we do this, you might become infertile and never be able to have children of your own,' he went on.

Dad made a scoffing sound. 'That'll be a godsend,' he said. 'She doesn't want them anyway.'

I noticed the doctor flinch.

'Are you sure you can't be supported by the father of your baby, Kim?' a nurse sitting next to him asked.

'She doesn't even know who the father is because she's a slag,' my father sighed.

I shook my head so they pushed the paperwork in front of Dad, who signed his name with a flourish.

Next came the request for the fee. Dad took a sharp intake of breath – he was a miser and didn't like wasting cash. Since his divorce from Alison, he often grumbled about money. He pulled the notes from his wallet but by the way he laid them on the table, I could sense how angry this made him.

I had to sign the consent form too. On it was a list of things which could go wrong, including me never waking up again. My hand trembled as I scrawled my signature because I'd never had a general anaesthetic before – this felt like my death warrant. The nurse took the form wordlessly before ushering Dad out.

He didn't look at me as he left, followed by the nurse. Alone, tears sliding down my face, I waited for it to be my turn for theatre. I had to wear a gown that opened at the back with nothing on underneath. Shivering and feeling so exposed, I had no book or TV to watch to take my mind off what was happening. Left alone with my thoughts, I closed my eyes and prayed I would survive this, but then part of me thought that if I died at least I could escape ever having to go home again.

Nurses came and I was whisked off down to the theatre. There, they put a mask over my face, told me to count backwards until everything went black.

I woke, shivering and felt raw. I was alive … except I wish I wasn't. My stomach felt as if it had been run over by a bus. I could feel someone had placed a big pad between my legs. When I placed my hand down there gingerly, I was soaking wet with blood. Turning my face to the side, I lay there sobbing, wishing someone, *anyone*, could save me.

When I opened my eyes again, Dad was standing over me.

'They're allowing me to take you home early,' he announced. 'Because I explained I'm in the medical profession myself. Get. Up.'

I slid my heavy legs over the side of the bed, but was barely able to stand. Feeling exposed, I clutched at my robe, but Dad was already sorting my clothes out to dress me.

'Whip it off!' he commanded.

With barely the strength to raise my arms, he roughly pulled them up for me to remove the robe and pulled on a top. I felt like nothing but a rag doll as he pulled on trousers and shoes. Then he dragged me out of the room by one arm, hissing at me to walk otherwise they wouldn't allow him to take me.

By the time we reached the car, I slumped in the seat, feeling light-headed from the anaesthetic. I was unable to stop sobbing.

'Shut up!' he snapped. Then he turned on the engine and roughly put the car into gear to reverse. Already I knew that I was for it when we got home.

The road was spinning in front of my eyes as he drove home at speed. That afternoon, my sister Susan was landing at the airport as she was coming over to start school at Hillcrest for her A levels. Dad was going to drop me off first before going to collect her. I'd almost forgotten but was so grateful. Although I couldn't tell her what had happened, just knowing she'd be here was such a comfort.

Back inside, Dad dragged me into the bedroom, where I could finally lie down.

The house fell silent after he went off to collect Susan. I lay there, thinking about my sister. I knew I could never tell anyone, including her: if I told my secret, Dad might kill me and he might kill her too. Deep down, I knew he was capable of this, but at the same time perhaps she could give me a cuddle when she arrived and make everything seem a bit better.

I managed to doze off, only waking when the dogs barked as they'd arrived home. I could hear Susan clattering in the hallway with her suitcase. She was taking the room nearest the lounge. I had the one between Susan's and Dad's (he was at the end) and Sean was going to have the one on its own on the other side of the corridor when he came home. After she made a fuss of the dogs, who were excited to see her, I could hear Susan's footsteps.

'Hey, Dad, where's Kim?' she said.

'Oh, Kim!' he boomed in a loud voice. 'She's in bed still.'

'Still in bed at this time?' asked Susan. 'What's wrong with her?'

'Nothing,' he told her. 'She's been drinking, just like her slattern of a mother.'

'What?' cried Susan.

I knew she wouldn't approve of this, especially because of Mum. The last thing either of us wanted was to end up like our mother.

'Yes,' said Dad. 'She had far too much to drink last night regardless of you coming. The amount of my whisky she downed … I couldn't stop her, you know. And now she's hungover.'

Susan opened my bedroom door to find me curled in a ball on the bed.

'Oh my God, Kim! Are you okay? You look terrible,' she said.

Tears smarted in my eyes when I heard her concerned voice but I forced myself to pretend all was fine.

'It's my own fault,' I said weakly.

I listened as Susan's footsteps disappeared off towards the living room as I lay there, more alone than I'd ever felt in my life.

As the afternoon progressed into the evening, Dad started playing his records as usual. Susan had brought him the latest Top 10 of singles as he'd requested. Pets and music were the only ways I could lose myself, so I listened intently.

Dad shouted down the corridor when 'Xanadu' by Olivia Newton-John came on.

'Come on out, Kim,' he said. 'Come and get something to eat.'

'Come on!' joined in Susan. 'You've not even said hello to me yet.'

*He knew full well I could barely stand.*

'Why won't she come?' Susan asked.

'Bone idle – stays in bed all day, if she can!' chuckled Dad.

The music died down around 9pm. Susan was jet-lagged and was off to bed earlier than usual so I heard her saying goodnight to Dad above the music.

Once the music was off, the house grew silent and dark again. I closed my eyes, willing more sleep to overcome me. At least tonight of all nights Dad was certain to leave me alone. Or so I thought.

I turned my pillow, damp with tears, over and felt the coolness of the fresh side on my cheek. Maybe tomorrow I could persuade Susan I had food poisoning and hadn't been drunk. I was starting to doze off when I heard the familiar padding sound of Dad's footsteps in the corridor and my bedroom door being opened.

I lay totally still, pretending to be asleep as I could feel the edge of my duvet being lifted. I didn't dare move a muscle as the heat of my dad began to press into my back. Then his familiar soapy smell enveloped the room.

I couldn't believe this was happening. Not tonight of all nights! I hardly dared breathe as he started touching me, moving a pad from in-between my legs.

'Touch me,' he growled, forcing me to turn over and look at him.

I wanted to be sick as tears gathered in the corners of my eyes again.

'The good news is, after this, there is no risk of me making you pregnant tonight,' he smirked.

Seconds later, he was raping me from behind while I whimpered in agony.

Once he had finished, he ordered me to clean up the mess, then left and shut the door.

After that, I lay completely still for hours. I was in so much pain, physically and psychologically, a strange numbness set in.

The day had been so traumatic, it was hard to believe it had even happened.

*My father had attempted to abort his own child.*

# Chapter 11

The next morning, I felt so weak, I could hardly stand. However, I was starving, so I shuffled to the table for breakfast – I knew Dad wouldn't serve me any in bed, so I needed to get up for it.

Susan's face lit up when she saw me.

'Oh my God, Kim! Was it a one-person party?' she joked.

I could feel tears prick my eyes.

'You'll need a strong coffee,' said Dad, pouring me one. He smirked as he passed it to me.

I thought of him and the three-day whisky diet he had put me on, but I didn't say anything – it wasn't worth it, Susan wouldn't believe me anyway. Miserably, I ate some toast. Dad told me I had chores to do so I knew I'd have to act like nothing had happened and carry on.

Over the next couple of days, as my body gradually grew stronger, my mind grew more depressed. I felt as if life wasn't worth living anymore. I was trapped in this nightmare cycle of abuse every day, with no end in sight, no way out. The abortion had been such a traumatic experience, but I couldn't talk to anyone about it. Dad was the only person who knew what had happened and he was the last person I could trust to care about how I felt.

A week or so later, when I was having a bath, I looked up at the shelf next to me, where Dad had left his razor (he used cut-throat razors, rather than safety ones). I picked it up, gently running my finger along the edge of it. I considered shaving my legs, something my father wouldn't let me do as he thought it would attract boys.

The coolness of the blade felt inviting somehow. I wondered what it would be like to cut my skin with it. Taking a deep breath, I imagined a teacher seeing these cuts and working out something was wrong; I imagined Dad seeing my cuts, and be racked with guilt, knowing that this was all his fault, and vowing from then on to leave me alone and be a normal, proper dad.

Studying the veins on the insides of my wrists for a while, I started pushing the edge of the blade over them. Willing myself to do it harder and harder with each stroke until I had made some red scratches. I badly wanted to have the courage to strike my arm and do it properly, but I didn't. I took another deep breath, willing myself to be braver. But, as the scratches began to sting, I started to cry. I didn't have the guts and besides it was purely to make my father wonder why I'd done it.

*Dad was right, I was useless.*

Lost in my own thoughts, I hadn't noticed the door was open, with Dad standing behind me. Before I had a chance to react, he yanked me out of the bath water by my shoulders.

'I was right,' he yelled, 'you're mental, just like your mum!'

He dug his fingers into my skin as he dragged me, naked and shivering, from the bath.

'You're so selfish!' he yelled once more. 'How could you even do this? If you ever hurt yourself again, I will hurt you more.'

By the time he'd finished, I went to get dressed, smarting with pain all over my body, feeling so stupid. I had hoped he would notice. Listen. Care about the pain I was in. Ask why I'd done it. But, of course, he didn't: he was furious with me and it only made things worse.

*I finally understood something: Dad wanted me to survive this not because he cared and loved me, but because I was his plaything.*

The next day I woke up, feeling worse than ever. I knew I couldn't live like this anymore, but it seemed there was no way out. I felt so stupid about what I'd done in the bath. I really wasn't trying to kill myself, just to get my father to sit up and take notice of me and my feelings. Already there had been years of persistent physical, emotional and sexual abuse at the hands of this middle-class man who appeared on the surface to others to be a charismatic and intelligent lecturer who had drawn the short straw in having to bring up his unruly daughter because her mother was incapable. I was still only fifteen. Girls of my age were out partying with their friends, not trapped in an incestuous relationship with their biological father.

Over the next few weeks, I virtually stopped eating. I was not anorexic, though. Monitoring my weight was the one thing I could control, or so I thought. Dad taunted me about this, persistently telling me I was fat, so I ate as little as possible. Other times, he would tell me that I was an anorexic. But now all food tasted like cardboard. I had no appetite – none for life and certainly not for food. The years of abuse were seemingly endless and I struggled to remember what it felt like not to be abused. I dreamed of escape once I'd reached adulthood.

*I was only fifteen; could I really survive this until I was eighteen and free to live my own life?*

At school, I hid my feelings as well as my body.

One of my first lessons back was swimming and I knew I couldn't go as the tops of my thighs were still covered in tiny bruises the size of Dad's fingerprints. Luckily, I had a friend who hated swimming too, so she used to write my excuse notes for me and I'd write hers. Usually mine was something about periods or a stomach bug.

Thankfully, our teacher never thought to question it. By now I also hated wearing a swimming costume anyway. Thanks to Dad, I felt fat, ugly and revolting in it – I'd learned to hate my body as much as he lusted after it.

Meanwhile, I slowly became good friends with Keg (Anthony Kegode). We had met outside the dining hall next to the washrooms, near the school kitchen in the quadrangle area (we called it the 'Quad'). He came up to me and because I was very shy and naïve, Keg did all the talking and the chatting up, but to my surprise, I found him attractive. He was Kenyan, with the most beautiful deep voice, and he had such a handsome, open face that when he came over to say hello, I couldn't help but smile back. I hoped we might become friends. Every time I saw him around, he always took time to chat to me. He lived down the road from us so we got off at the same bus stop and often he'd walk with me until I got home.

As always, outside of school, I kept my head down and avoided boys in case Dad spotted me but there was something so sunny about Keg's personality, I didn't have the heart to stop our conversation as we ambled down the road together.

'Do you like records?' he asked one day. 'I'd love to play you some of mine. Who do you like?'

I told him that I particularly liked Dr Hook, but didn't expect he'd have that album as it didn't seem the sort of music he'd listen to. To my surprise, he had it in his collection and so we excitedly made plans for us to listen to it together.

My eyes lit up. There was something about Keg that reassured me everything was going to be okay, so I found myself agreeing to go to his house.

Keg's family home had white-washed walls and was built on the steep side of Loresho. To get to the front door, we had to walk through a garden gate and down some steps. The house was split-level, with a sunken living room. He lived with his father, mother, brother and two sisters.

Up in his room, Keg was very complimentary about the way I looked. I blushed with embarrassment, but he insisted it was true.

'You are really beautiful, Kim, you just don't realise it,' he told me.

He tried to kiss me but I brushed him off. Kissing was the last thing I wanted. But I was flattered all the same and he was a lovely guy who made me laugh.

Slowly, Keg and I started becoming an item. One of the girls at school warned me that he was not after a relationship purely for friendship – 'Be careful, Kim,' she said. 'He'll want a great deal more than just being friends.' I was shocked – Keg didn't seem the type and this did send shivers down my spine. But I liked him and I knew I'd have to handle the situation if he tried to take things further. I wasn't ready for that kind of relationship and I didn't want him finding out about Dad.

The next time Keg asked me to join him, I said no. As if he guessed why, he reassured me nothing would happen.

'I just like spending time with you, Kim,' he said. 'You're fun.'

'Okay, then,' I agreed.

I didn't trust many people but as I've said, there was something about him. True to his word, we had a lovely afternoon sitting on Keg's bed, tapping our feet to the music he was playing. There were the Dr Hook songs 'When You're In Love With a Beautiful Woman' and 'More Like the Movies'; also, a brilliant one we would go on to play all the time, 'Papa was a Rollin' Stone' by The Temptations.

Keg seemed the perfect gentleman, but when he asked me out on a date, my face clouded.

'I … I … can't,' I stammered.

'Why not?' he asked, in his lovely deep, smooth voice.

'My dad wouldn't like it,' I admitted.

Anthony looked at me with his brown eyes with a sympathy I rarely saw in anyone.

'But nobody needs to find out,' he said.

I shrugged him off and went home, but over the next few days he wouldn't drop the subject. We always ended up chatting together on the bus and I felt so comfortable in his presence, I decided perhaps if we were careful never to be spotted by Dad then we could hang out sometimes.

Over the next few months things worked out well. Whenever I knew Dad was definitely busy at work, Keg cycled over. Being with him helped me through many a dark hour. He loved meeting all my pets or listening to records. I even let him in my bedroom for the occasional kiss. Initially, he was a gentleman and only tried to kiss me but as the months passed, he became more persistent. Each time I pulled away, or made an excuse. I'd jump up and say I was thirsty and needed a drink or I'd pretend I'd suddenly forgotten to feed one of the pets. Eventually, one day at his house, Keg asked me what was wrong.

'You're such a beautiful girl, Kim, I can't help but want to touch you,' he explained.

'Nothing's wrong!' I said brightly. 'I just …'

But I had run out of excuses.

'You don't like me?'

'No!' I cried. 'It's not that, Keg.'

He looked upset. I knew he was more experienced than me, but I couldn't face letting him get intimate, let alone sleep with me.

'I love you, Kim,' he said.

I stared at him in shock. Nobody had ever said that to me before. I giggled with embarrassment, but let him envelop me in a cuddle. Warm and safe in his arms, I wondered if maybe I loved him back a little bit too. Certainly, our friendship gave me a feeling of hope for my future. Somehow, I managed to get away with not having sex with him the whole time we were close. He'd become pushy and sometimes a bit angry, but I would laugh it off.

One afternoon, over at his house, Keg ran a bath after his PE lesson. I was sitting on his bed waiting for him to finish when he called me into the bathroom. Shyly, I opened the door, trying not to look at him.

'Come and sit with me, Kim,' he said, sitting upright, surrounded by bubbles.

I looked everywhere around the bathroom except at him.

'Please?' he asked softly.

Anxiously, I sat down on the closed toilet seat, still looking everywhere but at his half-submerged body.

'Kim, why won't you even look at my body?' he asked.

I could feel a redness spreading from my neck upwards. I loved spending time with Keg. He made me laugh like nobody else, he brought out my best side, he was one of my best friends, but how could I ever explain how I felt about sex? The idea revolted me.

'I don't know,' I said, trying to laugh. 'I'm just shy, I suppose.'

Thankfully, he let it drop and I told him I'd wait outside.

A few weeks later, Keg came home with me and as I fixed us something to drink in the kitchen, we heard the sound of an engine. Dad was home unexpectedly! I dropped my glass in the sink, almost shattering it, as I pushed at Keg's shoulder.

'Come on!' I cried, a feeling of rising terror taking hold of me. 'You've got to get out. Now!'

Keg was sipping his drink.

'What, now?' he asked, startled.

'Yes! NOW!' I screamed.

He could see the terror in my eyes so dropped the glass into the sink and ran out of the house behind me. As we left the front door, I could see Dad's car was already parked, but thankfully his head was in the boot as he collected a box of books.

'Quick!' I hissed. 'This way.'

We walked around the side of the house, so Keg could jump over the gate. But just as he got a leg up, Dad peered over his car boot.

'What on earth …?' he yelled. 'What's that black bastard doing here?'

He gave chase but Keg was too fast and vanished before he got close. Then he turned to me, his face twisted with hate.

'Sneaking boys in, are we? Come here!' he screamed.

Frozen to the spot, he grabbed my elbow painfully and frogmarched me back indoors. He told me no matter how educated black people could be, they were never to be trusted. What's more, they carried lots of sexual diseases and he didn't ever want to see Keg back here again.

'What would my friends from work say if they knew my daughter was seeing a black man?' he yelled. 'He's only after one thing, like all boys. Stay away from boys, they're all bad news!

'You're just like your mother,' he sneered. 'She used to throw herself at all the n—— in Nigeria. Prefer a bit of black to white, do you?'

After this, Dad often returned home suddenly without warning after school. Bringing Keg back became all too dangerous for both of us.

Weeks later, after the dust had settled, it didn't stop me from going to Keg's house myself. It felt like a place of sanctuary. I had started to trust him more and more. He was so gentle and respectful of me, plus he made me laugh like nobody else.

I was at his place after school one day. I was wearing a skirt, and as I reached up to take a book down from a top shelf, my skirt rose up, exposing my thighs. I heard Keg breathe in sharply, and when I turned to look at him, his face was shocked.

'Kim!' he gasped. 'Whoa!'

I looked down to see what he'd seen and there, at the tops of my thighs, were tiny bruises.

*Purple and blue fingerprint-like bruises left by my father.*

'Yes,' I said dumbly, unsure how to respond.

'What's happened to you? What's happened here?' he asked.

Keg looked truly appalled. I felt my throat constricting as I struggled to respond.

'Have you been raped or something, Kim?' he whispered, taking my hand.

I didn't pull away from him.

'Kim … Has someone older done this to you?' he said softly.

I shook my head.

'Was it your dad?' he persisted.

Hearing someone speak the truth, his words cutting through all the years of secrecy, lies, torment and torture, felt like a miracle. So, I gave a tiny nod.

'Yes,' I said simply. 'It was.'

How could I lie to my trusted friend? Deep down, I wanted him to know why I couldn't get intimate with him, why my father didn't like him. But would he even believe me?

# Chapter 12

Keg's mouth dropped open as he rubbed the back of his head in shock.

'Oh, good God, Kim!' he said.

He looked so horrified, I almost felt guilty. I didn't mean to upset him like this; I didn't want anyone's pity either as nobody could do anything about it, or at least that's what I thought.

'Don't tell anyone,' I said quietly. 'You mustn't tell anyone or my dad will kill us both.'

Keg stared at me, obviously not knowing what to say. I knew I looked emotionless – I was so used to hiding my feelings. But I was also self-aware enough to know this probably wasn't a normal response to what I'd just admitted.

Keg was just a sixteen-year-old boy from a loving, normal family. This sort of depravity wasn't something he'd ever come across, let alone knew what to do about.

I turned away as if to shut the subject down. Deep down, I knew our relationship was probably over as Keg sat back, clearly shell-shocked.

He reached out and took my hand. I looked down, appreciating its warmth, his caress, but slowly, I took it back. Neither of us knew what to say, so I gathered my things to go home.

'Kim,' he said, softly, as I paused at the door. 'I am here for you, you know.'

I knew he meant it. Despite his youth, I knew he was a deeply caring person. He could easily have run a mile, he wasn't getting any sex after all, but it made me realise I meant more to him than that.

I felt tears smart behind my eyes but quickly left before they fell.


The next day, when Keg saw me he didn't mention anything. I knew then he was going to respect my wishes to keep my dark secret. I knew he'd want to help me, that was in his nature, but there was nobody he could tell. He'd understand no one was likely to believe either of us. Dad was so well thought of. He was a lecturer who lived in a lovely district. A rich white man, a prominent person in the community. Going to the police was pointless – they wouldn't believe he was capable of something like this. As much as Keg would have liked to have done something, he didn't.

*Until I made the next nightmare discovery.*

Dad suspected something was wrong and forced me to do another pregnancy test. To my horror, the strip turned positive. Numb, I braced myself for an angry outburst so I averted my gaze to the floor, waiting for it. But I was met with silence.

'Oh, Kim,' he told me calmly. 'You're pregnant again.'

He sighed loudly then gave a weird, wry smile. I looked at

him properly, wondering what on earth was going through his mind. There was no anger now, just a wistful look on his face.

'This time, Kim, you can keep the baby. We can have a family together,' he told me.

I stared at him in absolute horror, physically recoiling as I sat perched at the end of the bath.

'We can live a proper life. We can move away, live as man and wife,' he added.

*What was he talking about? Was this some sort of sick joke?* I felt that familiar wave of nausea as he paced the room, his eyes roving over my body as he painted castles in the sky.

'We could escape all this, go and live somewhere remote. Just you and me and the baby.'

I still don't know what Dad meant by this comment. Maybe he was just being sarcastic or trying to get a reaction from me. Perhaps he didn't want to pay for another abortion. I wanted to be sick, but squeezed the edge of the bath to hold everything in. He took my silence as acceptance of his sick plan.

'It's going to be fine, we can bring this baby up together.' He beamed.

Thankfully, the phone rang and he left the room to answer it. I took deep breaths to steady the terrible knot that had formed in my stomach. I knew my dad was crazy, yet this madness was a whole new level. Here I was, pregnant again for the second time with my biological father's baby. Again, this was out of my control. He'd dictated what contraception I was to have, he never used a condom and he was still ad hoc with the contraceptive pills he was dishing out to me. He'd drink so much, he'd forget what he was giving me. I had to do something – the very thought of his baby growing inside of me for the second time made me want to claw at my body to get it out.

In a daze, I quickly got dressed for school, then forced myself to say goodbye to Dad calmly as he dropped me off at the bus stop. As I sat down on the bus seat, my mind was racing. I had no idea what I was going to do, who I could turn to. An abortion was the only way I could escape this madness. I didn't want this baby and there was no way I could keep it. Luckily, as soon as he got on the bus, Keg spotted the strange look on my face and sat down next tome.

'Are you okay?' he asked, concerned.

I shook my head, trying to hold my tears in. Then I forced myself to smile.

'Ah, just a bad morning,' I said. Then I made a joke about getting out of bed the wrong side. All day long, I forced myself to seem more cheerful than usual. But Keg wasn't fooled. That evening, he asked me over to his house after school – Dad was working late, so I agreed.

We were in his bedroom, having a kiss and cuddle, when he slowly undid my shirt. I started crying.

'I'm pregnant,' I sobbed.

'What? What do you mean?' he said.

I snatched at my buttons to do them up again. Then I turned my face away from him, tears sliding down my cheeks relentlessly. There was nothing he could do, nothing either of us could do. Then his jaw set with a look of determination I'd never seen on him before.

'Right,' he said, his eyes wide with shock. 'Leave this with me, I am going to sort this out for you.'

I didn't ask him what he could do. He was a kid just like

me. He had no money, just like me. But he was the only person in the world I could trust. After all, he'd never mentioned Dad abusing me again. Now I was trusting him with my life.

I had no idea what the plan was. All I knew was a few days later Keg told me to pack a change of clothes and meet him at the bus stop as usual in the morning. He told me not to eat anything the night before because I'd need an operation.

*Another abortion.*

I tried not to eat anything for breakfast, like Keg had warned me, but Dad started asking me why I wasn't eating so I ate some pawpaw, which seemed to satisfy him. The plan was that after my father had dropped me off at the bus stop as usual for school, I was to wait for Keg and he'd pick me up. As I stared down the road, an old blue Renault drove slowly up with Keg behind the wheel.

'Get in,' he said, anxiously, opening the car door for me.

I sat in the passenger side and stared at him incredulously.

'This is my dad's car,' he said, answering the question I couldn't ask. 'And yes, we're going to have to drive fast.'

As we roared off, I barely had time to put on my seatbelt. I felt in a strange sort of a daze, as if none of this was happening to me.

'Where are we going?' I asked.

'To hospital,' he said. 'Kim, I have it all sorted.'

'Where did you get the money from?' I gasped.

Abortions were very expensive and also illegal, but people were still able to get them in private hospitals under certain circumstances and if they paid for them. Dad was so angry about the amount the last one had cost him.

'I stole cash from the till at Dad's garage,' he explained. 'But don't worry.'

Every night, Keg's dad, Joshua, used to cash up the till and keep the float at home after a day's work. Keg had stolen all of it – 30,000 shillings – and had paid for the abortion upfront. I didn't know what to say. He'd gone to such lengths and could be in such trouble, but he knew I needed this to stop it from ruining my life.

'Keg, you've done so much for me …' I began.

'Shhh, let's just get through today,' he said reassuringly, although in retrospect, I'm sure he must have been very frightened himself.

Keg guided me gently from the car to the waiting room. Inside, doctors asked me to sign various forms.

'Have you eaten today?' asked one medic.

Keg looked at me anxiously as I admitted, yes, I had.

'Ah well, you shouldn't have.' The medic tutted.

For a moment I thought they were going to cancel the operation, but thankfully, they didn't.

The rest of the afternoon passed in a blur. At least this time I knew Keg would be there when I awoke. Sure enough, he was. I have blanked all this from my mind but he recalls what happened next. After the termination, he calmly helped me back to the car and drove me to his house as he knew everyone would be out – I could sleep soundly in his bed he'd covered with towels.

When I woke up in pain, Keg was there to hold my hand and tell me he loved me. My dear friend looked after me all day, even changing the pads as tears slid down my face.

All too quickly the hours went by and it was time for

me to go home. A reluctant Keg knew I needed to be back before Dad was home from work and had even planned what I should say to him.

'You tell him you had a miscarriage and a friend took you to hospital to have it confirmed,' he suggested.

The next time I saw Keg, we never talked about what happened that afternoon. I knew he'd got in trouble about stealing the money – his father was furious and had quizzed him and his siblings, but Keg stayed quiet. He was such a loyal, decent person.


By now, my sister Susan had settled in and had started Hillcrest to finish her A-levels. It felt incredible to have my sister living with us. Finally, I had a true friend in the house and I felt less alone. Still, Dad carried on raping me most nights. He was careful to wait until Susan had gone to bed – she didn't seem to suspect a thing.

Susan was also treated completely differently to me. She was allowed out after school and at weekends. She was also allowed boyfriends and school trips. I was jealous, but equally glad for her sake she wasn't going through what I was.

Susan was envious of me too as Dad often bought me clothes to wear and nothing for her. He'd take me on shopping trips, picking out fancy outfits. Nothing I ever actually liked, but things that made me look like a thirty-year-old woman. When I returned with clothes wrapped in tissue paper, Susan made comments.

'Why is *she* always being bought stuff?' she'd ask Dad.

But he'd just laugh it off or change the subject. He even told her I couldn't be trusted to choose my own clothes.

Susan saw me as the favourite daughter whereas I was envious that she had a better lifestyle than me. After all, she could go out and have boyfriends and she was allowed to go on school trips. There was some normality in her life. But I loved having a sister around. I hoped we'd see more of Lucy too, who said she wanted to come for holidays. It never occurred to me that either was at risk of Dad – I assumed he targeted me because I looked most like Mum. At least that's what he had told me.

My older sister had a very similar temperament to Dad, so they would often clash over silly things, for example, what Dad said she should be eating, about bringing boys back to the house (for some bizarre reason, he thought they'd fancy me), her school grades, how long she might be staying out. Occasionally, he would shove Susan backwards out of his way during a row but he never struck her. She would run to her room in tears and stay put for hours.

It never occurred to me to tell her what he was doing. She was my sister but had no power, least of all over our father, who controlled everything.

Every Saturday, Susan and I would spend the day together, sunbathing or baking, but always chatting. To feel like a normal teenager for a couple of hours was a huge treat. She was a little bigger than me, but Dad never mentioned this. Instead he focused all his criticism on me.

'Look at Kim,' he'd laugh, over breakfast. 'She is mentally deranged as she thinks she's fat.'

'Aw, Kim, you're anorexic, more like,' Susan would chip in. 'You should eat more.'

My sister was unaware I had developed a borderline

eating disorder because of Dad's taunts over the years but she rebelled with me against our father in secret. Once, when he was out, we quickly made biscuits together, eating them off the baking tray while they sizzled so we could have our fill before he came home. Giggling, we waved our hands in the air so he wouldn't be able to smell the delicious treats.

*Any tiny act of rebellion like this helped keep me going.*

Even an innocent comment could land me in trouble whereas Dad wasn't so vigilant with my sister. There was a boy in Susan's year who I had always liked and once he told her that he was 'infatuated' with me. I hadn't heard that word before, so later that evening, when Dad quizzed us about our days, I naïvely asked him what 'infatuated' meant.

'Who says they are "infatuated" with you, Kim?' he boomed, his face clouding with fury.

I recoiled, mumbling something about someone at school.

He grabbed the weighty copy of *The Oxford English Dictionary* and slammed it on the table in front of me.

'Look. It. Up,' he spat. 'Find out for yourself.'

My fingers trembled as they turned the pages.

'Infatuation, noun, an intense but short-lived passion or admiration for someone or something,' I read.

I didn't know if Susan was right about the boy in her class, all I did know was it made Dad very angry.

Years of sleep deprivation and trauma meant my concentration levels in class and exams were never good. I also went into my end-of-high-school exams with the attitude I was thick and would fail. After all, that's what Dad had been telling me for years.

He'd long given up teaching me anything and taunted me for my low grades. Even on the day of the exams, he kept me up until 3 or 4am, raping me. It didn't matter that I'd have to get up, exhausted, by 7am and then go to school and take an exam.

On results day, unsurprisingly, I only scraped a couple of passes. I'd had my mocks in January/February 1981. One of my teachers commented in my report, 'It'll be touch and go whether Kim passes Chemistry O-level. If she is to sit the exam, she must continue to make every effort.' My grades had been mainly poor, showing Cs and Ds, and as expected, I did poorly, achieving only 2 GCE grades in English language and English literature.

Dad used it as another excuse to mentally torture me. He screamed at me for being stupid; he'd tell me that I was the thickest out of all four of us, that I'd only ever get a job in a supermarket, that all my friends would go up a year while I would stay down. He'd tell me constantly that I was just like my mother. But I barely reacted because I knew what was coming – I knew my father was secretly pleased I'd failed; it meant his control over me continued.

Dad ordered me to stay at school and retake the exams. If he was already controlling my life, he was about to take it to another level. I depended on him for travel, for money, for absolutely everything. He had total control of my life, my education, what I did during the day, what I ate, what I drank, where I was allowed; he controlled my body too.

Meanwhile, Susan finished her A-levels and achieved grades that allowed her to get into Huddersfield Polytechnic, back in Yorkshire. Sean was in England, finishing at Woodhouse Grove School and due to join us in Kenya to do his A-levels.

We hardly saw him, although he'd come over for holidays now and again.

Dad already had plans for me for what I should do for a career: a BTEC in Animal Husbandry at ILRAD – the International Laboratory for Research into Animal Diseases. He knew someone at ILRAD and got me on the course there. It suited him as he could drop me off and collect me. Other times, he made me go to work with him. For hours I'd sit in a baking-hot car in the polytechnic car park with the windows down as there was no air-con. It was red-hot in Nairobi. When a song came on the radio, I loved it immediately and turned it right up, blasting it round the car park. The song was 'Billie Jean' by Michael Jackson. When Dad got back to the car, I mentioned it to him excitedly.

'If you want the record, you can have it, Kim,' he told me and he actually bought it for me.

Without asking me, he also signed me up to attend a local veterinary practice to watch the vets at work. This was just another way of him controlling me – he knew I couldn't walk anywhere from the vets as there was nothing around. He knew exactly where I was and what I was doing at all times. I loved animals so I hated watching them having treatment and in pain.

The vet was a white man who had been born in Kenya. He tried to make conversation with me on the first day but I was so shy and lacking in confidence I was barely able to say anything except nod my head. I hated it, because I felt so completely stupid.

Every day for weeks, Dad dropped me off and picked me up there so I'd have to spend hours standing in the theatre watching animals have operations or being put to sleep. I saw one poor dog react badly to being put down, so they ended up placing the needle in his heart. I watched it move back and forth like a metronome until it slowly stopped. Another time, I patted a dog with suspected rabies because he seemed so friendly – the vet was furious with me.

In late 1981, Susan left Kenya to go to Huddersfield Poly. When we said goodbye, I held on tight to her, unable to stop the tears. I knew I was going to miss her terribly. I had placed a little note in her case for her to find when she arrived home, telling her how much I'd miss her. The fact was I'd have done anything to join her. One day, I vowed, I would.

We stayed in touch by letter and she told me she'd met a guy called Gregory, a lad from Northallerton in North Yorkshire. I was happy for her, but also envious as I wanted the freedom she enjoyed – I just had no idea how this would be possible.

Around this time Sean returned to Kenya to start his exams at the Hillcrest. He seemed older, more reserved, and definitely took it upon himself to avoid Dad whenever possible, staying over at friends' houses, often all weekend. Dad encouraged this – it left him free to continue abusing me without interruption.

Sean and Dad clashed increasingly as my brother grew older. I think he was now more confident, having gained his independence at boarding school away from Africa. Once, when he visited during the holidays before Susan left for the UK, we were having dinner (Dad, Susan, Sean and I). Sean had left some food on the side of his plate and Dad told him to eat it up. An argument ensued, which ended up with Dad beating Sean up because my brother had told him to 'F-off'. After that, we didn't see a great deal of Sean.

# Chapter 13

One day, during a literature re-take lesson, I'd been revising with another lad in the group called Luke. He was nice enough, there was nothing romantic at all between us, but he gave me his phone number in case I needed help at home. Grateful for any extra help to improve my grades, I took it, aiming to call him when Dad wasn't around. Unfortunately, he wasn't in and by the time Dad got back, the phone rang and he got to it first.

'Kim!' he screamed. 'There's a *boy* on the phone for you!'

My heart sank. I knew I was for it. Dad stood, holding the receiver as if it was an unexploded bomb, watching me as I had to go through the charade of chatting to Luke as if nothing was wrong.

'That's great, thank you for helping me,' I said at the end of the call, dreading hanging up. My father had been standing over me the entire time. Waiting.

As soon as I put the phone down, Dad grabbed the receiver and lunged for me, whacking it as hard as he could across my face. I spun around, screaming, as he caught the edge of my jaw. White-hot pain seared across my jawline as my teeth vibrated with a sickening crunching sound. I fell to the floor, moaning in agony.

Dad loomed over me, his anger already satiated because he saw how badly he had hurt me. I hated him even more for this. He didn't even try to hide his satisfaction when I was in pain but just sent me to my bedroom, where even crying made the pain worse. For the next two weeks I could hardly open my mouth even to eat or drink. I just pulled my hair around my face, kept a roll-neck on and avoided looking anyone in the eye at school. If anyone had noticed anything was wrong, they never asked – most of my friends had left school for college now anyway.

Keg was the only person who noticed when I saw him at the weekend. After O-levels in 1981, he'd gone to college in Canada for his A-levels and was doing well. His brother was already there and his father had wanted him to join him. We didn't get to see each other as often as we had done, but he still cared for me deeply. I told him the truth and his face filled with such sympathy, it nearly broke my heart.

'There is nothing you can do,' I managed to whisper painfully.

As my jaw healed up after about six weeks (I never found out whether it was broken), I carried on studying. Dad made me re-take my English and biology exams until I had passed with a grade he thought was acceptably high enough.

At first, he seemed pleased with me for 'following in his footsteps', almost as if he was a normal father with normal fatherly pride in his daughter. I clung to these precious moments of normality, where he talked in a calm voice, showed genuine interest in my day and appeared to care for me. It was on these days I'd even allow myself to fantasise the abuse was over: perhaps he'd just stop one day; maybe he'd tire of it or realise it was wrong?

Since I was eleven years old, my dad was the only real parent I had so it was perfectly possible in these odd moments to feel affection for the person whom I was most reliant on. He controlled everything from how I travelled and what I ate to who I saw. I loved him like a prisoner ends up being in love with their jailer as they know no different, but sure enough, I was always wrong about any real reconciliation with the evil he possessed. Whenever I dared imagine my dad could be anything different, he would carry out another vicious drunken attack.

Looking back, our neighbours in Kenya must have thought it was weird that Bernard Beaumont was always with his middle daughter Kim. I went everywhere with him, including short trips to the shops and the poly on some days.

Despite being incredibly tight, Dad began to splash out on fancy meals, including visits to Kenyatta, International Convention Centre the famous rotating restaurant where you can view the whole of Nairobi from up high as it takes an hour to revolve 360 degrees. Some lunchtimes he took me to the Bacchus Club, where he'd buy me one of their signature cocktails and we'd eat fancy nibbles on silver trays. Waiters would often call us *Bwana* and *Memsaab*, meaning Mr and Mrs.

Over these meals, Dad would chat in a knowledgeable way about music, plants in the garden and cooking. Often, I even found the conversations interesting. I had few friendships or other relationships with other people so I had no choice but to get on with him on occasions like this.

One evening, around this time Dad made another request. He asked me to pluck all of the white hairs out of his scalp and then put them on my arm afterwards so he could count how many there were.

I stood behind him while he sat on a chair with the record player going (most likely the *Double Fantasy* album by John Lennon and Yoko Ono, he played it a lot at that time). Dad's dark hair was scattered with white now, so this was going to take a while. In fact, it took about an hour before I'd finished. He grabbed my arm and looked pleased. As soon as I could, I ran to the bathroom to wash the sticky hair follicles from my forearm, feeling absolutely revolted.

Another evening, he had a different demand: he wanted me to dye his hair dark with Grecian 2000. He insisted on leaving it on for longer than the packet suggested, so I didn't argue. When I rinsed it out, I had to rush out into the garden so he couldn't hear me giggling. It had almost bleached his hair white so he looked greyer than he had before we started. He was furious but there was nothing he could do. When I watched him go off to work the next day, I laughed my head off as soon as the door closed behind him.

But if Dad thought he was getting away with parading our close relationship, I began to suspect the neighbours had guessed something was very wrong. During one of the last lunch parties he threw for them many were left feeling very uncomfortable by his temper.

On one particular day I was told to make a fish dish, with

potatoes and string beans. Dad stood over me all day, criticising every move as always. By the time I'd finished, I was exhausted and the guests hadn't even arrived yet. People sat around the table, impressed at how I'd made such a huge dinner.

'Yes, she's good for some things,' my father chuckled.

As I brought the dishes out, people cooed at the food, commenting on how delicious it smelled while Dad glared at me. At first, I assumed no one had noticed the way he was looking at me – I was so used to his deadly hard stare, it was the norm anyway. But as I brought the hot plates through so people could help themselves, I noticed the polite conversation had quietened. Dad was drinking more than usual too, his voice becoming louder.

'Come on, Kim, bring it all through! We're hungry here.'

When I brought the boiled potatoes through, I spotted guests shifting uncomfortably in their seats. Everyone was silent as they ladled food onto their plates. I sat down to join them at last, when suddenly I remembered I'd forgotten the French beans so I dashed back into the kitchen to see I'd forgotten to turn them on. Quickly, I boiled the water, just for a minute as I could hear Dad calling me, drained them and brought them through.

*Perhaps nobody will notice they aren't cooked if I don't say anything?* I thought anxiously. Kicking myself, I wondered how I could have forgotten the veg. In reality, I'd been concentrating so hard on pulling the string off in one movement just as Dad insisted, I'd forgotten to cook them. Eager to pretend everything was okay, I ladled an extra portion of beans onto my plate.

'It all looks delicious,' said one guest. 'Well done to you, Kim.'

Dad took a bean himself and bit into it before removing it from his tongue as if it was poison.

'These aren't even cooked!' he said, then turned to his guests. 'Kim's head is elsewhere at the moment. She has all the brain and memory of a very old person.'

'Actually,' I said tentatively, 'I like beans done this way.'

Our guests looked at their plates and a few shot me a look of sympathy as Dad scraped his dining-room chair backwards to come to my side.

'Here,' he said, tipping the whole bowl of beans onto my plate. 'If you find them so delicious, you can eat them all!'

I tried to give a watery smile as I started crunching them one after another. By now everyone was totally silent, not knowing where to look.

Shame burned my cheeks as I worked my way through each bean, forcing myself to smile.

'Hmm, they're nice raw,' I said weakly, trying to defuse the situation.

But to everyone sat around that table it was obvious: Dad was a violent bully towards his own kids. This was a far cry from how he was viewed as DJ in the Woodley Club years ago, but he didn't seem to care anymore.

Around this time, one afternoon, our neighbour called Christine Layman popped in when Dad was out to borrow something – as an excuse to talk to me. Christine was a remarkable woman as it was known she'd had a son called Colin, who was the result of her being raped. Unusually, she spoke about this openly and without shame.

Although by now rape was a daily part of my life and had

been for years, I didn't equate what had happened to Christine with what was happening with me. Perhaps it was denial or I had just shut down about it, I don't know, but I admired this family all the same.

As we chatted about the hot weather, Christine gave me a concerned look. Her eyes locked onto mine. It made me uneasy so I glanced at my feet, mumbling about needing to get on with dinner.

'Kim,' she said, carefully, 'there is something about your dad I don't like. Please let me know if you need help.'

She seemed to be digging for information. I was so taken aback, I averted my gaze again. Then I quickly made my excuses and asked her to leave. She didn't push it, but simply said something like, 'Okay, I'm sorry to bother you.'

Afterwards, I never dwelled on this missed opportunity to finally tell someone the truth. It simply didn't seem possible any adult would ever believe me.

# Chapter 13

When Dad insisted I follow him to work, I found the days long and boring as I trailed around watching him mark papers, or was made to watch the lab technicians do dull experiments. Afterwards, he would bring home piles of textbooks, forcing me to learn exercises by heart. I didn't understand what all of this was for until one day he suddenly announced I was to teach his students a lesson by myself. I was terrified. Aged only seventeen, I didn't have any teaching qualifications and barely understood the subject myself as I'd only just begun my own course but none of this mattered to my father as he'd decided I was to play teacher.

Trying to make me understand his subject was another excuse to get angry at me too.

'You have to try harder,' he screamed, banging his fist onto the table. 'You mustn't embarrass me in front of my pupils. They look up to me as I am the best lecturer in this field.'

Time and again, he warned me I was turning into my mother.

'She did nothing with her life. If you leave me, you'll

turn into her. You need more experience and qualifications otherwise what are you going to do? You're out of options for a career because you keep failing your exams.'

I sat in tears, desperately trying to absorb the information. The evening drink Dad poured me was the only time I felt relaxed and by now I had been drinking regularly since I was a young teenager.

On the day of the lesson I wanted to run away as I watched all of these older students taking their seats in class. I was painfully shy anyway so this seemed like such a humiliation to pretend I could teach anyone anything, but Dad watched from the sidelines, a smirk on his face throughout.

I managed to mumble my way through the lesson, barely able to look up. Not only was I ashamed of being Mr Beaumont's daughter, I was ashamed of pretending to do his job.

For my eighteenth birthday, on 26 March 1983, there was no acknowledgement of it being a big birthday. I had a cake and was allowed to go to the cinema, but Dad appeared to want to play it down. Perhaps it's because he knew I was an adult. Officially and legally, I could have walked out of the house and never looked back. Except the reality was, I had no money, few qualifications and no way even of driving to the nearest town. Nothing had changed: whether I was now an adult or not, I was still dependent on him. I tried planting the seeds there was nothing in Kenya for me now but he didn't seem to appreciate this.

A few months later, Lucy came to live with us. She had been asking to come and join us for ages. I think perhaps Mum was under the impression that she was only coming out for a holiday. Although we hadn't grown up together, I loved having my little sister around. She was different to Susan, quieter, but soon settled in. Like our older sister, she was allowed a boyfriend and to go on school trips. By now I was used to being singled out.

Around this time, Dad answered an advert he'd spotted at his polytechnic. It was for extras for a new film called *Out of Africa* starring Meryl Streep and Robert Redford to be filmed in various locations in Kenya. The story was based on the memoirs of a Danish author called Karen Blixen, who recounts events of living in Africa for seventeen years.

When he asked if we'd be interested in taking part, both Lucy and I jumped at the chance. We signed up straight away but to my disappointment, Dad did so too.

'I'm not letting you do it if I can't,' he warned.

Over the last year he had become more and more reclusive. He'd stopped inviting friends over, long stopped DJing at the Woodley Club and only ever wanted to spend all his time in my company. He even began hiding when neighbours knocked on the door. One neighbour – Sean's best friend's mother Zoë, from a lovely Jewish family – saw straight through him, I could tell. When they did cross paths, I could see she hadn't fallen for his cut-glass accent and she'd question him about the things he said.

'That bloody woman,' he hissed at me after she left. 'Tell her I'm out next time!'

He only ever left the house for work or to take me out to dinner. Beforehand, he'd pour me drinks after dressing me in something he'd selected himself, like a burnt-orange knee-length skirt and high heels. He'd always choose a place slightly out of town so none of the neighbours spotted us and the Africans serving us would assume I was his wife. Often if they called me *memsaab* (the title for a woman in authority), I always tried to correct them before he spoke over me to hush me up. By the time the food arrived, I'd feel too sick to eat, just thinking about how we appeared like a couple.

But despite Dad wanting to be involved as usual, I couldn't resist the chance of being on a film set. I loved watching films and listening to music. They were the two rare occasions when I could pretend life was different to how it really was.

Lucy, Dad and I went to the audition and all won parts as background extras. My sister and I were to play the roles of colonial women, so the wardrobe department fitted us with incredible costumes from the pre-war era. Then we spent several days on set, being ushered from one location to another, trying to catch glimpses of the big stars. Wherever I was asked to stand, I always found Dad just at my elbow. He was constantly watching me, prepared to pounce if I so much as glanced at another extra other than my sister or him.

By the end of the first week, in a rare moment when my father wasn't around, an assistant director approached me.

'Hello, Kim, isn't it? Thanks for taking part. We've been watching you and wanted to ask if you'd like to play another role?' he said.

'Sorry?' I said.

I had such little confidence in myself, I wondered if this was a joke. But the look on this director's face told me it wasn't.

'We'd like to ask you if you can swim. Because if you can, we're looking for someone to play the stunt double for Meryl Streep,' he said.

Absolutely stunned, I opened my mouth to reply but the words came out as a garble.

'Yes,' I managed to splutter. 'But why me?'

'You look very much like her from the side angle.' He smiled. 'Similar bone structure.'

I was so flattered, I didn't know what to say but agreed to talk about the opportunity again the next morning. As I walked away, I felt as if I was walking on air. I touched the side of my face, wondering if they saw the same fat, ugly person I saw in the mirror. Maybe not?

That evening, I fizzed with excitement as I told Lucy and Dad my news. Surely Dad would be proud of me now? But, as I excitedly told him, I immediately guessed what his reaction was going to be.

He glared at me with his penetrating stare and sneered.

'You? Playing Meryl Streep's stunt double? I don't think so, Kim!' he mocked.

'But why not, Dad?' I asked.

I never normally bothered to try and argue with him but this was such an amazing opportunity. Couldn't he be happy for me just for once?

'Because you're not to be let out of my sight,' he snapped. 'As if you could ever do it anyway without messing it up. A stunt double indeed. How fanciful!'

Tears plopped silently down my face as I tried to eat dinner that night. The disappointment of knowing I'd have to say no the next day was too much to bear.

Although Lucy had quickly settled into life in Kenya, I could tell something was wrong. She was losing weight very rapidly and was tiny. She'd always been petite, and was by far the prettiest of us all, but this weight loss was too much.

Dad began taunting her for being anorexic, one of his favourite insults. I was either anorexic or too fat according to his mood. Neither of us had healthy relationships towards food.

Like Susan, Lucy was also allowed freedoms I wasn't, like making friends and staying over at their houses. She had boyfriends and could choose what she wore. A very pretty, vivacious girl, she quickly found a circle of friends yet I began to fear for her. One afternoon, the school rang Dad to make a complaint. In a cookery class, allegedly, where they were making chocolate cake, Lucy had taken a bite out of everyone's cake at lunchtime then made herself sick. I was worried that she was showing signs of bulimia. Dad's reaction to it, predictably, was one of anger: he'd try and force-feed her at dinner time, calling her mental, and as she grew thinner, taunted her for looking 'disgusting'.

Lucy soon hid her body with baggy clothes. I hated seeing her like this, but she never wanted to talk about it. Dad had also started to force her to make the Sunday lunches and jam instead of me. I was desperate to help her but he warned me off. I knew if I tried, he'd punish me. To Lucy, it looked like I was being lazy, leaving her to do it all, but in fact I was terrified and feared for her too.

During the uni holidays, Susan came over to visit and brought her boyfriend Greg with her. Greg was a lovely guy, but predictably, Dad was horrible to him: he was rude and followed him around the house like a shadow. He even told him he was not allowed to stay even one night in our house, so they left. I was so embarrassed – Greg had done nothing to warrant Dad's behaviour towards him.

Dad liked to give the impression I was a man-eater who would seduce any male who stepped foot over the threshold when the reality was, I was so shy, I could barely look anyone in the eye, let alone flirt with them. As always, having Lucy with us or someone over to stay, made no difference to Dad's routine of raping me most nights. It also never occurred to me to tell Lucy either – I was utterly within my father's control and after six years couldn't remember a time when I wasn't being raped.

In 1984, Dad bought me more new pets – a pair of Basset Hounds, a brother I called Hector and sister I named Annie (her full Kennel Club name was Annabelle of Ehrenkreutz). I adored these animals and decided to train them as show dogs, though it soon became clear that Hector didn't meet the breed standard for showing. Like Annie, he was tri-colour, but slightly darker where she was tan. He had the right temperament and appearance but his occipital bone was not prominent enough and his ears fell just short of the official standard length. Dad made me sell him to another expat (sadly, a month or so later, she told me he'd been bitten by a snake in their garden and had died). I was very sad about this, but I threw myself into training Annie.

Showing dogs was a hobby I absolutely loved and it gave me a chance to get out of the house. Dad always accompanied me to every single event, never letting me out of his sight, but I managed to get to know other dog owners and even won a few medals. Taking care of my dogs and taking pride in how they looked gave me another focus away from the horrors of Loresho Grove.

By the summer of that year, I'd finally finished my hated course in animal husbandry. I'd done as Dad had insisted and passed. The only pleasure I still had in life at this point was showing my Basset Hound, Annie (who went on to become a champion in January 1985). But even when I was going to dog shows or meetings at other people's houses, Dad would be there, right by my side, and he made sure that I only spoke to other women or elderly people. It was also becoming increasingly clear there was no real future for me in Kenya. We lived in an isolated place, I couldn't find work at the poly with Dad and there weren't any jobs suitable for a young woman with few qualifications.

My frustration began to spill over into conversations with my father, especially after I'd had a few drinks at night. He saw how hard I'd been trying, he knew I'd struggle to find work here. There was part of him that clearly cared about this, I could see it in his eyes.

*My brutal father still had a glimmer of sympathy for me.*

It was about this time that we moved from our lovely big bungalow in Loresho Grove to a small maisonette on Ngong Road. Dad never disclosed the reason for the move and it seemed very strange to me. He made sure that his room and mine were the only ones that could be accessed on the outside to each other's as they were joined by a balcony. He used this to his advantage as it meant he could come and go from and to my bedroom without anyone inside the house noticing.

I'd spend long days at home, cooking or cleaning, looking after the various pets and taking the dogs for a walk. Dad was becoming more and more of a recluse, preferring to spend every evening alone with me, yet I wouldn't let him off the hook for keeping me captive. One day, I dared to speak out in the hope he might relent.

'Dad, it's not fair that everyone else has got jobs but I'm stuck at home. Is this what you want for me? To lose the chance to further my education? You don't really want that for me, do you?' I'd said over dinner.

For years, he had screamed at me for being thick and now I was the one pointing out that he was holding me back. I chipped away whenever he was in a good mood or not too drunk to listen.

Around this time, Lucy's weight was more of a concern to me. My heart went out to her, but she refused to talk about it or even acknowledge it. Dad often bullied her about it, making her shrink into herself even further. He'd call her 'Twiggy'. Always, he was laughing at her. Away from the house, she was still a popular, seemingly happy person, so I wasn't overly worried about her.

After many months of my nagging about my lack of future prospects, Dad came home with news for me.

'I have booked you a place on a course,' he announced. 'To study Animal Technology, a two-year national certificate.'

My heart sank. I hated all the courses he'd suggested or forced me to do so far.

'It's at the North-East Surrey College of Technology,' he continued.

'In the UK?' I said, barely concealing my surprise.

'Yes,' he replied.

I was careful to look impassive though inside I was fizzing with excitement.

*Dad was actually going to let me return to the UK? On my own?*

'Okay, thank you, Dad,' I said calmly.

He nodded and then told me to go and pour him a glass of whisky. I did as I was told, knowing what was coming next, but what made it bearable was to know I wasn't going to endure this forever now.

That night after he raped me, I lay there listening to the sound of his breathing becoming heavier so I could escape to my bed. But even in my own bed sleep was impossible, as I thought about returning to the UK. I couldn't believe he was letting me go. I'd no idea how Dad was going to behave if I was living away from him.

The next morning, I woke vowing to keep calm. I knew he couldn't see me looking happy or excited or he'd change his mind.

As the date drew closer, Dad's moods seemed more volatile. Things in life were in flux now. He knew his contract as lecturer at the polytechnic was coming up and it might not be renewed. The political situation in Kenya was becoming increasingly volatile too, with clashes between the one nation state and political opposition parties. It was no longer a safe haven for expats to live and we often saw neighbours selling up and moving away. As much as Dad longed to maintain the status quo between us, he must have known time was running out.

My Animal Technology course was due to start in September 1985, in about three months' time. Dad explained he owned a house he rented out in Guiseley, West Yorkshire, where I could live with my sister Susan initially. He also said he'd apply for a bursary for me for college. I had no idea how this would be paid for and he took complete control. I almost didn't care – as soon as my plane landed in the UK, this nightmare would be over as far as I was concerned.

Dad told me he'd booked me on a flight for mid-July. He gave a date and told me to pack for it. For the next few weeks I was very careful never to show any emotion of excitement to him. If I ever said anything about being happy I was escaping, I feared he would cancel the flight. I ticked off the days in my head like a prisoner etching his final few days until freedom on a wall.

On the final night, I was so ecstatic, I could barely sleep. Dad made sure I couldn't anyway. He started to rape me, but then fell asleep due to the booze. I crept to my bed, only to be woken by him an hour or so later. As I closed my eyes, wanting to scream as usual, I tried to comfort myself with thoughts of stepping off the plane into the cold air of Heathrow before my connecting flight to Leeds. Then it would just be a short journey and I would be back home again. I couldn't wait to see Mum and Susan again. Yes, I was sad about leaving Lucy behind, but I hoped she might join me soon. As soon as she finished her A-levels, she would follow me.

In the morning, I woke up groggy as usual through lack of sleep but I had a spring in my step as I packed my case. I only had a few records and clothes I actually liked to wear so it wasn't much, but already I was planning what I'd do when I arrived. I needed a new wardrobe to rid myself of the hideous outfits Dad had chosen for me. Maybe I'd even have a haircut too, the first one in years. I had no money at all, except for a few coins saved from pocket money, but decided I'd worry about things one day at a time. The plan was I'd go and stay with Mum at first and then move into the house in Guiseley, a few miles away.

There was only one person I was truly sorry to say good-bye to: Annie, my beautiful dog. She was so precious to me. Dad promised he'd take care of her but I didn't believe him. He shouted at her when he was in a bad mood and I'd even caught him kicking her in the face. I dreaded to think what might happen if I wasn't there. As I knelt down and pushed my face against hers, Dad caught me with tears in my eyes.

'Ah, you see, you'll miss the animals, won't you?' he said.

He'd often used the pets as an excuse to tempt me home when I was at Hunmanby Hall. And he was right, they always made me feel loved.

'Yes,' I admitted.

I gave Annie one last stroke and picked up my bag.

'Ready?' said Dad.

I tried not to smile as I walked to the car but really, I felt like punching the air.

As my father drove me to the airport, I squeezed my knees together to stop them from trembling with excitement and kept my face impassive. As we approached the car park, he was quiet so I kept silent too. He helped me with my bag to the waiting area for the flights.

'Stay here,' he ordered. 'You're on a last-minute flight so you need to wait to be called. I'll go and ask at the desk.'

I wasn't sure why he needed to ask, but I hadn't seen my ticket yet so I assumed he was picking it up then.

After half an hour, other travellers started to gather their belongings as the flight I was supposed to be on was called to the gate. I began to shift uncomfortably in my seat.

*Surely Dad would be back soon with my ticket?*

Finally, his face emerged from the queue. He was shaking his head.

'Sorry, Kim. You're not on this flight.'

'What?' I said.

'I had you on standby, you're not guaranteed a seat,' he explained.

I swallowed the immediate lump that had formed in my throat to hide my reaction.

*The tight so-and so! How could this be happening?*

He shrugged. 'No room on this plane for you so off we go back home,' he smirked.

I was totally confused as a hot redness crept up my neck. I wanted to howl with disappointment but instead blinked furiously to prevent tears as I followed him back to the car.

*This was a nightmare.*

On the way home Dad chatted about his work as if nothing had happened. When we pulled into the driveway, he told me he would sort out another flight for a few weeks' time as if we'd had a simple holiday postponed.

Back at home, I tried to deal with the disappointment of still being stuck in Kenya with the man I hated most in the world. I felt a new wave of numbness wash over me, because the pain of knowing escape had been within reach and then snatched away was too awful to bear.

# Chapter 15

A few weeks later, Dad was true to his word and we were driving back to the airport. This time, he said he'd make sure I made the flight. I had no reason to disbelieve him so I contained my sense of desperation as we walked calmly into the Departures lounge.

He made me wait in the seating area as he approached the check-in desk. I could see him having an animated conversation with a smart air steward, who was frowning and checking a list. As he walked back over, his face was an unreadable mask.

'They don't have a seat for you,' he said, simply. 'Back home it is again, Kim!'

It never dawned on me to ask what he'd said to Susan. He'd told me that she would be picking me up from the airport, but if I was meant to be on all the other flights, why didn't he tell her? I believe I was only booked on the flight when we attended the airport the last time. I never mentioned it to my sister when she met me at Leeds Bradford airport – I didn't want to say what Dad had been up to. She never mentioned anything either about cancelled flights so he was obviously playing some kind of game with me.

I didn't know if this happening twice was better or worse. I willed my body to put one foot in front of the other, back to his car.

A week later, when Dad said we were going again for the third time, I almost didn't believe him. He blamed the plane being overbooked, but looking back, I think it had become yet another game of control for him.

Dad found us a seat at a rickety table below the board announcing the gate number and went to the airline desk to see if I was on the flight. I barely bothered to look out for him as he returned, waving a ticket. I glanced at it, resisting the urge to snatch it from his hand.

'There it is, Kim,' he said. 'Your ticket to the UK.'

I reached out calmly to take it, half-expecting him to snatch it back and say it was a joke. He looked at me carefully as I held on to it.

My eyes roved over the details: it was valid for that day. It confirmed I was flying from Nairobi to Heathrow, then on to Leeds Bradford.

*It was a genuine ticket.*

Pressing my lips together, I willed myself not to smile or show emotion. Dad was studying my face. He told me to follow him to the gate, so I did, sheep-like, trying to control my breathing.

*Is this it? Am I finally going?* I wondered.

It was impossible to believe.

In the next queue, I found myself fumbling for my passport. I checked and triple-checked it was valid until I feared the numbers might magically change into the invalid ones. I put it back in my pocket, patting it numerous times to make sure it was still there. To keep calm, I focused on the number of people in front of us in the queue. Holding my breath, I flashed my ticket as we were allowed through to a lounge.

I could barely believe this was going to happen as he said he needed to speak to the stewardess again. Once again, a numbness overcame me as he disappeared. I might have my ticket this time, which hadn't happened before, but I knew he could be taking me home once again.

*This could be another false alarm.*

He returned, his face inscrutable. Then he patted my arm.

'You are on this flight, Kim,' he said, finally.

As I looked my father in the eye, I felt light-headed. To my shock, I could see tears forming in his eyes. Eyes that often sent terror into my heart now wept with sadness; I started to cry too.

This man was my abuser but he was still my father. He was the only person who'd provided for me for almost a decade. I was dependent on him for everything. Now we were saying goodbye. I stared at him, unable to comfort him in any way. As I opened my mouth to say something, nothing emerged so I nodded, acknowledging his upset. He nodded back at me as I realised to the outside world, for once, we looked like an ordinary father and daughter saying an emotional goodbye.

The gate number was called over the tannoy. It was time to go, so I took my bag, half-expecting him to pull me back. My heart was beating so hard like a drum, I feared he'd hear it, see I was excited and stop me from going at the last second. Carefully, I arranged the features on my face so I betrayed nothing.

Holding on to my ticket for dear life, I pecked my father goodbye on the cheek then I began walking through the security gate, the point of no return. Each step, I kept thinking, *He's going to call me back. I'm going to find out this ticket is void. He's suddenly going to join me.*

I stepped through the metal gate and turned my head to make sure I was alone.

And I was.

Dad was waving, tears streaking his face. I waved until I was finally out of sight, then broke into the biggest smile, gave the biggest sigh and only just stopped myself from sobbing with joy.

*This was it, I was finally escaping!*

It was 22 July 1985, nearly nine years to the day since Sean and I had left England for what we thought was going to be a week's holiday of a lifetime. I was only twenty, but I'd been forced to grow up so fast in those nine years. I walked onto the plane as if walking on air. Part of me believed perhaps Dad was still going to appear by my side as he had done for so many years. But as more passengers crowded behind me, the fear began to vanish. I clicked my seatbelt around me and gazed out of the window onto the runway. This was the moment I'd spent years longing for. I watched the luggage handlers throw bags into the hold as a range of emotions coursed through me. Inside I was punching the air, jumping for joy and laughing my head off all at the same time. This was a heady kind of ecstasy I'd never experienced before; it was better than any drink.

As the plane taxied down the runway and the engine roared into life, I allowed my shoulders to relax. Dad still hadn't jumped on board, he definitely wasn't coming.

I landed at Heathrow to grey, drizzly skies but to me it felt like a new dawn. The blast of the fresh cool air as we disembarked, something I'd experienced on every visit back, smelled pure and clean.

Knowing my father was thousands of miles away made life appear sharper, more colourful. Catching sight of myself in a glass window as we walked though Security to get my next flight to Leeds Bradford, I realised how much of an expat I looked, with my dark tan, strange clothes and long style-free hairdo – I had lots to do to change so that I could fit in.

As I walked through Arrivals after landing in Leeds Bradford, my sister Susan was behind the barrier, looking for me. Her face broke into a big smile as I walked into her swift hug. Greg was standing by her side with a camera.

'Take a picture of us.' She grinned.

He took a shot of the historic moment. Tired, but brimming with relief, my smile could not be more genuine or wider. As we walked away from the airport, I found myself still looking over my shoulder every now and again. I half-expected Dad's thunderous face to emerge from the crowd, telling me it was all a mistake and frogmarching me back onto the next Nairobi-bound flight. But even if I saw him in every middle-aged man with greying hair, he wasn't here – he was far, far away.

We drove straight to Mum's house. I'd not been there for so long and she was living in a new three-bedroom council house in Markham Avenue in Rawdon. When we arrived, she was there with her arms open, ready for a big cuddle.

As usual, it was freezing cold inside. It seemed darker than it was because of the net curtains at the window. No longer white, they were more of a yellowish grey and the place reeked of Mum's favourite cigarettes but it was lovely to see her all the same.

'Hello, Kim, love, it's so good to have you back,' she said, breathing into my hair.

I tried to hug her tightly but was afraid I'd break something. Her fragile shoulder blades jutted through her cardigan, which hung off her. She had the body of a woman much older than her forty-something years.

'Sit down, sit down,' she fussed. 'Tell me all about the flight home.'

I began to respond but she didn't listen for long. On every visit, Mum was always the same. She'd make an initial fuss of you on arrival but then you'd have to make your own tea – that's if there was any milk in the fridge or it was in date.

Susan went to get something to eat but returned to say the smell of the fridge put her off.

'I'll go get something from the chippy,' she said.

Mum was sitting in her usual chair, staring at me as if she couldn't believe I was there.

'You've got a beautiful tan, Kim,' she repeated.

Looking down at the side of her chair, I saw a drink in a chipped mug. There was wine in it rather than tea. I quashed worries about Mum's escalating drink problem when Susan returned with some food. We sat eating, chatting about what I was going to do next. My course started in six weeks.

Until then, I wanted to get new clothes, a haircut and settle back into life in the UK. Mum immediately gave me some money.

'You need to treat yourself,' she said.

I took it with thanks. I knew money was tight for her, so I was grateful. Dad hadn't given me anything to come over here with. I half-wondered if he did that on purpose to make it harder to settle back in. I couldn't imagine him wanting me to choose my own outfits or take pride in my appearance in case I attracted men. He'd already warned me to stay away from them. His plan hadn't worked, however, as I planned to go shopping and get my hair sorted out as soon as possible. But first, I booked an appointment the next day to see Mum's GP. I wanted to register there, but also, I wanted to do something else. The pain of the secrecy surrounding Dad's abuse had always been kept locked inside. Even on my first day of freedom, the burden of the secret felt unbearable. Now an overwhelming urgency to tell someone, *anyone*, meant I had decided to take action.

I couldn't tell Mum, I didn't know how she'd react, if she'd believe me or even if she'd be so upset, she'd get drunk and do something stupid. And I couldn't tell my sisters. Lucy was still over there. Susan, well, I loved her to bits but feared she wouldn't believe me and I didn't know what her reaction would be. I couldn't tell Sean either – we'd grown apart since he'd moved away to boarding school. Again, I feared he'd never believe me. I didn't even contemplate telling the police. I had no doubt they would think I was lying. Dad always had a way of talking to people to make them think he was the cleverest person in the room. He'd charm them, convince them I was mad. I wasn't going to put myself through that for nothing. Besides, there was another reason I didn't want to tell the police: a big part of me simply didn't want to get him in trouble. I'd feel so guilty about it. After all, he was still my father, the only one I'd ever had. Could I really bear to watch my own dad being led away in handcuffs? It frightened me. Maybe he wouldn't cope in prison or he'd think even less of me for putting him there.

So, my only option was to tell a stranger or better still, someone in authority. A local doctor was the only person I felt comfortable telling because they had to maintain patient confidentiality. I could say whatever I liked, unburden myself and walk away, knowing my secret was shared, but without consequence. At this stage that was all I wanted to do.

I booked the appointment the next morning to see Dr Booth from Mum's surgery. I caught the bus there. As I sat in the waiting room, watching people coughing or sitting with a bandage around a finger, I wondered if the GP would have encountered a patient with a 'problem' like mine before. I put my hands in my lap, knowing I'd been forced to live the most disgusting secret, but I believed this would somehow make it better.

As I crossed and uncrossed my legs, fidgeting in my seat, I wondered if the doctor would want proof. No. I just needed to blurt out this secret so someone, somewhere, knew what had happened and then I could get on with my life.

*Kim Beaumont!*

I almost missed my name when it was called by the receptionist. I stood abruptly as if pushed off my seat by an invisible force, and followed the doctor into his room.

The doctor, a man in his early forties, sat behind a desk, peering at notes.

'You're a new patient, Miss Beaumont,' he said matter-of-factly. 'So, how can I help?'

I shuddered at his words, which took me back to seeing the doctor in Nairobi when I was pregnant, but I was here now, so I took a deep breath and began to speak.

# Chapter 16

'I ha–have … something to, er, get off my chest,' I stammered. Tears formed in my eyes, but I tried to ignore them. This was much harder than I'd expected. My hands sweated as I took a deep breath, willing myself to form the words. I was determined finally to speak the truth.

'You mustn't tell anyone,' I added, clearing my throat, 'but my father … he raped me for years.'

If the doctor was surprised or shocked, he didn't show it. Instead he blinked at me.

'I see,' he said slowly. 'Have you told anyone about this?'

'Only one friend.'

'Have you told your mother?'

'No.'

'Why not?'

'I didn't want to burden her with this. She isn't very well herself, she wouldn't understand,' I replied, staring at the pile of notes on his desk.

The doctor gazed at me with a look of sympathy I'd never seen before as he scribbled notes down.

'Have you had any help?' he asked.

'Help?' I replied, shaking my head.

I really didn't know what he meant. I knew I was damaged. I understood a great wrong had been done to me yet it had happened in the past and nobody could change that, could they? As Dad had told me a hundred times, nobody would believe a man like him could do such a thing.

Dr Booth pondered for a moment, obviously wondering what the next step should be.

'You cannot tell anyone,' I said more forcefully.

As if this clarified things in his own mind, he nodded.

'Okay, Kim. Well, I have made a note of this. Should you want to tell me anything else, please make another appointment. My door is always open to you.'

I stood up, my limbs feeling much lighter. I'd done it! I'd told someone and he'd obviously believed me. There was no way I could ever contemplate telling the police. They'd never believe me over Dad and I had no evidence; this was the next best thing. I thanked the doctor, even gave him a smile, and walked away. Nothing had changed what my father had done, but telling someone else made it that bit easier to bear. I walked home, breathing deeply, thinking I should move on. There was nothing more I could do, except focus on the here and now.

Three days after I arrived, Susan invited me to a birthday party. Greg's brother Jonathan was having a do to celebrate his twenty-first at his dad's house in Northallerton, where he still lived.

'You need to let your hair down, Kim,' she said. 'You really haven't lived yet. It would do you the world of good.'

'I can't go anywhere looking like this,' I said, pulling at my dress. It was a horrible patterned one, something Dad had bought for me in Kenya.

'Then we'll sort that out too,' said Susan.

The next afternoon, I went shopping for some new clothes with the money Mum had given me. I bought a pair of jeans and a top. Understated but fashionable clothes to make me feel less like a freak. I had my hair cut and asked for soft curls. Afterwards, I stared in the mirror to see Deirdre from *Coronation Street* staring back with the short hair and light perm, but too embarrassed to say anything, I thanked the hairdresser and went home to Mum's. She told me it looked lovely, but by then she was sitting quietly in her chair, drunk, so I didn't believe her. I thought it was awful and when I saw Susan later, she laughed but in a nice way.

The next day, we went to Jonathan Chown's party – an unusual surname, Chown originated in Kent in the twelfth century and means 'Son of Chun'. Anyway, when I walked into the large lounge of their smart house packed with family and friends I didn't know, I fought the urge to run away. Susan introduced me to Greg's siblings – Jonathan, Andrew, Daryl and Joanna – and to their father and stepmother, who their dad had married after their mother passed away in 1982, aged forty-eight, due to ovarian cancer.

I was completely out of my depth at such a social gathering. It was okay for Susan as she had Greg there and already knew the Chown family whereas I felt like a third wheel. But I could see why she thought they were so special. They were an ordinary well-to-do middle-class family; Jonathan teased his stepmother with a silly sense of humour. I watched this ordinary, easy-going family with a mix of fascination and envy. I had no idea what it must feel like not to live in fear. To laugh and joke with family members without worrying about a change in atmosphere. Standing in their living room, with their comfortable clean furniture and loving family photos on the walls, I felt like a stain on the sofa. With my strange new haircut and clothes, I was far from comfortable in my own skin.

At one point, I saw Jonathan sitting opening his presents with enthusiasm. He turned, nodded an acknowledgement and then turned back. I noticed he hated being the centre of attention. I had never had a birthday party as big as this and wondered what it felt like.

*He's probably wondering who the hell I am*, I thought miserably. Wanting to keep out of the way, I sat on a three-seater settee, watching everyone nervously. *Could they be laughing at my Deirdre Barlow haircut?* I thought self-consciously. I hated my hair but there was nothing to be done about it. There was party food everywhere. I was hungry but hated eating in front of people. Even if Dad was safely in another country, I still felt anxious around food. His voice echoed around my head, telling me I was fat, ugly and shouldn't eat anything nice.

'Hey, don't jump in my grave so fast, will you?' a voice said suddenly.

I looked up and a guest was laughing at me.

'That's my seat,' said a young man.

I stammered an apology and wanted the ground to open up and swallow me. With Susan busy with Greg, I reached for a plate for party food to find something to do with my hands. Already, I wondered what time I could leave.

As the evening stretched out, everyone went on to a nightclub to continue the party and Susan encouraged me to join them. On the way there I thought of my life back in Kenya and felt a sudden pang of loss. I missed Annie and my thoughts turned to home.

By the end of the evening, I'd shrugged off my shyness, thanks to visiting the nightclub bar. The next morning, with a bad hangover, Susan told me how much Jonathan had liked me. I laughed it off – the last thing on my mind was finding a boyfriend.

That afternoon, Susan and I were invited along with Greg, Jonathan and Andrew to a caravan in Runswick Bay. The brothers were a good laugh and we happily joined them for drinks in the local pub to continue the birthday celebrations. As we sat down, Jonathan chatted to me properly for the first time.

As we chatted, we began flirting. I liked his silly sense of humour. He had such a kind, handsome face too and he made me feel comfortable as he gently teased me about my accent.

'I can't work out if you sound American, Australian or South African, but you certainly sound colonial,' he laughed.

'That's thanks to the elocution lessons Dad made us have.' I giggled, making it sound like I was from a normal family with a normal father who cared and that felt good.

Jonathan had been to university to study law but had to abandon the course following the untimely death of his mother. He now worked in the family window joinery business with his brother, Daryl. He was young, but I was impressed by his work ethic and found him attractive. Best of all, I didn't feel threatened by him, which was unusual when it came to men.

When it was his turn to get a round in, I spotted him flirting with the barmaid and felt something I'd never experienced before: jealousy. It was then I realised how much I liked him.

Afterwards, we all returned to the caravan to continue our evening. When I needed to use the loo, I was embarrassed to be using such a small space, so close to everyone. I hadn't been in a caravan for years either. Not since 1981 when Dad got a small caravan somewhere on the coast for a weekend for the two of us.

Once the beer was finished, Jonathan brought out a bottle of whisky he'd been given for his birthday.

'I can drink you under the table with that,' I laughed. 'I love whisky.'

That wasn't strictly true, as it reminded me of Dad. But I knew I could impress the lads with a drinking game.

'Well, whisky is my favourite drink, so I bet you can't,' Jonathan grinned.

'Just try then,' I said.

Giggling, we matched each other, downing the throat-burning liquid one shot after another.

Triumphantly, we finished the bottle before I staggered off to bed, hoping I'd covered up my shyness and lack of confidence. The next morning, I vowed never to touch the stuff again as I felt so sick in the car on the way home to Leeds. After I'd recovered, I asked Susan about Jonathan.

'Has he got a girlfriend?' I asked.

'Why, do you like him too?' she teased.

'Maybe,' I said coyly.

'Great!' she laughed. 'I'll set you two up on a date together.'

True to her word, a few weeks later she arranged for me to meet Jonathan again. We got on even better by ourselves, sharing a similar sense of humour and a love of a drink or two. After a couple of weeks, we were an item. Best of all, he didn't mention or even suggest any intimacy, which I took as a mark of respect for me. Also, he kept telling me how much fun I was, which I loved. For once I could be the person I'd always wanted to be, not the fearful child terrified of her father's next move.

A week or so later, Susan and I moved into the Guiseley house Dad owned, a few miles away from Mum. The place was bare, with little furniture, but Dad was keen for someone to look after it. We didn't mind either as neither of us liked staying at Mum's – it was always dusty there and very cold. Mum smoked a lot too and our clothes would smell. Although the house in Guiseley belonged to Dad, I wasn't worried about him being there. After all, he was busy with work and had no plans to return to the UK.

For the next few nights I was hardly able to sleep as I couldn't believe how fast my life had changed. Jonathan and I were getting to know each other and I was living an independent life – a life I'd only ever dared dream of.

On one of our early dates, he and I jumped in a car and drove to the nearest fair. We drank bottled beers and went on all the rides.

'Kim,' said Jonathan, as we sat together, 'you're honestly the most fun and relaxed girl I've met.'

I snuggled up to him, feeling so happy. I was glad he

thought so. Jonathan need never know the truth about my family, especially my dad. It was bad enough he'd met Mum, but I explained that away as her being a drinker. He had already heard Dad was a bit of a nutter after his brother's visit to Kenya, but none of that seemed to matter in our blossoming relationship.

I'd been living at the house for several weeks when one morning, the front door opened when I was in the kitchen. I wasn't expecting anyone but turned to see Dad's face smirking at me. Clearly, he enjoyed paying this surprise visit.

'Hi, Dad,' I said. I found myself edging backwards as he walked towards me, arms outstretched.

'Kim! How are you settling in?' he asked, his eyes flashing.

I forced myself to look and sound calmer inside than I felt.

'Oh, fine! Dad, how are you?' I replied. 'Didn't know you were popping in.'

He pulled out a kitchen chair and sat down heavily; he looked tired. He started talking about the flight, then began slagging off Mum, who he'd also been to see.

I didn't say anything. Being alone with him had changed the air in the room. I remained standing as I clutched the work counter behind me. As if reading my fear, he got to his feet abruptly. Moving up closer to me, I turned my face away. The familiar scent of his stale cigarettes made my stomach twist. He hugged me, his nose in my hair.

'You smell wonderful, Kim,' he said.

*It was the same nightmare all over again.*

He grabbed me by the arm, pulled me upstairs and raped me on my bed. I'd been unprepared for this attack.

Afterwards, he went downstairs as I lay there crying, unable to believe what had just happened, knowing there really was no escape. Even if we lived in different countries, it didn't matter – Dad still had total control, I'd always have to be on my guard.

I managed to gather myself and got up to have a bath and wash him off me. I knew I couldn't tell anyone, least of all Jonathan – he'd never want to be with me if he knew my dad was forcing me to have sex with him.

I went back down to find my father sitting at the kitchen table with a glass of whisky, an overnight bag by his side.

'I'm staying here for a week,' he smirked.

I knew then I'd face multiple attacks. I almost blamed myself for making things worse by not trying hard enough to resist his attack.

'You know, we could still run away together,' he said, pouring another drink. 'I still want you, Kim.'

I didn't want to hang around, so I grabbed my coat and left, telling him I was off to meet a friend in Harrogate. I had nowhere to go, except to meet Jonathan later on at Leeds station for our date, but I just needed to get out.

Later, when I met Jonathan he told me he'd bumped into Dad earlier at the house when he'd dropped off a surfboard he was lending his brother Greg. In a bid to make polite conversation, Jonathan had asked Dad where the station was, even though he knew perfectly well. Dad guessed he was meeting me so he sent him in the opposite direction.

'Your father is a bit odd, isn't he, Kim?' he observed.

'What do you mean?' I asked, not wanting him to guess what Dad had done to me.

'I mean, he doesn't smile and didn't seem very pleased to see me,' he said.

Of course, Jonathan had heard all about our weird dad from Greg but he'd never seen it for himself.

'That's just Dad, I guess.' I shrugged, then changed the subject.

All I hoped was that Dad was going back to Kenya soon. Already I was dreading going home that night because I knew what I faced.

# Chapter 17

Dad might have temporarily lost control of my day-to-day life, but I was still signed up for the two-year course in Animal Technology in Epsom that he wanted me to do. After settling back in Leeds, I didn't want to go at all. Clearly, Dad did, as he didn't want me around my family. He often warned me not to tell anyone about our secret, but he didn't need to worry.

*Despite having told my doctor, I still didn't think anyone would believe me.*

In September 1985, I said a sad goodbye to Jonathan, who vowed to come and visit me, and left to live on my own in digs in a house in Stoneleigh, a suburb of south-west London. Dad didn't pay a penny towards it and I had to have a grant to cover for the accommodation. I had only a few pounds from Mum when I arrived, no other money.

Thankfully, after a couple of weeks Dad returned to Kenya to sort out his affairs. He was still lecturing at the polytechnic, but I think he'd applied for jobs elsewhere and was considering another one at Brunei University. Lucy was still with him. As long as he didn't return to live in the UK full-time, I didn't care where he went.

For the first time I was living independently and should have felt free but instead I was out of my depth and somewhat abandoned in this strange new place away from everyone. My confidence had hit rock bottom, especially since Dad had raped me again. I couldn't help but blame myself for not escaping him completely.

While this disturbed my mind and my sleep, I also had more pressing things to worry about. After a day or so, I'd spent all my money on a few bits of food and clothing. I didn't have a bean and without anyone to turn to, I began to panic. I could have asked Jonathan but I didn't want to, as he had little money himself and I didn't want to be a burden so I looked for a part-time job straight away. After an afternoon of not finding anything, I was very worried. I literally had nothing at all and had eaten the last of my food.

Without anyone to turn to, I went to visit the Department of Social Security. Benefit applicants had to book an appointment to see anyone but in desperation I stood outside their office and begged anyone going in for help. Eventually someone took pity on me and let me inside, so I could speak to staff.

'You're a student, apply for a grant,' a blank-faced official told me from behind the counter.

I began to cry, explaining I couldn't get one in time. It would take days to apply and I couldn't even afford to pay for a stamp for the envelope. (I was later told officially and Dad also told me that I was not entitled to any benefits or a student loan as I had not been a full-time student in the UK for the last three years. I was waiting for money to come through for accommodation, but that was all. Dad wouldn't give me any money either.)

'I don't have a single penny,' I sobbed.

Thankfully, he took pity on me and gave me a pound to buy something to eat.

On the way home, I asked in every pub I passed for a job until one agreed to take me on for a trial shift. It was right next to the railway station in Stoneleigh. I was so grateful, I could have hugged the landlord.

I bought a loaf of bread and butter, then went home and ate it alone on my bed. This wasn't the fresh start I'd been hoping for.

The next day, I began my new job and worked every evening alongside my college course. I had just five pounds a week to live off. All I could afford to eat was one pitta bread smeared with chicken paste but it was better than nothing. I was always hungry but knew I had to finish this course. I feared what Dad would do if I missed a single lesson or, worse still, failed.

In many ways it didn't matter that my father wasn't physically present to tell me what to do – he lived inside of my head. Often, I could hear his opinion as if he was on my shoulder, commenting on how I looked, the way I studied, what I was eating. Sometimes I had to take a breath and remind myself firmly he wasn't *actually* here. In theory, I could do what I wanted now – except somehow I couldn't. The rapes in Guiseley had proven this. This became maddening and the only time my thoughts stopped rattling around in my head was when someone bought me a drink behind the bar or I was asleep. Dad also kept me controlled by not giving me any money and sending two letters a week. There was always an undertone to them and although it was not spelled out in the letters, I knew what he was getting at. He'd be careful not to write anything that could be used against him, but still slipped in the odd phrase to subtly show me he still 'wanted' me. For example, he would say, 'Your room is just the way you left it, it still smells of you.'

I'd put them in the bin, feeling nauseous.

Dad had such a domineering presence that when he visited the UK, it was like an overbearing whirlwind ran through our family, especially as he was so opinionated about what everyone else was up to. Like me, I believe Susan, Sean and Lucy all craved his validation. Even Mum still cared what he thought. Despite him slagging her off to us, he'd often drink and laugh with her. Afterwards, when I was alone with him, he'd slag Mum off again.

When Dad wasn't there, his name always cropped up in our conversations on my visits home. It was either what he was up to, when he was coming over again or what he'd said or done on his last visit. I was so disappointed in myself. Even alone in my bedsit, thousands of miles away from him, I couldn't stop thinking about my awful father. What was wrong with me?

Thankfully, Jonathan was true to his word and came down to visit frequently. His easy-going nature meant that he was always happy to do what I wanted. Often, I suggested going to the pub, but even if we didn't, I always found myself going to the local shop to take some booze with us wherever we were going.

Jonathan had so much respect for me and let me take things at my own pace. I felt very lucky to have found someone like him. Everything between us happened so naturally and unfolded as it was meant to.

Once again, just as I was beginning to relax into my new way of life, Dad burst my bubble. I was visiting Mum's house one weekend when he called on the phone.

'You're coming over to Kenya for Christmas, Kim,' he announced abruptly. He didn't need to ask if I wanted to or pause to hear what I thought because he wasn't interested – he was telling me, not asking me.

I bit my lip, grateful he couldn't see my face.

'Okay, Dad,' I said calmly.

'Tickets will be in the post. Don't miss that flight now,' he said.

I replaced the phone, feeling sick to the pit of my stomach. There was no way I could decline this invitation. In fact, it didn't even occur to me it was *even possible* to say no. After years of being controlled, I instantly said yes to everything he demanded. I was still in his power, he still controlled me. If Dad wanted it, I did it, no questions asked – I couldn't even imagine any other choices.

I knew I was walking back into the lion's den but aside from being under his spell, part of me naïvely clung to the idea that things could be different. After all, on rare occasions, Dad went weeks without attacking me. I imagined that I could perhaps fend him off. A large part of me clung to a fantasy he might even stop doing it and we could have a normal relationship, especially now I had a boyfriend. I wanted to believe he'd changed and he wouldn't rape me or treat me like he used to.

*It might seem madness to return to my abuser but the reality was that for me there wasn't a choice.*

Sure enough, a week later, the plane ticket from Leeds Bradford to Heathrow to Nairobi arrived, along with a note, asking me to pick up the Top 20 singles for my dad.

'We still can't get the latest chart singles here,' he'd written. 'And it would be nice for the party we're having. I enclose the money for them.'

I closed my eyes at the thought of what I was facing. Dad getting drunk. His music blasting out of the stereo. Just the thought of some of those old songs took me straight back to him raping me. If I ever heard Pink Floyd's *Dark Side of the Moon* or 'Telephone Guy' or music from *The Rocky Horror Show* on the radio I always switched it off as fast as possible. Even hearing the first notes of those songs sent my heart rate high, my head spinning. The thought of setting foot in Dad's house with him there, always around me, his breath smelling of fags, the way he controlled me through food, the fear at night-time … it made me want to weep helplessly.

As I held the ticket in my hands, I stared at the 'return' part of it. At least I had a return ticket. I could hide it in my bedroom to make sure he didn't take it away from me. I also thought of my precious Basset Hound, Annie. I missed her so much. Instead of thinking about Dad, I decided to focus on seeing her and my sister Lucy again.

On the day I left, Jonathan saw me off at the airport. After we kissed goodbye, I smiled broadly, pretending I was a normal daughter going home to see her family at Christmas.

'Make sure you keep in touch,' he said, holding me tightly. 'Ooh, do you have a number I can reach you on?'

I looked at him helplessly. My first instinct was to say 'No, sorry' but then I realised how oddly this might come across. He knew my dad was strict and a bit strange but I couldn't ban him from calling me for weeks. So, despite knowing my father would be furious, I quickly scribbled down the landline in Kenya.

'It's expensive,' I warned. 'You won't be able to ring too often.'

'Nothing is too much for you, Kim,' he said, pecking me on the cheek one last time. 'Love you.'

As I walked away from him, I fixed a smile on my face to try and stop myself from crying. My lovely boyfriend had no idea what a twisted world I was travelling back to – I never wanted him to know either.

As I settled into my seat on the plane, it felt as if every part of me was screaming 'Don't go!', yet I had forced my body to take the steps onto the plane, buckle up, sit back and try to relax. Somehow I managed to doze off and all too quickly it was time for the plane to land. As if an automaton, I walked off the plane through Security, collected my suitcase and met my father in Arrivals.

'You're back, Kim.' He beamed, pulling me roughly into a hug. 'I've missed you.'

I felt like a prisoner being led back to her cell as I climbed into his car to be driven to the maisonette on Ngong Road.

Dad took me inside to show me back to my room.

'This is yours again.' He smiled.

His room and mine shared a balcony, which meant he could slyly creep into my room without anyone noticing.

When he offered me a finger of whisky to 'welcome me home', I knocked it back.

*Oh God*, I thought. *Why did you ever come here again?*

The only good thing was having Annie in my arms again. As soon as I walked into the lounge, she ran straight over to me. She had lost weight and her coat didn't look shiny anymore, but at least she was still here.

Lucy emerged from her room soon after I arrived to say hello. I returned her hug but was afraid I'd crush her with any pressure. Her bones protruded from her shoulders and her arms were so thin. I desperately wanted to say something, but knew better than to upset her.

With both of us there, Dad quickly poured more drinks, smiling. He put his arm around my shoulders and I tensed my body to stop myself from instinctively pulling away.

'So, Kim has a boyfriend now, did you know this, Lucy?' he said in a creepy way. 'Both my girls have boyfriends.' He had a weird smirk on his face, so I changed the subject.

I spotted Lucy looking down at her drink in her hand. I wondered what was going through her mind. Not for the first time I wondered if Dad was now attacking her as he did me, but I never could bring myself to say anything, the idea was completely taboo.

We had dinner together and Dad played all the records I'd brought over. We even had a drunken dance around the room. It felt good to see Lucy smile again. She had an air of sadness about her I'd not noticed before. When it was time to go to bed, the old fear quickly returned. I found myself shutting my bedroom door and wanting to put a chair behind it, but also, I felt resigned to coping with whatever was going to happen. I knew I couldn't stop Dad, he had control as usual – I'd just have to survive this attack, like all the others. I lay in bed waiting for any sound, either footsteps or his heavy breathing at the door.

It didn't take long before the sound of the door opening came and it was as if I'd never been away. Within seconds of the attack, I went limp, as always. Any fantasy about things being any different or me being able to defend myself soon vanished.

I cried with pain but also deep guilt. It felt like I was cheating on Jonathan. I was riddled with shame, wondering how I'd face him – I never wanted him to know what my dad did in case he ended things with us.

On the fourth day, the phone rang at home: it was Jonathan. I knew Dad would view this as an act of defiance and I was right.

He picked up the phone, eyeing me as Jonathan asked to speak to me.

'She's not here,' he said bluntly and put the phone down.

Jonathan didn't give up. He rang a few times over the next few days, but Dad always put him off. Eventually he did get through and I managed to chat to him for about ten minutes, pretending everything was fine. There was no way I ever wanted him to know what happened.

Dad waited until Lucy went to bed and then quietly crept into my room via the balcony. I felt like the little girl in Kenya again, miles away from anyone who could help. Besides, who would believe me? Especially as I was an adult and had seemingly willingly returned.

I'd never been so happy to be going home. On the day I left, I calmly said goodbye to Dad and Lucy, pretending it was a shame to leave. I genuinely felt for my sister as we had one last hug, but she had become very distant, spending more time on her own in her room. She looked blank when Dad teased me about my hair, saying it was ridiculously short and made my face look fat. Dad told me I was piling on the pounds and looking beefy.

When we arrived at the airport, I felt bad for her again.

'See you soon,' said Lucy, her face impossible to read. 'Come back for my birthday, won't you?'

She was turning eighteen that April, the same year I would be twenty-one, and wanted us to have a joint party. I dreaded the thought of having to return in just a few months but smiled tightly and said nothing. I could sense she didn't want me to leave.

Dad clung to me too tightly as he said goodbye too.

'I'll miss you,' he said, breathing into my hair. I couldn't stop myself from pulling away as he tried to grasp my arm. 'You need to come back, Kim,' he added, as if reading my mind. 'I won't give you any money for college otherwise.'

'Yes, Dad,' I said.

But he hadn't given me any money on this trip either, so I suspected this was a lie.

For the next few months I tried not to think about my next trip to Kenya. Instead I focused on finishing my boring college course and worked as many shifts as possible in the pub. Money was still a huge problem as I barely scraped by and had to live off credit cards. Despite his promises, Dad refused to give me a penny and insisted he would only hand over cash if I came back for the Easter trip. He also kept begging me to return to Kenya, telling me I would be happier there. On my loneliest days I was even very slightly tempted as life was so hard struggling to make ends meet without knowing anyone while doing a course I hated. I felt so alone. Of course, I spoke to Jonathan on the phone whenever I could, but it wasn't the same as having him nearby.

Often at weekends, I'd watch families in parks or walking to shops and feel so envious: I had nobody. More and more, I found myself reaching for a can of Carlsberg Special Brew lager – a full-bodied strong beer with a percentage volume of 9 per cent – to take away the pain. I hated the taste but just one can gave me the hit I needed. When my landlady was out, I even pilfered some of the spirits from her bottles, always careful to top them up with water afterwards.

Easter was early in 1986 and my twenty-first birthday that March was fast approaching, but I wasn't looking forward to it. Lucy had begged Dad for Mum to come over too as a treat. It was a joint birthday present for Lucy and me – Dad would pay for Mum's flight (I think Sean was away travelling, maybe Tanzania, after he finished A-levels).

I was also hoping that travelling to Kenya and feeling the warm sun on her skin and experiencing a different lifestyle to her current one might prompt Mum into making some radical changes to her own life. I was so worried that if she was to continue smoking and drinking to the extent she was doing then she wouldn't be around for much longer.

*Maybe this trip would give her a much-needed wake-up call?*

Knowing Mum was going to be there too made me feel slightly more relaxed about going back to Kenya. Surely Dad wouldn't attack me with her there?

All too soon, the time came for me to go again as another plane ticket turned up in the post. Jonathan was sad I wasn't going to be around for my birthday, so he made me a special mix tape of Dire Straits songs which he handed me with my present, a new Walkman.

'You can listen to the songs while you're in Kenya and think of me, Kim.' He smiled.

No one had ever bought me such a personal and special present before. When I put the earphones on my head and switched 'play', I felt overwhelmed.

There was little doubt I was falling in love with Jonathan. The love I had with him felt real, the respect we had for each other was mutual. It was important to me that he never knew what Dad had done to me. I didn't want him to view me as a victim. He loved me as the person I always wanted to be. He saw my happy-go-lucky side, the person who made jokes and worked hard and enjoyed life. The Kim I'd always wanted to be.

On the flight over to Kenya, I settled into my seat, listening to the first song on Jonathan's mix tape, which was 'So Far Away'. The lyrics brought tears to my eyes. He was so thoughtful. I didn't feel as anxious this time. I hoped Dad knew better than to try and attack me again. Part of me even tried to fantasise about a new beginning. Maybe we could all pretend it never happened? Perhaps he would start behaving like a normal dad and we could all move on? Of course, I could never forget what he'd done but I just wanted him to see me as his hardworking daughter who always tried her best – the real me rather than a sex toy.

Dad chatted amiably as we drove back from the airport to his house. He seemed to be in a good mood.

'Come in, come in,' he said, waving me into the room where Lucy was.

I was horrified by how thin she had become. She'd lost even more weight than when I last saw her.

'Are you okay, Lucy?' I asked, guessing she was no more than six stone.

She scowled at me, as if I'd said the wrong thing.

'Fine, how are you?' she asked.

I smiled in response and gave her a hug. Her weight was off limits.

'Where's Mum?' I asked.

'Oh, she's coming a bit later,' said Dad, opening a bottle of whisky.

Mum was often late and chaotic but also Dad had bought her ticket to come later, probably controlling things so he had time with us on his own. I only hoped it wouldn't make an attack more likely if she didn't arrive for a few days.

Thankfully, the whisky did its job, blurring the edges a little as I caught up with Lucy. Then Dad put on 'Super Trouper', his favourite ABBA record, singing along loudly to it – he seemed so happy we were there.

I carried on drinking, already longing to go home. All I could hope was nothing would happen that night. But as the evening wore on, Dad began to make more comments.

'Oh, Kim, remember you're in the room next to mine, won't you?' he smirked.

I changed the subject, ignoring him.

That evening, I had a few drinks and was desperate to go to bed but Dad made us stay up with him. Lucy was the first to go, after dropping off to sleep on the sofa. She seemed so small and fragile as she slept, and it brought tears to my eyes. I quickly blinked them away, not wanting my dad to see. I questioned him about Lucy's health, but he laughed it off, saying she was anorexic. I stared at him in disbelief. His face showed no emotion whatsoever. It dawned on me that he couldn't care less about Lucy, me or anyone else for that matter. All he cared about was himself!

Dad seemed pleased we were left alone and poured me another whisky.

I gulped it down, said I was tired too, and went off to bed. My heart was pounding as I shut the bedroom door. I listened and waited before sliding into bed. *Maybe he was leaving me alone?* I closed my eyes, exhausted.

Just when I began to relax, I heard the door creak open.

'No, get off!' I said, pushing him away. 'I've got a boyfriend, remember, Dad.'

But he slid into bed, pressing himself up against me. He smirked. 'Oh, come on!' he said.

'Get off me!' I snapped. I was so petrified, I was trembling, but also furious. I was nearly twenty-one now, I had a boyfriend. How could he think he could carry on and do this?

He grabbed me like he always did so I allowed my body to go floppy.

*Just let him get it over with*, a familiar voice told me. It was then I realised this voice was the one that had helped me survive a whole decade of this – and it wanted me to survive one last time.

Dad grabbed me, pinned me to the bed, raped me and then passed out. Lying in the dark, listening to his snoring, I cried and cried. Why had I come back? Why had I done what he'd told me? Why did I ever think it could be different?

As I curled into a ball, I vowed then and there never to return to Kenya. Whatever Dad said or threatened, I couldn't put myself through this again.

# Chapter 18

In the morning, Dad was up bright and early, offering orange juice before my coffee. Like he'd always done, he acted as if nothing had happened again.

Desperate to get away for a few hours, I contacted Keg, as I still had a number for him. Despite Dad trying to cut us off, I had reconnected with him as a friend. After completing A-levels in Canada, he was back in Kenya for a short time before leaving to go to Harvard University to study Liberal Arts. He was so happy to hear from me. We managed to arrange a secret meeting at the Fairview Hotel, which was right in the middle of the city, but in the lush, leafy part of Upper Hill.

When he saw me, he wrapped me in a warm hug.

'You look like you've been eating lots of McDonald's, Kim,' he teased.

He was right, I had filled out since we'd last met. Without Dad constantly taunting me, I felt more relaxed about my weight back in the UK.

'But you're happier, right?' he asked.

I nodded, telling him all about Jonathan. Keg was genuinely happy for me even though he admitted he still had feelings for me.

'They'll never go away, you know, Kim.' He sighed. 'I will always love you.'

I was touched but changed the subject, asking after his family and for an update on what he was doing. I knew we would always be friends.

We only spent an hour or so together. It never occurred to me to tell him what my dad was doing and Keg never asked. Now I was twenty-one, I guessed he assumed it wasn't still happening.

Over the next two nights Dad attacked me and then in the morning pretended nothing had happened. I noticed he was less vicious, perhaps, I thought, because he had mellowed. Or maybe he was afraid I might tell someone. I didn't know, but weirdly felt grateful he hurt me less than usual.

Thankfully, a week before I left, Mum finally arrived. Instinctively I knew while she was there, I'd be safe.

I'd never seen Mum and Dad together for any length of time since they'd split up. I half-expected there to be a scene, or for Mum start a row, but she didn't. In fact, she looked as if she couldn't be happier to be on holiday. She had bought new clothes, a couple of sun dresses and short skirts so she could go home with a tan, and when Dad offered her a glass of whisky, she didn't hesitate.

Within hours of her arriving, the pair of them were pissed together. Lucy and I watched as our estranged parents laughed and giggled away, topping up each other's drinks. By the end of the evening, Dad acted as if they were good old friends again.

Dad didn't rape me as Mum was there but he whispered how he wanted to when she was out of earshot.

'You ruined everything by leaving me,' he snarled.

I managed to get through the next week, pretending all was fine to Mum and Lucy. That night, I slept fitfully, but my door remained shut the whole time.

In the morning, I woke desperate to get safely on the plane home. I also wished I could take Lucy with me. She looked so unwell and had been quiet and withdrawn on this visit. As Dad drove us to the airport, I brought up the subject.

'Dad, can't Lucy travel back with Mum? I bet she'd love that, even if it's for a short spell,' I begged him.

'Absolutely not, she has schoolwork to focus on,' he replied.

Lucy didn't say anything, but I felt very emotional when we said goodbye. Not for the first time, I dreaded to think what she was going through behind the scenes.

On the flight on the way home, I tried not to think about what had happened over the past few days. I had to go home and block it all out otherwise I'd go mad.

When I got back, I pretended to Jonathan that the trip went well and it was lovely to see my family. I badly wanted him to think I was from a normal family just like his. My sister Susan did too. She respected the Chowns, seeing them as a middle-class family to aspire to.

From the outside everyone thought our well-spoken, educated father was a decent fellow. This was a mirage Susan was eager for the Chowns to believe too. She rarely had a bad word to say about Dad outside the house. However, she had plenty to say about my relationship with Jonathan.

'I found the Chowns first, Kim,' she told me one day. 'It's

odd us seeing two brothers so I think you should end it. I honestly didn't think your relationship would last otherwise I wouldn't have encouraged it.'

It's true, history was repeating itself – Mum's sister had married Dad's brother. But I wasn't having any of it. The moment I saw Jonathan waiting for me at the airport, I walked straight into his arms.

'Good to have you back, Kim,' he said, kissing my forehead. He had no idea how good it was for me too.

In 1987, I finally finished the course Dad had forced me to do. I managed to pass, but had hated every minute and vowed to get a job in a different industry.

Dad still rang regularly, asking what I was up to. He continued to berate me for not doing well enough or not finding a job fast enough. He never did give me any money or help with my finances either.

With no spare cash, I moved back into Mum's house in Markham Avenue in Rawdon and quickly found work as a trainee manager for Safeway in Chapeltown. It was a long bus ride away, but I was determined to assert my independence. Finding a good job with prospects was one way of doing this.

Living with Mum made me realise her drinking had spiralled beyond all control. She didn't work and lived off benefits, spending most of her day sitting in an armchair in front of the electric fire. Despite her alcoholism, her chatty and flirtatious nature hadn't changed and she had met a new boyfriend, a neighbour in his seventies called Alan (she was by now in her late forties). He had had his own joinery business in Yeadon, but was retired now and had passed this to his sons. Mum told me that they had said she was after his money (this wasn't true) and that she drank too much. But Alan was a nice guy, who seemed to genuinely care for Mum, even though she was often unfaithful to him.

I couldn't do much to help Mum, so I left her to it while I focused on my new job. I enjoyed working with customers – it gave me a chance to learn better people skills, something I discovered I was good at. I always had a positive approach to any problems; nothing was too difficult for me to sort out. By now I had the approach to life that nothing was 'that bad' because for me, this was the reality. Not being attacked every night and being allowed to sleep made me feel so grateful for normal life.

But my attitude was helped along by something else too: drinking. Every night I stayed up with Mum, drinking our latest tipple: Special Brew with a really strong cider mix and blackcurrant, a homemade super-strength snakebite which was cheap and tasted good. We'd often watch TV together or sit chatting, although Mum usually veered the conversation towards herself.

Every morning, I'd wake up at 5am terribly hungover but always made the bus on time. Usually, it would take me until mid-morning before I'd feel normal, even if I always kept a smile stuck to my face for colleagues and customers. By now I was so good at 'carrying on' despite everything. After all, I'd lived like this since childhood, pretending not to have emotions.

As the months wore on, however, I found life with Mum increasingly hard to cope with. She began ringing my workplace, asking for me.

'Why are you leaving me alone for so long, Kim?' she demanded during one seven-hour shift. 'When are you coming home?'

'Mum,' I hissed, aware my senior manager was listening nearby, 'I am at Safeway, working. You know where I am!'

'But when will you be home?' she cried. I could hear her slurring her words, pissed by lunchtime again.

From then on, she rang almost every day. She didn't stop even when I asked her to. Once she even told my senior manager she was a sick woman and I'd left her home alone to fend for herself.

'Why are you leaving a woman who is so unwell and unable to look after herself alone?' a colleague asked me.

'She's a woman in her forties who drinks too much,' I replied with honesty, furious anyone should think badly of me for this.

But the calls didn't stop. Just weeks after I started, the interruptions got to the point where my manager pulled me aside.

'Kim, this cannot go on. Your mother needs to stop ringing the store,' she said.

I felt embarrassed and ashamed. Back home, I rowed with my mother about it.

'Don't you care about me, Kim?' she sobbed, pouring another glass of snakebite. 'Do you want one?'

'No!' I yelled, wanting to knock the booze from her hand.

'Another thing, Kim, when are you paying your rent?' she slurred.

The irony was although Mum harassed me about working, she was also insistent I paid her rent. She was very tight, never allowing me to pay it late, yet she wanted me to pander to her all day and not work.

The pressure on me in the supermarket was obvious and my supervisors didn't like it. After one call too many from Mum, they decided to let me go.

Devastated, I came home and cried. It felt like my family had messed up every aspect of my life. I had no other qualifications aside from Animal Husbandry, so little choice about where to apply. Dad quickly stepped in and put me in touch with one of his old contacts, who found me a job back in London. The way I got it was typical of him – the first I'd heard about the job was when they contacted me to arrange an interview. I hadn't applied for the post – Dad had done it and forged my signature. Even from this distance, he exerted his control over me.

Despite loathing the idea, I went to the interview and got the job. It was at Hammersmith Hospital, breeding and working with mice in SPF (specific pathogen free) isolators – meaning the mice were and would stay germ-free. They offered me day release to High Barnet College to do a Higher National Diploma in Animal Technology. This felt like a step backwards, but I also felt pressured by my father. Once again, I had to say a sad goodbye to Jonathan and return to a lonely life, but I was pleased to have a break from Mum.

Meanwhile in London, Dad announced he was moving to Brunei with Lucy. He had got a new job there, but he was over in the UK and was leaving for Brunei from Heathrow. This was before I left my job in Hammersmith and he asked me to meet up with him and Lucy in London. He also asked me to see them off at the airport that week, saying I might not see them for years otherwise.

'I'd love you to come with us,' he said.

When I arrived at the airport to say goodbye, Dad offered there and then to buy me a plane ticket to go with them. He made it sound so appealing: 'You'll have everything you need, Kim,' he said, smirking. 'You need never worry about money again. I'll pay for everything.' It was indeed a strange offer and besides how could I just drop and leave everything without saying a word to anyone?

I could see in Lucy's eyes a silent plea. A part of me wanted to say yes for her sake and also because I was skint and hated London, hated my job and didn't relish the prospect of being with Mum. Despite this, I would never have gone because I knew that I couldn't put myself in the same position with my father again.

While waiting for the gate to be announced, Lucy began pleading with me to go with her.

'I will miss you so much, I want you with us,' she begged.

My heart went out to her and I found myself wavering. I felt so alone in London and all my money went on rent. I could hardly afford to eat, let alone have any fun. Around this time, I was only seeing Jonathan every two weeks so who knew what future we had?

Lucy shuffled to the edge of the chair she was sitting on, hanging on my answer. I desperately wanted to pull my little sister away from Dad, take her back home with me. We'd have no money, but we'd at least have our sanity. But I knew even as I thought this, that it was an impossibility.

'No, Dad,' I said firmly. 'You go.'

'And make sure you come back soon,' I whispered to Lucy, tears falling down my cheeks.

As I waved them off, I was heartbroken for my sister. Saying goodbye made me feel awful inside. I remember crying even more once I had said goodbye and turned away.

Jonathan and I talked endlessly about my job in London and our future. I hated watching the cruelty to animals, so while I was worried about Dad's reaction to leaving the job he had found for me, I resigned and moved back up north to be closer to Jonathan again, even if that meant living with Mum for the time being.

I found work as a hostess at Sun Alliance, an insurance company in Leeds. It was hardly my dream job, pushing a trolley around, offering free coffees to the office staff, but I was only there for a short time and pleased not to be in the animal labs.

As time wore on, things got worse at home. Despite being an item with Alan, Mum had met another guy called Mike and brought him back to the house. The noise of their rowdy nights, with music on or them arguing incessantly drove me crazy until one evening I lost my temper and called Alan to tell him.

'You'd better come over to see what Mum's up to,' I said.

He came round, catching her in the living room with Mike. After a huge barney, they split up and Mum blamed me.

'Why did you tell Alan, is it because you fancy Mike?' she yelled. 'Get out!'

I'd never heard anything so insane – with all I'd been through with Dad, middle-aged man with a beard wasn't my cup of tea. She told Alan I'd invited Mike over but Alan knew what Mum could be like when she'd been drinking and he marched off back home.

In her fury, she pushed me out of the front door. I banged hard on it to be let back in, but she ignored me. It was freezing and I didn't even have my coat on. I knew Mum was probably passed out on the sofa, so I walked off to find somewhere to shelter. It was snowing and soon I was soaked through. Catching sight of myself in the reflection of a shop window, I felt shocked. I'd sobered up by now but looked exhausted and bedraggled. Luckily, I had a few coins in my cardigan so when I spotted a phone box, I called Jonathan.

'Oh, Kim, I'm so sorry,' he said. 'Can you come and stay here?'

'No,' I said, quickly. I knew I couldn't as I had no transport and it was very late. 'The last thing I want is for your dad to see me like this.'

'He won't judge …' Jonathan began.

'It's fine, don't worry, I'll find a friend's sofa to sleep on,' I said brightly. 'Sorry, I can hear the pips. See you soon!'

I replaced the hand receiver, pretending I'd run out of money. The snow was falling harder now on the roof of the phone box, so feeling defeated, I crouched down in the box, pulling my cardigan more tightly around me. Closing my eyes, I willed the dawn light to come quickly.

The next day, I stood up, stiff and aching with cold. It was freezing cold and snow was on the ground; I couldn't even feel my feet. I hurried back to find all my belongings in bin bags on Mum's front lawn – I just had to hope she would let me in so I could throw on my uniform and get to work. My bedroom window was wide open, a black bin bag hanging from it, where it had got stuck. Shoes were scattered over the lawn, where they had spilled out, and everything was dusted with snow. Mum was still in bed, but thankfully she let me in begrudgingly, so I rushed upstairs to change and get to work. When I left for the bus, I noticed the remains of my birth certificate lay in the sink, where Mum had burned it – I think she must have been drunk when she did that and when she put all my things outside in the black bag. (Later, I applied to Somerset House and got a duplicate birth certificate but not the full-length one.) Anyway, that day I was late, but I pretended our washing machine had leaked – I didn't want anyone to know how chaotic my life really was.

Every night after work, I'd go home and Mum would reluctantly pour us both a drink – she didn't like to share. I struggled to have a proper conversation with her as she always stuck to boring gossip about neighbours or friends. She rarely took an interest in me or what was happening in my life. The only other subject she liked talking about was Dad. Often, she talked about the past, the drunker she got.

One evening, she began to bring up how abusive Dad had been to her throughout their marriage. She told me crazy stories I'd never heard before, like how he had slept with her cousin Joyce and even got her pregnant.

'They called their little girl Ellie, which was the name I wanted for Susan originally,' she said, staring into the fire while I looked on with horror. 'He also slept with one of my sisters.'

I didn't know what to believe, but knowing Dad, it didn't surprise me.

'You know, your dad wasn't a nice man to live with in

Nigeria.' She sighed, taking a big sip of drink. 'Once I caught him having it off with our maid so I sacked her. You kids were too young to remember, but he frightened me. I couldn't wait to get back to the UK, he was so controlling.'

I picked up on her description of him. Boosted by the feeling of confidence the drink was giving me, I wanted to share my experience too. Dare I tell her? I pondered.

'Mum, Dad was controlling and aggressive to us too in Kenya. He beat us up at the slightest thing we did,' I confessed.

Her gaze slowly moved from the bars of the electric fire to mine.

'Oh, sorry about that, love,' she said. Quizzingly, she looked at me.

As the warmth of the fire and the alcohol flowed through me, the words seemed to follow. Quickly, easily, I carried on talking.

'He abused me, Mum, as well,' I blurted out. 'Dad raped me. He got me pregnant twice, you know,' I continued.

Her gaze moved back to the bars of the fire.

'Aww, love, I'm so sorry,' she said. 'That must have been awful for you.'

I stared at her.

'Well, you know he used to be aggressive to me too.' She sighed.

My mouth fell open – it was as if my words hadn't sunk in at all.

'Mum!' I said, sitting up in my chair. This time I spoke more clearly. 'Dad abused me, he *raped* me. He was my dad and he made me *pregnant*. Do you understand what I'm saying?'

She looked at me again, tears streaming down her sunken

cheeks. I wanted to shake her, make her react appropriately. Like a mum who cared.

'Mum, Dad sexually abused me,' I repeated, this time more loudly.

Her face creased as the tears fell faster down her cheeks.

'Doesn't surprise me,' she said at last. 'How could he do this to me? How could he cause all this upset? It's too awful! Oh, I feel terrible now!'

My mouth fell open in disbelief as I suddenly felt sober again. I had finally plucked up the courage to tell my mother my deepest, darkest secret and all she could talk about was herself? She'd not even asked me how I felt or how I was coping. How could a mother, any mother, react in such a way? It was staggering and I was lost for words.

So, I sat in silence as Mum sniffed into a tissue, crying for nobody but herself.

She soon fell asleep in her chair as she always did, so I put out the fag she still had held between her fingers, turned off the electric gas fire to be sure nothing accidentally caught alight, before slipping out. A familiar feeling of emptiness washed over me as I went up to bed. This was a sensation I'd grown up with. It was a horribly sad feeling of being betrayed, let down and not heard by anyone who was supposed to care for me.

The next day, I vowed to concentrate on my future without Dad in it. To move on, I knew I had to try and forget the past. I'd done what I could. I'd fought him off. I'd told a GP. I'd confided in Mum. I'd even told Joanna, Jonathan's sister. She had wanted me to go to the police, but I swore her to secrecy. But other than Joanna, nobody suggested helping.

Nothing more could be done, nobody would believe me or nothing would be done even if they did.

*Raking over the past would only hurt one person – me.*

# Chapter 19

Little did I know, Mum wouldn't view my confession as something to handle sensitively. One weekend, a few weeks later, I met her in the pub. Sitting in a dingy corner behind a haze of cigarette smoke, she singled me out as I walked through the door. I wasn't sure how many drinks she'd had, but she didn't need that many these days as she kept her alcohol levels constantly topped up. One thing I did know was that her personality changed after a few drinks. When sober, she'd give us her undivided attention but when drunk, she became selfish and self-aggrandising. Everything was about her and everyone was either against her or she'd been dealt bad luck.

'Here she is,' she slurred. 'My Kim, the daughter I was telling you about. The one who was raped by her dad, my bastard ex-husband. It's so awful what he did to me, isn't it?'

She began sobbing as the men on bar stools next to her all raised an eyebrow. I turned heel and walked away, out the back entrance. This was unbearable.

The next time I saw Mum – at her home – she started talking about it all over again.

'I can't believe what he's done to me,' she cried. 'Honestly, Kim, it's just so shameful! How could he hurt my own kids like this?'

'Mum, it's not about you!' I snapped in the end, but there was little point in trying to make her see this.

Soon afterwards, Jonathan was round at Mum's house for dinner. He didn't come round very often as he lived over an hour and a half away, so when he did come to see me, I'd cook his favourite dish: ox heart fried with onions. It wasn't something I liked, but I loved cooking for him. We'd been together for two years by now and were very much in love.

I'd served up the plate and brought it through to the lounge when I noticed his face.

'Oh, what's the matter?' I asked. I glanced at the plate of food – I'd made it just how he liked it. 'Is there something wrong?'

Mum sat pulling hard on her cigarette, unable to look me in the eye. Instead she was staring at the back of Jonathan's head in sympathy. All the colour had drained from his face.

'Your mum just told me about what your dad did to you, Kim,' he said quietly. 'Oh God, I'm so sorry!'

'What?' I said.

'I just don't know what to say,' he said, his face whiter than a sheet.

He looked so confused and upset, my heart broke. I didn't know what to say either. I glared at Mum, unable to believe she had just blurted out something so sensitive. How dare she? This wasn't her secret to share. Jonathan pushed the plate away as if food might make him choke.

'Sorry, Kim, I can't eat now,' he muttered.

'Just go then, Jonathan,' I said quietly. 'We'll talk later on.'

I felt a huge pain in my chest as I watched him disappear out the door. Mum poured herself another drink, so I went back in the kitchen to clear up the mess – I didn't know what to say to her either.

The next day, Jonathan came to meet me in a pub. His knitted brows and haunted look told me how upset he was.

'Kim, I've never even heard of this sort of thing before,' he said, wiping the tears with the back of his hand to try and hide them. 'I can't believe your own dad did that stuff to you.'

I didn't know exactly what Mum had told him, all I knew was that I hadn't wanted him to know any of it. His family were nothing like mine. How could he understand something like this? It wasn't part of his world.

'It's okay, Jonathan,' I soothed. 'I'm okay now. Really, I'm over it.'

'You're always so happy-go-lucky, Kim,' he cried. 'I would never ever have guessed something like this had happened to you. It seems unreal. Your dad is such a bastard! I knew he was weird, but could never guess he'd do something so awful.'

He broke down again, clutching my hand in his. If I could have turned back time and stopped Mum from blabbing everything to him, I would have done.

Jonathan had never encountered anything like the pain Bernard Beaumont had brought to our family, and why should he? Most parents loved and cared for their kids. It was only my family that was so unnatural. I put my arm around his shoulders.

'It's okay,' I said. 'I don't expect anyone to understand.'

He looked at me with such pain in his eyes. 'But I *want* to understand. I don't want us to have secrets from each other. I love you.'

Now it was my turn to start crying. 'I know you do,' I whispered.

I explained I didn't want to go into details. Where could I even begin? I didn't want to tell the man I loved all the awful things my own dad had done; I was ashamed. I felt sickened by it, so God knows what he'd think. Maybe he'd even suspect I enjoyed it – after all, it had gone on for so long.

'I want to leave it in the past where it belongs,' I said, firmly.

'Kim, you don't have to tell me if you don't want to,' he said, obviously sensing I didn't want to talk about it and respecting this boundary.

The last thing I wanted was for it to come between us.

'I don't want you ever to mention this, Jonathan. Ever again. It's in the past now, it's over. Dad can't, and won't, hurt me again,' I told him.

'I know he won't,' muttered Jonathan darkly. 'Because I won't let him.'

A few days later, Susan invited me out for a drink and I had a feeling Mum might have told her. I assumed she was going to offer me a sympathetic ear, so for the first time in my life, I steeled myself to be honest with my sister. But when I arrived, the look on her face told me otherwise.

'Why are you going around telling everyone what Dad did to you?' she said to me before we had even ordered a drink. 'What are you playing at, Kim?'

I was so taken aback, I could hardly get my words out. As

I stammered an explanation, I could hear how unconvincing I sounded.

'Bu–but, Susan, it's, it's true, he did do stuff to me,' I replied.

'Kim, what are you doing?' she sighed. 'Think about it. You're ruining the Beaumont family name. I don't want the Chowns to know about this. It's private and needs to be kept private. God knows what they'll think of us if this gets out. You're tarnishing everything. You need to forget about this. The past is in the past, leave it there.'

I was stunned into silence. Watching my big sister wave away sympathy for me for fear of tainting the nice middle-class Beaumont façade was an insult I'd not expected. But I didn't argue with her, I was too hurt. First, my father abused me. Then my mother made the pain her own. And now my own sister wanted to keep me quiet. Yet again, it was another conversation where I walked away with the desolate feeling of betrayal.

If I'd hoped that would be the end of it, I was wrong. On our next date, Jonathan brought up the subject again.

'I just think something has to be done,' he said. 'Your dad can't be allowed to get away with this. Please let me try to speak to Susan.'

We discussed her reaction to the news I'd spoken out. I told him in plain terms she just wasn't interested in helping and he must *not* in any way breathe a word of this to his family.

'I've embarrassed her,' I explained. 'Apparently, I've brought shame on the Beaumont name – not Dad, but me. Susan doesn't think I should go to the police. I know it's not just up to her, but I do care what she thinks.'

'Please let me try then,' he offered.

I loved him so much for wanting to help. A small part of me hoped he could, but within weeks, any hopes were dashed. Jonathan spoke to his brother Greg and Susan, but neither wanted to help. Horrified as Greg was to hear what had happened, he followed Susan's lead and she didn't believe the right thing to do was to tell the police.

*My secret was to become the elephant in the room for many years.*

Now my secret was out, my relationship with Mum felt more strained than ever so when her boyfriend Alan, with whom she was now reconciled, offered me a room to stay in, I jumped at the chance. It was on the same road as Mum so I didn't have to move far. His house was warmer too. Meanwhile, I moved back into the house in Guiseley temporarily as Dad had offered for me to stay there for free. As much as I didn't want to set foot in there again, I had little choice because I had no money.

The months passed, with me dividing my time between the Guiseley house and Alan's place. I got another job working for Bradford Golf Club, where I did my Silver Service waitressing course. I enjoyed the social aspect of working in the food industry and was relieved to have escaped the work in animal labs. I felt free of Dad too; now he was abroad, I rarely saw him.

When one Saturday morning I heard the front door key turn in the lock unexpectedly, I was more horrified than ever.

'Hellooooo!'

Dad's voice boomed into the house, carefully enunciated as usual. I stood up, clutching my mug as he appeared in the doorway, looking tanned and relaxed. History was repeating itself yet again.

'Kim!' he smirked.

He stepped across to me, leaving me only a split second to put down my mug as he drew me into an uncomfortable hug. The familiar scent of stale cigarettes on his breath made my stomach lurch. I frantically glanced around, expecting to see Lucy, but she wasn't there – he must have dropped her off at Mum's first.

'Hi Dad,' I replied.

'How are you doing? Come on, put the kettle on. I'll have a tea, please. Bit early for a whisky but I'm guessing you didn't know I was coming so won't have any in. Or do you?'

He started laughing, his eyes roaming my body.

'I can see you've put on weight,' he said. 'Still looking gorgeous but you need to be careful about eating the wrong things.'

I ignored him and crossed my arms over my chest.

The radio was playing and for a few minutes we had a relatively normal conversation about the chart hits we liked. He told me he was over to sort out the house. I think he was intending to sell it. I even allowed myself to relax a little. But as soon as I let my guard down, the atmosphere in the room changed. I didn't need to look at him to know he had that look in his eye: a cross between a glare and sick lust. A look I knew too well. I stepped backwards until I felt the edge of the kitchen worktop on my back.

'I've missed you, Kim,' he began. He moved to my side and

slid an arm around my shoulder, then leaned into my hair. 'You smell lovely,' he murmured.

I pulled my shoulder away. 'Stop it!' I said. Already, hot tears pricked my eyes as that familiar creeping sensation of nausea swept over me.

'Upstairs to the bedroom,' he ordered.

I knew what this meant. A rising sense of helplessness gripped my throat as he clutched my arm, trying to drag me to the hallway. I knew what he wanted, I knew what was going to happen next, but something bigger than my fear of him kicked in. I had no idea where it came from, but I couldn't stop myself: this had to stop.

'Get off me, Dad! I've told someone, I've told the police too!' I lied. 'So, you'd better stop! I'm not going through this anymore.'

My words hung between us in the air as if, for a few split seconds, neither of us could actually believe I'd said this.

I'd finally stood up to my dad. I had told him 'no'. I had threatened *him*.

He dropped my arm as if it was a hot poker.

'You what?' he yelled. 'How dare you! No one would believe you anyway so why should I believe that you've told someone? Who have you told beside the police? You stupid girl, you've just signed your life away by doing that!'

I knew I was sailing close to the wind and my heart was racing. 'It doesn't matter who I told,' I said, 'but they're aware now, including the police.'

Frantically, I looked around in order to locate my nearest exit, should I need to make a run for it. I began walking backwards around the kitchen table. He followed me, standing over me and drawing himself up to his full height, telling me what he was going to do.

But Dad must have believed me for he immediately said, 'You are going to go to my solicitor to retract the statement.' His voice was icy. 'I will make an appointment right away. Do you really think anyone will believe you over me? Of course they won't!'

My whole body was trembling as what I'd just done was sinking in: I'd managed to say no to my abusive father. Of course, I faced a punishment for it, but going to a solicitor felt like I was getting off lightly. I didn't even consider not agreeing to it at once. Dad ranted and raved for a few minutes more. I stood there watching him, then realised he wasn't going to stop me from leaving as I edged towards the door.

'Get out then, but before you go remember this,' he spat. 'I'd think seriously about what you've done. Remember how I said I could dispose of you? Well, you'll be sorry about this and better put it right!'

I ran as fast as I could to the nearest bus stop. Seeing other people waiting for the bus made me feel safe, so I sat down on the bench with them, waiting for my heart to return to a normal beat. I spent the rest of the day wandering around and only went back when I was sure my father had left.

The following day, Dad was true to his word and called a solicitor for the next available appointment, which was the week after. He rang and told me he'd attend with me and if I didn't turn up, there would be hell to pay. I believed him too – the viciousness I saw in his eyes that afternoon scared me witless.

Later that evening, I told Jonathan about Dad's demand. He was appalled.

'But, Kim,' he said, quietly, 'you can't do this. You should go to the police and tell them everything. That man needs bringing to justice for what he did to you. You can't protect him.'

I swallowed hard. He was right on one level – but the reality? That was different. I knew only too well how persuasive Dad was. He was so well spoken, so believable. I wouldn't even know where to start if I tried to tell someone what I'd endured over the years. Besides, what proof did I have? The bruises had long cleared up, I had normal periods now. I didn't have any photos, letters, witnesses. Nothing! Dad was an esteemed lecturer at universities around the world. I'd been sacked from a supermarket job. The years of emotional, physical, mental and sexual abuse had worn me down. I didn't like what I saw in the mirror. I was fat, ugly and stupid. Dad was right: I was a nobody. I hated myself and suddenly regretted standing up to Dad the way I had.

I started to explain some of this to Jonathan and the look on his face told me he'd not thought of the implications.

'Jonathan,' I said, 'I know none of my siblings will back me up on this. Susan has told them not to talk about it. Sean rarely has much to do with us. As for Lucy, poor Lucy, she's still living with him and under his spell. They're more worried about bringing shame on the family. I have no proof about what he did to me. I just can't bear going to the police and not being believed. Can you imagine how awful that would be?'

Jonathan rubbed his eyes. I hated seeing him upset over me.

'Come on,' I cajoled. 'If I just do what Dad says, we can all move on.'

'But, Kim,' he persisted, 'that man deserves to be in prison for what he did to you. God, if only I could put him there myself! Every time I even think about what he's done ...' He clenched his fists.

'Shhh,' I said. 'Jonathan, this is my business. This is the decision I have made for myself. I know what's best for me and what I need to do to get through this.'

The next day, Jonathan came over to see me, and Dad was in the kitchen. I could see him tense his fists at his sides so I quickly ushered him out of the house – I didn't want any trouble.

Dad had asked me to tell Jonathan to drive us to the solicitor. At first, I refused but then agreed. I knew Dad's plan: it was to make it appear as if he was innocent but once again, I felt under his control.

Jonathan looked horrified when I suggested this as we went for a walk. 'But it's like I agree with what your dad has done if I drive you there,' he said, helplessly. 'And, Kim, nothing could be further from the truth.'

I gave him a hug. 'You're not doing it for Dad, Jonathan, you're doing it for me. If you don't take me, I'll just go alone.'

On the day, he came to pick me up and Dad got in the back of the car. I could see my boyfriend twitch and glance in the rear-view mirror at him as they nodded acknowledgement. Jonathan gripped the steering wheel as if he wished it was my father's neck. Dad noticed this too and calmly spoke up: 'Thank you for putting yourself out, Jonathan. Kim has seen the error of her ways and I have forgiven her – she is prone to making up lies.'

At this, I felt Jonathan tense up more and feared he might explode. I patted his arm. 'Come on, let's just get over there,' I said softly. 'For me.'

We drove off in silence, Dad staring out the side window as if we were on a day trip but I could tell he was seething inside. Jonathan focused on the road, as if resenting every corner he turned as we sped our way there. By the time we arrived at the small solicitors on the high street in Guiseley all the colour had drained from his face. Quickly, I unbuckled my seatbelt just as Dad was already opening the car door.

'Won't be long,' I told Jonathan.

He briefly touched my arm. I knew exactly what he wanted to say: *Don't do it!* But I had to – I couldn't look him in the eye.

'Won't be long,' I repeated.

I didn't dare contemplate ignoring Dad's request: he was due to fly back to Brunei soon and he'd be furious if he had to extend his trip. I just wanted him to go back and leave me alone. Signing anything he wanted was the quickest way of having him out of my life.

Inside the solicitor's we sat silently in the waiting room before a man in a suit ushered us into an office. The solicitor was an elderly man with an ill-fitting suit and an officious manner. Rustling papers on his desk, he then hunted around for an extra pen for me. He behaved as if he was expecting us and wanted this business concluded as swiftly as possible.

'We have drawn up a statement here as requested by Mr Bernard Beaumont regarding allegations made by Kim Beaumont in relation to an alleged assault Miss Beaumont has lied about …' He spoke using legal words I barely understood. The only thing I needed to understand was in this situation I couldn't be less powerless. My hand trembled when I felt my dad's eyes on me as I picked up the pen.

'Sign here,' ordered the solicitor. 'Here and here.'

I thought it was so strange the solicitor never asked to see me on my own. He was asking me to sign the paper in front of a man I'd accused of rape. But who was I to question this? He pointed at the dotted lines. Relieved he'd finally stopped speaking, I scribbled on each line. Then I sat back in the chair, defeated.

*You're signing any chance of justice away*, I thought to myself. *That's it.*

Dad's face had softened into someone smirking with enjoyment at a small victory.

'Thank you kindly,' he said to the solicitor, pumping his hand up and down in a handshake. 'Your assistance in this matter has been greatly appreciated.'

Once again, my father looked and sounded like an upstanding member of society, while I felt like trash.

The solicitor looked equally pleased with himself, as I shrank into my chair. I desperately wanted to go home now.

Dad opened the door, allowing me to walk through first. He stood slightly too close to the doorway, forcing me to edge away from him as I left the room. Then he waited until the solicitor was out of earshot before he said firmly through gritted teeth: 'Now that is an end to it, Kim. Nobody will ever believe you.'

# Chapter 20

Jonathan looked pale as I climbed back into the car. We drove off in complete silence. He dropped Dad back at Mum's house. He didn't look at him as he emerged from the car, but my father turned to him.

'Think carefully about staying with Kim,' he warned. 'I'm sorry you've been roped into this.'

I desperately bit my tongue, wanting to lash out.

'Thank you,' he smirked at me. He slammed the car door as hard as he could and Jonathan pressed the accelerator as soon as it was safe to do so.

'I can't believe you made me do that,' he cried, close to tears. 'It's all so wrong, Kim. Your dad is an evil monster!'

'You did it for me,' I repeated in a low voice that I hoped he realised he couldn't argue with. 'I honestly had no choice; you don't know what he's capable of.'

We continued on, driving back to his house in silence. I felt wretched but had nothing left to say. Jonathan was so upset and I felt dreadful for getting him involved with this.

Jonathan did drop the subject, but then a few weeks later, he suggested I might have some counselling.

'I just really want to help you, Kim,' he explained. 'Nobody can get over something like this on their own.'

I'd never considered talking about it to anyone else before. What was the point? But gently, slowly, Jonathan persuaded me to go and see someone in Leeds. His dad even offered to pay for it as he had told his family what had happened.

So I went along, prepared to try, but found it pretty useless. When I told the counsellor what had happened, she just listened, while constantly glancing at the clock on the wall behind me to check whether my hour was up. There was no advice or empathy. I didn't see the point in bringing up old memories for what appeared to be no good reason so I stopped going.

In May 1988, Jonathan and I both found jobs working together in a pub, The Royalty in Otley on the Chevin. He wanted a break from working in the family company and we even dreamed of going travelling together.

'We could do whatever we like,' I said excitedly. 'We're both young and free, aren't we?'

For the first time, I imagined this was true for me. I was so desperate to leave my past behind.

It was a lovely pub, and working alongside the person I adored every day was a bonus. Finally, I had found someone I could have a laugh with, someone who wanted to understand what I'd been through, someone who believed in me, who told me I was pretty, intelligent, slim – the opposite of things I had heard about myself for a great deal of my life. I trusted

Jonathan like I had trusted no one else before, except for Keg. I longed for us to have a future together, but still didn't have the confidence to tell him that, so we just went with the flow. We ended up living together in a little caravan for six months, which felt very romantic. I loved it being just the two of us and away from my family.

Of course, what happened to me was always at the back of my mind. The flashbacks to my past occurred almost every day. For instance, if I heard certain music I was taken straight back to Dad's old house. I suppressed all these memories as far as I could in order to get on with my life – I didn't want to be defined by what happened to me or destroyed by it. For example, my love of music has remained even while some of it reminds me of being abused. On the other hand, some music takes me back to Kenya and the good memories I had there – there were some happy times and music helped me cope – and to this day my love of music is very strong. But while I tried to stay strong, memories kept intruding into my mind. I didn't feel I could talk to anyone – not even Jonathan – about them so they made me feel very lonely.

Working in the pub meant easy access to drinking too. Regulars often bought me a drink or two during my shifts and often we'd sink several glasses of wine or beer after work too. Jonathan also liked a drink, but nowhere near as much as I did. He never noticed an issue, however, as it was as much a part of our routine as working and going out with friends. We had a few drinks some evenings and weekends but never anything especially excessive.

After six months we had to move out of the caravan and moved in together to Alan's house (Mum was happy about this because we weren't using up her heating, etc.). We were a couple very much in love and talked constantly of our future. One day we wanted a place of our own and maybe even a family. I was on the contraceptive pill again, even though I became very nauseous taking it and I tried to block out the memories, but once again it felt as if my past was ever-present.

Just before Christmas in 1988, I realised I'd skipped a period. My periods were very erratic, but I thought, just in case, I'd do a pregnancy test. As I sat on the loo watching a firm line appear, flashbacks from earlier years clouded my mind, but I squeezed my eyes shut, telling myself this time it would be different. The idea of being pregnant was terrifying, especially as I knew I'd want to keep the baby. But I forced myself to smile and determined to put on a brave face for Jonathan and pretend to be over the moon.

*Hiding my true emotions came naturally to me.*

First of all, I wanted to confirm the result was right, so I made an appointment to see the GP that afternoon. Quickly, another test confirmed it was correct. As we talked through my irregular periods, the doctor asked about dates.

'You're about two months pregnant,' he said.

First of all, I called Susan. She was still my big sister and I was desperate to share the news with someone. Albeit reluctantly, she was now used to Jonathan and I being an item.

'That's amazing,' she said. 'When are you going to tell Jonathan?'

'Straight away, I suppose,' I said. 'Even if it's going to be a Christmas surprise.'

That evening, I rang him after Mum had gone out to the pub.

'Merry Christmas!' I cried, smiling down the phone. 'You're going to be a dad!'

I don't know how I expected him to react – this wasn't our life plan at this stage – but his first words told me this wasn't the reaction I wanted.

'Er … are you sure?' he said.

'Yes,' I replied.

He was stunned into silence.

My heart sank as I replaced the phone receiver back in the cradle. I didn't know what to expect, but not this. I had to leave him for the news to sink in.

Later on, Jonathan agreed to meet me to discuss things over a drink in the pub. I'd already began to feel nauseous, so for once I didn't want my usual glass of white wine. He was honest and said he wasn't sure if we could afford a baby or whether this was the right time, but the smile on his face told me he was happy about it.

'Sorry about my initial reaction. Whatever happens, Kim, we will make this work,' he said.

I was so relieved. I'd been worried Jonathan wouldn't want this but he admitted he'd just panicked. For the first time in my life, I felt I had something wonderful to look forward to. We set about finding a place to rent and set up home properly together in Darlington.

When our baby was born in July 1989, my life was turned upside down from the first moment I held Harry in my arms. I was so happy and felt a profoundly protective love towards him. My determination that my own children would never ever suffer what I had done was overwhelming.

We had bought a little two-up, two-down terraced house in Rockingham Street in Darlington, County Durham in north-east England. It was far enough from Mum so that she couldn't pester us daily but not so far that we couldn't visit her occasionally. Rockingham Street wasn't The Ritz but it was ours. It was a cold house with no heating apart from an open fire in the dining room. The bathroom was downstairs at the end of the kitchen and it was freezing. I had no tumble dryer so I had to dry our washing on a clothes horse or drape them over the banister. If Jonathan got up to go to the toilet in the night he'd often step on a slug but because he slept in his socks he wouldn't notice until the next day! But I didn't care about any of this as this was our house. Not even my dad could change how happy I felt.

By coincidence, the small yard of our house backed onto the yard belonging to one of the mums I'd met in hospital. It was a lovely surprise so we started hanging out together during the day. We both had little money, so we went on trips to the park or museums, anywhere to break the monotony of our days.

Naturally, trips to the pub were a thing of the past, but I began to buy two small bottles of cider – either Diamond White or Merrydown – to drink during the day because it felt like a treat I deserved. I'd not drunk regularly since having Harry and it perked up my mood no end. It was never enough to make me drunk, just enough to get me tipsy.

I wasn't thinking this consciously as I was so happy to be a mum, but increasingly my mood did need to be lightened.

Although we rarely saw Dad now, he still occupied a lot of my thoughts. I often heard about what he was up to via Susan. At Christmas time we saw him very briefly as he was at Mum's for the day.

Jonathan wouldn't let him anywhere near Harry aside from a brief look when we arrived. I stayed chatting to Lucy, Susan and Mum. Sean didn't come – he was doing his own thing, travelling, etc. – and we didn't hear from him very often either.

Lucy still lived in Brunei with Dad. She never spoke much about her life over there but, apparently, she had a boyfriend so I hoped things were okay.

I avoided Dad completely as every time he got me on my own, he said the same thing: 'You ruined everything between us.'


Jonathan and I loved being parents so much, we quickly decided to try for a second baby.

Our daughter Clara was born in January 1991 and when she was six weeks old, we moved to a large three-bed terraced house in Harrowgate Hill in Darlington. It had a long garden and the house was so much warmer than our old place in Rockingham Street! Jonathan was now working at the family window company again and I felt so lucky, I had to pinch myself. To have a boy and a girl was a dream come true and to bring them up in a beautiful home was amazing.

Susan helped out enormously when Harry and Clara were first born. By now, she was living with Greg in Macclesfield and worked as a sales rep for a large pharmaceutical firm. She was an absolute rock and genuinely loved the children and helping out – having them for weekends and buying them clothes. I was so pleased my big sister was a part of their lives and hoped she always would be.

However, alongside the extra responsibility came fresh fears. As soon as I had my little girl in my arms, new flashbacks began to appear uncontrollably. I couldn't stop thinking about terrible things happening to her or how my parents had failed to protect me. Worse still, not only did my dad not protect me, he abused me in the worst ways imaginable. It was unbearable to think anything like that could happen to my daughter.

Once again, I didn't tell anyone what was going on in my mind. I simply focused on one day at a time and told myself to concentrate on the future.

Jonathan proposed and we were married less than five months later on 15 June 1991 at St Andrew's church in Darlington in a beautiful wedding ceremony in front of all our friends and Jonathan's family. It was such a wonderful day. Mum, Susan and Sean all came. Dad wasn't invited. I didn't tell him to stay away, but as he was still in Brunei, it was assumed he wouldn't be there (he turned up for Susan's wedding a couple of years later, though, and was also at Sean's). He sent me £200 and told me to spend it wisely. As Lucy was with Dad, she didn't come either. Once again, I told myself to focus on our wonderful future rather than think about the past.

With two small growing children, money was tight. I returned to work in the evenings with various part-time bar and supermarket jobs to supplement our income, but we still lived hand-to-mouth. Any jobs I took had to be in the evenings so that Jonathan could come home and look after the children but I was always home by 11pm. One day I sat down with him to try and decide what I could do with my life, work-wise.

'I'm qualified for nothing, really,' I said. 'I hated working in those laboratories.'

We sat up with a pen and paper to brainstorm ideas. As my main qualifications were science-based, it seemed nursing was an option. This appealed as I liked working with people but my self-esteem was so low.

'I don't know whether I'm capable of passing a proper nursing qualification,' I told Jonathan.

'Why?' he asked.

'Because I'm pretty thick, you know,' I said, reinforcing what I'd always been told by my father. In the end, I'd come to believe it myself.

He wrapped his arms around me.

'Oh, Kim, you're nothing of the sort!' he said. 'You're brilliant with people. You're such a kind, caring person too – you'd make an amazing nurse.'

Not for the first time, I felt so lucky to have found such a supportive man.

Despite the kids being so small, I applied to start a three-year course in adult nursing at Teesside University in 1993. To my surprise, I enjoyed it and threw myself into working as hard as possible. Finally, I was on the road to a career I had chosen as my own. At last this seemed like the fresh start I longed for.

Around this time, we suddenly heard the news that Lucy was back from Brunei and had given birth to a baby girl on 21 July 1993 (my nursing course began a few months later, in September 1993). Not even Mum had known she was in the

UK, let alone pregnant or had given birth, so this was a huge shock. Susan asked her who the father was, but it seemed to be a mystery. I feared the worst and hoped it wasn't Dad, but I had no proof he was abusing her.

Shortly after she gave birth, Lucy returned to Brunei with the baby, a little girl, and Dad. None of it made sense but I was relieved to hear she was coming back to live in the UK for good a few months later. Worse still, however, was Dad moved back to live in the UK permanently too as he bought a chip shop in Leeds. Of course, it was strange to go from being a lecturer to making chips but I didn't question his life choices – I just made sure to avoid the area where it was as I wanted as little to do with him as possible.

It didn't take long before I heard that my dad's new venture had failed. I learned he didn't get on with his customers as he told them chips were bad for their health. If they came into the chippie more than once a week, he'd tell them they were eating too much of the wrong stuff. He'd sold his house in Guiseley years before and then the chip shop, but squandered the money and was left broke.

Jonathan and I had no regular babysitter, which meant that we were often drinking more alcohol at home and it had grown into a habit. I didn't ask Mum to babysit often as she lived a good hour away and we'd have to collect her. Anyway, I was very reluctant to let the children sleep over at hers. It wasn't just the distance between us – I couldn't trust her as she always drank to excess and the children didn't always want to be around her as they didn't like the state she'd get in.

I found myself looking forward to Fridays, my day off from college, as I could drink earlier in the day. I never drank heavily around the children, but my evening drinks became earlier and earlier.

The more I tried to avoid thinking of my past, the more the memories seeped into my consciousness. In the early 1990s, there was a revival of *The Rocky Horror Show* in the West End and T. Rex's 'I Love to Boogie' was often played on TV adverts. Whenever I was on my own, I would quickly change the channel, annoyed at myself for the power those songs still had over me. If I was with Jonathan, I'd be careful to hide my upset – the last thing I wanted was for him to start trying to persuade me to go to the police again.

One afternoon, I flicked the radio on and nipped around the house with a vacuum cleaner to ABBA's 'Dancing Queen'. Clara and Harry were in school, so it was a rare hour to myself to get some tidying done before picking them up. As I hummed along to the songs and dusted our wedding photo frame, suddenly my heart lurched as the opening bars of the next song – 'Telephone Man' by Meri Wilson – began with the lyrics that talked about 'doing it' in the bedroom and the hallway.

Flashbacks of Dad pinning me to the wall in our house at Jamhuri Crescent and Loresho Grove entered my head. I could hear him singing along, placing special emphasis on the lines containing the innuendoes.

I heard a crashing sound as the can of spray polish fell from my hand.

Light-headed and panicked, I squeezed my eyes shut and felt for the carpet beneath my feet to remind myself where I am. With my heart in my mouth, I ran to the radio and switched it off and then there was silence.

Except for an uncontrollable sob that I realised was coming from me. Only then did I realise tears were dripping from my chin.

'Kim, you are going mad,' I said out loud to myself. 'What's wrong with you?'

Impatiently, I took a deep breath to steady my heart rate. Once again, the memories receded like the tide.

Until next time.

I needed to get a grip.

# Chapter 21

By now I was seeing Dad only about once a year and it was always with family around, never on my own. He lived alone in a dark and dingy two-bed council flat in Roundhay Park, Leeds (Lucy was now living in Bradford with her partner Ralph and had children of her own). Dad's flat only had one window in the lounge, which looked out onto a small garden, and the bedrooms were directly off the lounge, with no separate dining room. His curtains were always kept partially closed. There was a computer in the lounge and another in his bedroom on the dressing table. He took ages to answer the door and I thought he might be trying to hide things.

Each time Jonathan would beg me not to go, but I always insisted on doing it. Not because I wanted to see Dad, far from it, but because, as crazy as it might sound, there was still a nagging part of me which hoped things would be different and that we could have a normal father–daughter relationship. I felt sorry for him in that he appeared to be lonely. He had no friends and was stuck in that awful flat day in and day out. I thought how I'd feel if if was me. I still hadn't accepted that he would never change. Perhaps I should have realised it sooner, but I kept giving him the opportunity to start again with me and also to say he was sorry, but it never happened.

At one time, our family had been close, especially Susan and me, but Dad had started to turn my own siblings against me. He told them I was bad news, generally tried to stir things up between us all and kept me away from them, so his secret would be safe. I think he realised or had certainly become aware that I'd mentioned things about what he'd done to me to Mum (who still saw Dad and almost certainly brought it up when she'd been drinking).

Although he'd try and turn my siblings against me, he still couldn't help himself and would sometimes call me to have a whinge, usually about Lucy and her partner Ralph. He'd tell me things about them, saying he was useless and Lucy was too good for Ralph. He blamed Mum for introducing them too (she had been seeing Ralph's dad romantically before Lucy came back to England).

I'd also started questioning Lucy about why she left her children alone with Dad. The two youngest girls in particular often had sleepovers at his house and their brother occasionally stayed too. By this time my story about Dad was known to my siblings so they were all aware of what he was, even if they didn't openly admit he had done anything to them. Anyway, I started asking Lucy's children if they were okay and what they did at Grandad's house when they were left there with him. Sometimes they'd tell me he'd locked one of them in a cupboard under the stairs and how they played games on his computer in his bedroom.

I had a lot of rows with Lucy over this and I knew she

would have told Dad. Often, she said that Dad had told her to stay away from me and my family as we were a bad influence. He'd tell Lucy's eldest daughter that we were bad. Lucy also told me that Dad had said my daughter Clara was a bad influence on her children and she would lead them astray. At the time, Clara was just seven years old.

He held such sway over the entire family, though perhaps not as much power over me now as he would have liked. Everyone wanted to make him proud of them but Dad being Dad, he never once praised any of his children. We all did whatever he asked, it seemed, including my siblings' partners. Sean might have got a little bit of recognition but not much. It was as though we were all competing for his admiration. By now, Susan had married Jonathan's brother Gregory and they had three children, two boys and a girl. Sean was also married to a girl he'd met while studying at uni in Newcastle. He was now living in Stoney Stanton in Leicestershire and they had two boys but we rarely saw them.

On each visit, Jonathan would be on edge all the way there. Part of me hated putting him through it, while another part worried one day he might explode at my father, but I also trusted him to do the right thing for me. He was always so respectful of my wishes even if he didn't agree with them.

One thing we did agree on was keeping Harry and Clara well away from Dad. They were never allowed to sit on his knee or behave like most grandkids did around a loving grandparent. We watched him like a hawk, not allowing any physical contact or even a split second alone with him.

As always, Dad tried to control the situation. In one family photo of us all, taken in Knaresborough, near Harrogate, where

Dad was staying at the time in a static caravan, just before the camera clicked, he suddenly rammed an unlit cigar in Clara's mouth. She would have been about six months at the time.

'What are you doing?' I snapped as I pulled it out while he sniggered.

'Just a joke, Kim,' he said.

I could see he was getting irritated with me and then he picked up the cigar and did it again.

'Leave it there whilst I take a photo!' he said menacingly.

My instinct was to pull it out again, but he was so fast in taking the photo and I was taken aback by this sudden aggressive behaviour.

Dad wasn't pleasant to any of his grandkids. He was impatient and snapped at them all, especially our two. Whenever he saw me alone, even for a brief few seconds on the way to the kitchen or the loo, he made the most of it. He always told me he missed me. Once when I was at Mum's and went to put the kettle on to make a coffee, he followed me out to the kitchen to snatch a few seconds together.

'We can still run away together, Kim,' he whispered.

Often, I totally ignored him when he said this, pretending I hadn't heard him.

I tried to move out of the way, but he blocked my exit.

'You know your nursing course is just a Mickey Mouse training course for people too thick to become a doctor, don't you?' he spat. 'It's nothing more than wiping people's arses!'

I stared at the floor, waiting for him to finish. His habit of swinging from trying to 'seduce me' to demeaning me was something he'd done for so many years.

Harry and Clara soon grew old enough to realise their

relationship with their grandad wasn't 'normal' and started to ask questions.

'Why don't we see Grandad Bernard much?' asked Harry after we went to a family gathering one Christmas at Mum's house.

They saw Mum every few months and although she idolised the children, after she'd had a few drinks, she could get cantankerous. She often bought them presents and then teased them by taking them back and telling them they could only be played with at her house. But with Dad, it was even more odd. On a rare visit to his flat with Jonathan, Harry and Clara noticed he didn't have any photos of them up on the walls, despite having photos of their cousins, as well as Lisa, his deceased daughter. They asked me why that was and it was then that I made the decision to tell them the complete truth. At first, I talked it through with Jonathan. We didn't want our precious children to think such evil acts could be carried out towards them but at the same time we wanted them to be very wary of Dad, even though they were never left alone with him. Already they didn't like him very much. He was often rude with his 'jokes' and wasn't especially pleasant to be around. So, I sat them down and gently explained how I hadn't given him any photos because their grandad wasn't to be trusted and he'd hurt children in the past by touching them inappropriately. Then I explained what a paedophile was and told them that he'd hurt me when I was growing up. I used simple language a child could understand and watched their reactions carefully as my words sunk in.

Thankfully, they took the news in their stride and accepted their grandad wasn't a good man and should be avoided at all costs. As far as they were concerned, he was a bad-tempered man who snapped at them. With no real relationship between them anyway, there was nothing for our children to miss. After that, they decided they didn't want to see him at all.

In the summer of 1996, I finally completed my nursing course and we moved to a new house in Northallerton with a large rambling garden for the children to play in. All the long hours of studying, working and looking after the kids were worth it, despite my drinking, which now seemed to be a part of my everyday life.

Every single New Year for the past few years I always put 'give up drinking' on top of my list of resolutions and every year by mid-January, I would fail. However, I still managed to keep on top of day-to-day life and on the whole, it was working – in other words, and in language I wouldn't have used at the time, I was a functioning alcoholic.

On the day that I received my nursing diploma, I couldn't believe I'd actually done it. And for the first time in my life, I felt something I'd never felt before: a sense of pride. With my new qualification under my belt, I promised myself, yet again, I'd stop drinking for good. Although I was still drinking, it was not during the day. Jonathan and I generally kept it to one night a week apart from weekends.

When I looked for another job, I found one quickly enough at our local hospital in Northallerton, on the Orthopaedics ward. Jonathan was doing well with his work too – he was now a director at his father's company. We weren't exactly well-off, but we were comfortable and could finally afford weekends away in the caravan and holidays with the kids. From the outside, I had put my past firmly behind me. I looked and behaved like a middle-class professional, well dressed, with lovely kids, a husband and a home.

By then, Dad had given up with his chip shop and had gone to live in St Helena, a remote volcanic tropical island in the South Atlantic Ocean, off the West Coast of Africa. It was part of the British Overseas Territory and had such a tiny population of about 7,000 people. We had no idea what he was up to there, but believed he'd found work as a lecturer. He'd also lied on his CV, saying he was ten years younger than he really was. Dad told me himself he'd done that – he said he'd struggle to get in otherwise. Once again, I was so relieved there was distance between us, but in many ways, it didn't matter. On the outside everything seemed rosy, but inside I was a prisoner of my own mind as my drinking was getting steadily worse. I told myself I didn't have a problem because I was perfectly capable of going for weeks, even months sometimes, without a drink but I also didn't have an 'Off' switch once I started.

At first, determined not to drink, I poured all my energies into my new job, especially as life as a nurse was a challenging one. Far from it being a Mickey Mouse job as Dad had taunted me, the position was one of massive responsibility. I had to administer injections for people and make sure I gave correct advice and prescriptions. Above all, I had to believe in myself and my abilities but after years of having it drummed into me that I was stupid, this was a challenge too.

After the kids were in bed I'd run through the day's events, worried I'd made a mistake with someone's prescription or the way I'd taken a blood pressure. I found myself struggling to relax, so started having a drink again to unwind.

On Friday nights I began to secretly buy a bottle of white wine on the way home from work as I felt I deserved it and would binge drink the lot within an hour after the kids were in bed. Jonathan noticed I was drinking more than usual, but I told him it was all under control. Even if I woke up with a hangover, I'd hide how bad I felt.

Within months of starting my new job, my drinking escalated again. I tried to stick to the evenings and weekends, but often I'd tell myself I deserved a well-earned glass of wine – which was never just the one glass. I'd crave wine as soon as I got home from work. Meanwhile, I moved to another hospital and then on to a medical practice called Blueways Medical Centre.

In the early years when I first started there, I actually had long spells of sobriety. I'd mainly drink at home on a weekend, but not much through the week. If I ever finished work early on a summer's afternoon, I'd go out into the garden with a nicely chilled glass of Sauvignon Blanc before the kids came home from school, to soak up the remainder of the sun's rays. One afternoon, Jonathan came back to find me so pie-eyed I'd fallen asleep upstairs, having started to mow the lawn earlier. I'd left the grass half-cut while I was actually half-cut myself! Several times he sat me down to tell me I needed to consider what the drink was doing to me, but I always dismissed his concerns. Then I'd stop for several months to 'prove' to him and the kids I didn't have an issue. I never allowed it to interfere with looking after the children either – I always made sure I drank to excess when they were in bed or at one of their friends' houses.

I spent five happy years at the GP practice. I'd have the odd hangover and take the day off, but it was never anything serious. As I still managed to juggle all the balls, I thought I was getting away with it although I knew deep down, my drinking was fast becoming a problem. In 2004, I told Jonathan that I was concerned about my drinking and that I was going to see my GP. I went along to the surgery and the doctor referred me to a psychiatrist at the nearby hospital. Jonathan went with me to the appointment. I don't really know what I expected the psychiatrist to say, but I was shocked at what he said.

'You're an alcoholic, Kim,' he told me. 'You need to stop drinking and never drink again.'

'You don't even know me!' I retorted. 'I'm not an alcoholic, I'm just having to deal with a lot that's happened in my past.'

The doctor didn't seem bothered about the past although he took a brief history. He asked how much I was currently drinking so I lied and told him I was drinking only a bottle or so a day. Jonathan tried butting in to say I was sometimes drinking more but I snapped at him and told him to mind his own business.

The doctor gave me another appointment date and I walked out of the room. Angry, I chuntered all the way back to the car.

'How *dare* he call me an alcoholic, I'm not a wino who sits in the park, drinking from a bottle disguised in a brown paper bag! I'm not unkempt. I have a job, I have a car and house, how *dare* he!'

*I was a well-dressed, middle-class mum-of-two who worked as a medical professional. If I was really an alcoholic, how did I manage that?*

By 2004, I had moved to a new medical centre called Greenwood to further develop my nursing career. It was also a promotion but I wasn't as happy there. By that summer, my drinking had once again escalated but this time even when I wanted to stop, I found myself struggling. The one bottle of wine I used to drink had become two, then three. Not every day, but several times a week.

Jonathan had started to get openly angry with me for not stopping my drinking. Then I'd feel guilty, which led me to want to drink more to drown my feelings: it was a vicious cycle. Even I began to worry I couldn't control it, but I went to see my GP again even if, deep down, I considered it to be a waste of time.

*After all, if I really wanted to, I could stop drinking, couldn't I?*

This time the concerned psychiatrist at the hospital explained that I needed to take urgent action and accept help from the mental health team or my drinking would get considerably worse. He carefully explained that my behaviour was one of an alcoholic and if I continued like this, it would cause me serious harm, even death. I thought he was being way over the top,   and even thought he and Jonathan were colluding behind my back, but I continued to listen as he explained how he would like to prescribe me a drug called Disulfiram, also known by the trade name Antabuse, which acted as a deterrent for drinkers.

'If you were to have a drink while on this medication you would immediately suffer terrible unpleasant side effects, including vomiting, rashes and headaches – even death,' he explained.

It sounded awful, but also, I was determined to prove to my husband I had a handle on my drinking so I agreed to a prescription. To be honest, it was just to keep Jonathan off my back. I was getting very irritated with him by now. Like a dog with a bone, he kept nagging me about the drink.

Shortly afterwards, we toured Western Europe in our caravan for Jonathan's fortieth birthday. On the last night of the holiday, he already knew I was going to stop drinking when we got back and declared he would do the same. He knew I was going to start taking daily tablets of Antabuse when we got home and wanted to encourage me.

I was glad of his support, but assured him I wouldn't find it hard myself either.

'But, look, I've agreed to take the medication and will stick to it,' I insisted.

Deep down, I agreed to trying the Antabuse just to keep him quiet, but I knew it wasn't going to fix anything as at that stage I couldn't contemplate life without drink. Everything we did as a couple involved alcohol – socialising with friends, having meals, watching TV, going on holiday. I couldn't remember a life without alcohol. If I visited Mum, I wasn't offered a coffee, it was always booze. Besides, it was my head that needed fixing, not just my drinking.

Back home, all my assurances to Jonathan came under pressure. In-between the stresses of my job, nightmares I sometimes had about Dad, songs I heard on the radio or other things that triggered my anxiety, I found myself craving the warm release of a glass of wine. But alcohol made things so much worse than they were. It made minor problems become bigger ones and I was becoming so self-absorbed and self-loathing.

Soon I worked out ways of having a drink while on the Antabuse. I couldn't be trusted to take it under my own volition, so Jonathan would give me the tablets. Once he caught me spitting it out so he began crushing the tablets and watching me eat them with food. I knew where he stored them so I replaced them all with paracetamol so I could sneakily have a drink without him knowing while he was at work. They were of a similar size and were broken in half so he wouldn't notice. I remained under the care of the mental health team, who sent out a woman to breathalyse me regularly too as part of the plan. Once she found I was over the limit, but I insisted the machine was faulty to the point where she was convinced it was broken.

Because I was taking Antabuse (a drug at that time that could only be prescribed by a specialist in the field), I had to be carefully monitored. The therapy was purely in tablet form and not to tackle my underlying reasons for drinking. In retrospect, I should have had rehab in conjunction with this. I also needed a detox (Librium to help with any unwanted side effects of withdrawal) to start with as my drinking had got so bad, the only safe way to stop was to cut down gradually (impossible – how does an alcoholic cut down?). Like Antabuse, Librium is very carefully monitored and must be prescribed by a health professional. My initial dose was so high, I couldn't function for a week and had to gradually be weaned off it.

If Jonathan ever found a bottle of wine I'd hidden, he'd tip it down the sink and he took away my car keys so I couldn't do a supermarket run for more. I became even more inventive though and ordered taxis to bring me booze, asking them to drop it off at the bottom of the garden. When a taxi driver cocked an eyebrow at the amount of wine ordered, I told him sadly my husband was an alcoholic.

Deep down, I knew I was an alcoholic but I desperately wanted to be like other normal people – to be able to drink like them, enjoy going out, etc. In my eyes the psychiatrist had now made that impossible because he'd called me an alcoholic in front of Jonathan and now my husband was on my case! How could I ever lead a normal life without alcohol being a part of it? After all, it had always been there from when I was small. I simply refused to accept it and became more and more devious. If Jonathan was playing games, I could play far better games than him, I told myself.

One evening, I pretended to sleep while waiting for Jonathan to nod off. Then I went downstairs to carry on drinking in peace using bottles I'd hidden all over the house, places I'd think he would be unlikely to look and find them. Often, I couldn't remember where I had hidden all the bottles as I would hide them in a hurry, maybe when Jonathan or one of the kids walked in the door unexpectedly, or I'd simply forget because that's what alcohol did to me. In desperation, I'd search under piles of clothes on the bed, under mattresses, in the shed, behind the dog basket, anywhere!

Once, a half-glass of wine was only found because we needed the boiler servicing. When the boiler man opened the door to the boiler, he found the glass and brought it out to

Jonathan and I in the kitchen. I nearly died of shock. I didn't look at Jonathan but I knew that he knew it was mine, even when I said my mother had likely put it there as she was an alcoholic.

Sometimes I'd glug alcohol straight from the bottle just to save time. I hated myself for this, but it seemed the best way to manage it. I could quickly hide the bottle rather than hide a glass of wine and a bottle, should the need arise. Soon, hiding my drinking felt like a full-time job. I'd disguise the smell of alcohol on my breath with coffee or a mint before Jonathan came home. But this particular evening, I don't remember much of what happened next, except the deep well of sadness and hopelessness that seemed to wash over me until I felt consumed by it. All I wanted was for the pain to stop and befuddled by booze, I started eating the Antabuse tablets. It was more to see what would happen than anything else. I'd been on a forum where other alcoholics had said they'd been fine mixing it. Within minutes, I struggled to breathe and a rash appeared all over my body. Drink made me do stupid things, things I would never even contemplate while sober. Instantly regretting my decision, I ran upstairs to wake up Jonathan. He rushed me into A&E, where they admitted me for observation purposes until I was safe to go home. Hours later, I had recovered and felt deep shame for what I'd done.

Jonathan told my workplace what had happened when he rang in sick on my behalf. When I returned to work, they wouldn't allow me to dispense any medicines to patients and insisted I was breathalysed before work. They were awful! For a caring profession, they were far from caring towards me. I'd never gone to work drunk, I feared making a mistake too much, so decided to leave and returned to my old job at Blueways.

My former colleagues were totally unaware of my drinking. I knew them all pretty well, though – I'd worked there for five years the first time around – and they were lovely people. They thought I'd made a big mistake in leaving them in the first place.

After the A&E episode, I decided once again to focus on being teetotal. I realised how much upset I had caused Jonathan and the kids. He had been devastated so I wanted to make an effort for his sake as much as mine. When I put my mind to it, I could somehow resist the booze. It never lasted forever, but I'd manage to do so for weeks, sometimes months at a time. What I didn't realise, and what no one told me though, was that my alcoholism was a disease and it might not be so simple as just giving up the booze!

In order to gain promotion as a nurse, I knew I needed to go back to college. When the medical centre offered to support me while I did a Master's degree, I jumped at the opportunity. Part of me wanted to prove something to myself and if I'm being honest, to my dad too. After all, if I managed to get a Master's, it meant I wasn't so stupid after all.

I went for weeks without drinking, but then when I visited Mum, I often had a few drinks with her as we both liked drinking. She lived on her own and was incredibly lonely. Often, I didn't feel like going, but I felt it was my duty – she was my mother, after all. She'd get me to add Sanatogen to her coffee first thing in the morning when she was still in bed or she'd drink it separately – 'It's a tonic, love, it says so on the label,' she'd say. It was 14 per cent proof alcohol!

Although Mum constantly had a drink on the go, she'd nurse the same one for hours. A slow drinker, she was always keeping her alcohol levels topped up. Although she'd slur her words, unlike me she rarely drank to oblivion. When I was drinking at home I was afraid that if I didn't drink up fast or didn't drink while I could, then the alcohol would be taken away from me. Mum, on the other hand, knew her drink was safe as she lived alone. The only times she displayed erratic behaviour or pure drunkenness were when she was out, away from her home, and then she wouldn't be in control of her drinking.

A few times she came to visit us, but often the visit would end with her complaining about us not caring about her. I preferred to go and visit her alone.

Watching Mum's drinking worsen made me full of self-loathing for my own situation. When I found myself joining her on benders, I'd tell myself I wasn't as bad as she was. But this is an all-too-common excuse an alcoholic makes – we're not alcoholics as there are others worse than us! I was always looking for the differences, not the similarities.

Susan suggested that Mum go into residential care close to her in Embsay, near Skipton, as she was by now incapable of looking after herself. Her partner Alan had died in 1996 and she'd had another relationship with a man called Carl, but he too had died before she moved to Embsay, around 2004. Now she had no one. To be fair to my sister, Mum wasn't eating well and the toilet was upstairs, which often proved too much for Mum's weak bladder and failing legs to get there in time.

Once there, Mum confided in me that she hated it in Embsay and couldn't understand why she had been put there as her friends all lived near her old place in Rawdon. Susan argued Mum didn't have any friends as no one visited her, but to be fair, Mum did her best to settle in and made new friends in Skipton. She just longed for her old life, I think, and to be honest, it was easier for us to visit her before – Embsay was an awful place to get to.

Sean didn't appear to spend as much time with Mum as he should. Mum used to ring me, saying she'd not seen or heard from him in weeks or months and she found it very upsetting. He didn't seem to accept part of the responsibility of having her over as much as Susan and I did. Lucy lived about twenty-five minutes' drive away from Mum, but she herself didn't drive and by then she and her partner Ralph had four children so Susan and I didn't expect her to do as much as us.

Mum came to stay with us for New Year's 2005. She wasn't that happy coming to stay as she felt she couldn't drink what she wanted as Jonathan would moan at her, especially now he was watching what I was drinking too. In fact, he didn't want my mother there at all that night as he felt she was a bad influence on me.

Mum was in one of those moods where whatever I did, she made it known that it wasn't good enough. When she got like that, it was always down to something to do with drink. This time, we were going to the cinema and she was meant to come with us, but as she was in one of her moods, she said she wasn't coming. I knew this was because she wanted alcohol – and plenty of it – while we were out. She then started complaining of chest pains so much to her annoyance and Jonathan's too, I decided to stay with her.

'Oh, leave me in peace! I want to be on my own. Get me that bottle!' she snapped.

Jonathan had taken her case upstairs and she demanded I go and get her alcohol from it. Unbeknown to me, he had heard it sloshing about in her case, while he was carrying it. He looked inside to find the case was rammed with vodka and Stowells wine – I think he hid it because he didn't want me seeing it and he didn't want Mum drunk. So, it wasn't there when I went to look for it. At this, she went into the biggest mood possible and basically blamed us all for stealing her things (she didn't want to say 'vodka' as it would make her look bad, or to admit that her case had been rammed full of alcohol!). She might have told Susan and co. that we'd stolen things from her case, including her PJs, as my siblings fell out with me around this time.

Meanwhile, I continued the cycle I was trapped in. I still managed to hold down my job, look after the house and tried to stop myself from succumbing to benders. By now the kids were in their teens. Harry was doing well in his exams and planned to go travelling, while Clara was just fourteen and had started preparing for her GCSEs. I was so proud of our family. Despite all the ups and downs, my children were my greatest achievement, but they made looking at my own family even harder.

Every New Year, I made the same promises to myself: to stop drinking and try and recover from the demons of my past. In 2007, it was no different. I wrote down my resolutions and then broke them days later (at the time, I was still under the care of the psychiatrist and he was monitoring things). One resolution I did keep, however, was to write a letter to Dad, asking him why he'd abused me like he had.

I didn't want sympathy, I wanted empathy. I believed if he said sorry to me, somehow, I'd be able to cope better with the memories and could put them behind me. I longed for him to tell me it wasn't my fault and that maybe we could have a normal father-and-daughter relationship.

*There is always hope, isn't there?*

# Chapter 22

*Dear Dad,*
*I have been contemplating writing this letter for many*
*years and finally feel strong enough and confident*
*enough in myself as a worthwhile and well-adjusted*
*person to do so. The abuse (in all its manifestations)*
*that you inflicted upon me as a child has had a*
*profound effect on me through my teens and well into*
*adulthood. It has also had an effect on relationships*
*within our wider family (i.e. with siblings): we are all*
*treating the terrible wrongs in different ways: some*
*in denial; some perhaps feeling guilty about the past*
*because they could have done something to halt it, and*
*some trying to properly address it head-on. Inevitably*
*this has led to some suspicion and mistrust creeping*
*into our sibling relationships, which I find to be very*
*sad. Indeed, it is only over the last couple of years that*
*I have been able to properly start to confront my past*

277

*and look towards the future with real optimism and
anticipation.*

*Have you any idea of the suffering that you put your
innocent little girl through? Sometimes if I couldn't
sleep at night, I'd lie awake utterly dreading you
coming into my room to do your despicable deed: I bet
that you can't start to imagine what that felt like. I will
never know how carefully and cunningly you laid your
plans: was moving overseas a way of isolating us; to
move us away from our mum? Did you choose Africa
because there was less chance of you getting caught?
Do you remember what you did to me? Or, are you in
denial – like most abusers?*

I went on to list everything he had done to abuse me and
how I'd tried to have a 'normal' relationship with him. I also
questioned why he had chosen to abuse me the way he had
done, rather than my siblings.

I ended the letter with this:

*Bearing in mind what you've put me through, I feel so
very fortunate as many women who have experienced
what I have been through never overcome it. I don't
feel bitter, just sad that I never really had a father that
wanted me as a daughter in the proper loving way: we
are both losers in that sense.*

*Kim*

After I had finished, I reread my words a few times. I didn't
know how he was going to respond, but I knew how I wanted

him to. I wanted him to say sorry. To acknowledge my pain. To tell me it wasn't my fault and should never have happened. And maybe, just maybe, to let us have an ordinary father–daughter relationship.

To an outsider this may have seemed unbelievable that I'd even want to try reconciling with my dad and try forging a new relationship with him, but often when I got drunk, I'd tell Jonathan that having a normal dad was all I ever wanted. He was the only dad I had so I wanted to try and make him change.

I sent the letter by recorded delivery so I knew he would definitely receive it. The last thing I wanted was for him to be able to claim it got lost in the post.

By now, I rarely saw any of my family except for Susan and occasionally Lucy. A party was planned for Uncle Jake's seventieth birthday in October 2007 and the family were all together again, including Dad. I agreed to go but decided to stay well out of his way.

The days after I sent the letter turned into weeks. There was no acknowledgement of it. No reply. I wanted to confront Dad, but decided the party wasn't a suitable time. Besides, the pain of him ignoring the letter like that was too great. What I suspected was true: he didn't feel guilty or upset or hurt about what he'd done to me. Worse still, he didn't seem to feel anything at all. I just couldn't believe he could cast my heartfelt words aside – I had no choice but to take his silence as a 'reply' in itself.

Jonathan, Clara and I went to the party as a family. A lot of mum's siblings and my cousins were there. I avoided speaking to Dad and put on a brave face. He kept his head down, hardly speaking to anyone and left early. I tried to catch up with my siblings to be polite but felt a distance between us. Seeing my dysfunctional family was never a good idea and afterwards I struggled with drink for weeks again.

*Little did I know that this was to be the last time I would see my mum alive.*

On 14 December 2007, about eighteen months after her first heart attack, Mum called me to have a chat. She complained about Dad sending her a Christmas card without putting a stamp on it.

'He's always been a tight bastard,' she said.

As I listened to her, I wondered how many times I had heard her complain about Dad over the years. She'd started to slag him off more and more since learning new things about him. In particular, if one of us moaned about him, she would do the same. Now she vented her fury, whether or not it was instigated by one of us. He'd obviously hurt her over the years and she couldn't stand him.

How, after all this time, could he evoke such a strong reaction in her? Like us kids, she was clearly looking for some sort of validation from him. The hold he had over all of us was extraordinary.

Mum had been up late drinking with one of the other residents she'd got close to. She'd tripped and her wine glass had broken. Her hand was hurting, she complained.

'I smashed a glass when I landed on the floor,' she said, sounding stone-cold sober. 'Got shards of glass in my palm.'

*Typical Mum*, I thought. *Been on one of her benders.*

I didn't think it could be that bad as I'd have heard about it before.

I listened to her, offering my sympathies, but as I needed to get back to my list of jobs for the day, I cut her off after half an hour. Harry had been on a trip to Australia and was returning home that weekend and I wanted to sort out his bedroom for his homecoming.

'I'll ring you later, Mum, okay?' I said. 'Make sure you get your hand looked at. I'll call you in a bit.'

'All right, love,' she said. 'I'll look forward to it.'

Mum was waiting for one of the residents to give her a lift to the hairdresser's, where she was having her nails done too, so she didn't mind the phone call being cut short. She always took great pride in her appearance, her nails often matching the colour of her outfits.

Hours later, my phone rang: it was Mum's phone. I was in a café having a coffee with Jonathan.

'Hi, Mum,' I said. 'Is everything okay? I was going to call you in an hour.'

'It's not Mum, it's Susan,' my sister's voice replied. 'Are you on your own?'

I told her that Jonathan was with me.

'Mum's dead,' she said, crying.

Soon after we spoke, Mum had had another heart attack: she was sixty-seven.

For days, I felt completely numb. On the one hand, I had lost my mum many years ago when I'd left for Kenya as a little girl. But on the other, my longing for a 'mother' never went away. Although Mum had never really been there for me, and

I don't blame her for it, we'd often had some lovely chats. I suddenly felt so alone.

Mum had the most amazing personality. Despite her drinking, she could light up any room. Ask anyone who knew her. Yes, she could be miserable and have moods, but in general, especially when sober, she was incredible! She'd soon lift the mood in a quiet group of people and have them eating out of her hands in no time. Her personality was infectious. She was also incredibly funny. Even when drunk, she got away with things that many others wouldn't. 'He's nothing but a prick willy,' she'd say about Dad. 'Go tell him to shit and shut up!' Best of all, she once told me, 'I'll never trust him, you know. A tiger never changes its spots!' She meant a leopard, of course.

I'd be rolling about with laughter.

The grief I felt was darkly complex and something I couldn't understand. I went to see Mum's body in the mortuary: she looked peaceful at last. When I glanced at the palm of her hand, it was a strange colour. Then I noticed the lilac polish on her fingernails. Although still pristine in general, there were a few chips on an occasional nail. I remembered our last conversation about her being on her way to the hairdresser and having her nails done. She never made that journey and had died on the way there.

I couldn't stop crying. It was a hand I longed to hold as a little girl. Drink had broken Mum, causing so much pain to her and everyone around her. How different things between us could have been.

I slipped a ring off Mum's right hand and passed it to Susan.

'Add that to the collection,' I said, 'keep them together and we'll sort everything at a later stage.' Unfortunately, I never received any of Mum's jewellery. I was offered some of the cheap costume jewellery after I questioned its whereabouts. Still to this day I'm heartbroken that all my mother's favourite jewellery has passed me by … I only ever wanted one piece that I could have worn, something to keep Mum close to me and to remember her by.

Susan invited Dad to Mum's funeral. I was upset as it wouldn't have been her wish but Susan and Sean were executors of her will so they had control over everything.

Mum didn't have a lot in the way of savings, but she did state in her will that any money was to be split equally four ways (between the four siblings). Unfortunately, this was not the case and I believe it was split five ways to include Dad although he was not written into her will. I was notified after this happened, but I couldn't be bothered arguing about it. What I do know is that Mum would definitely not have wanted Dad to have anything.

With Mum gone, I saw less and less of everyone. I only kept in touch with my siblings via phone and rarely saw Dad. For the first time in years I managed to feel some relief. This made abstaining from drink easier too. I enjoyed my work as an advanced nurse practitioner and was happy to see Clara and Harry doing so well. By now, both were at university (Clara was studying for a BA (Hons) in Business & HR Management and Harry was doing a degree in Human Geography & International Politics) and leading the busy lives of twenty-somethings.

The only time I heard from Lucy was when she wanted a chat so we often talked on the phone. Occasionally, she'd bring the children to stay for a few days – I'd pick her up and drop her back or her partner Ralph would do this. Dad was not at all happy about her coming over to see me. He'd try and persuade her not to, saying I was a stirrer, best avoided (Lucy always told me what Dad said). Lucy's eldest, who was close friends with my daughter Clara, would say Grandad thinks we're all odd and best to keep away. I knew the reason for this – he must have worried about us siblings getting together and me telling them everything he'd done to me. The possibility of a knock on the door from the police must always have been on his mind.

Often, when Lucy came to stay, she would want to drink so I'd join in, keeping it away from Jonathan. By now, in my opinion, my little sister was drinking far more than me, which made me feel better about this. Gradually, as usual, I started to drink more heavily at the weekends, or whenever I had a day off work as niggly day-to-day stresses mounted up. I desperately tried not to let it interfere in our everyday life, but Harry and Clara soon noticed my benders became more regular when they moved back home after university. If either of them got upset, I'd stop for weeks, sometimes months at a time, before something else would trigger my drinking and I'd sneakily begin again.

My drinking was always erratic until it became a bigger problem later down the years, although I managed to curb it significantly for a few years while studying for my Master's degree.

Despite my on-off benders, by 2011, we were doing well. Jonathan continued working in the family business, a wood window joinery and manufacturing business in Northallerton. His father and grandfather had established it in 1965 (his older brother is the MD and Jonathan became a director in the nineties). We moved to a lovely house – a new barn conversion in a village on the outskirts of Darlington. For the first time in years, I hoped once again that I could perhaps finally put the past behind us. I made an extra effort to curtail my drinking for the umpteenth time.

Dad was also out of our lives. He still lived in his council house in Leeds but had met a Filipino woman called Julie online and gone to the Philippines to see her. Without telling any of us, he had married her out there (we only found out when one of my nieces saw some photos of Dad and his new bride). She was around twenty years old then, younger than my daughter, so there was an age gap of about fifty years.

Dad had always ranted about anyone who wasn't white and made directly racist remarks to my old friend Keg. It didn't make sense. He had sent Lucy a photo of himself surrounded by young girls over there. When she showed me the picture, I recognised his familiar smirk and felt nauseous.

*Why did he choose the Philippines and why a very young Filipino?*

He spent months at a time out there, which made me even more concerned. But I couldn't do anything to stop him living a depraved life, so tried desperately to put it out of my mind.

Meanwhile, life felt good – fun even – as we enjoyed several lovely holidays and I was picked as a volunteer nurse for the 2012 Olympic Games. While working as a medic in the international broadcasting arena for two weeks, life was wonderful and I forgot all about my past. I loved the experience and the optimism the whole country felt about its future was infectious.

Sadly, my optimism wasn't shared by the new medical practice I had joined. By now I had worked at several different places and this new practice didn't approve of me taking time off to volunteer at the Games. Once I returned to work, I was called into the office. The practice manager and another member of staff told me they'd have to let me go. I still don't know the reason behind it and although I was upset at the time, these events opened up new doors for me career-wise. I do believe things happen for a reason in these situations and as one door closes, a new one opens and this was the start of my aesthetic business. I'd already been dabbling in my spare time while at the surgery. It never got in the way of my main job and once I had left, I could put my all into it.

Quickly, I cleared my desk drawer and left, without even saying goodbye to anyone. I got back in my car and sat in silence, my head reeling.

*How on earth do I tell Jonathan?* I wondered.

That evening, before my husband came home from work, I sat and drank as much wine as I could. The pain of losing my job felt too awful and I didn't know how to tell him, so I drowned my sorrows instead.

Jonathan returned to find me passed out on the sofa. I woke to find Clara by my side in tears. By the time I sat up, confused and feeling sick, I was also desperate for another drink. I couldn't stand the looks of pity and shame they were giving me. I confessed I'd lost my job and they immediately told me it wasn't important. My husband and kids agreed my health meant more to them and they begged me not to start drinking again. But it was too late: I'd pressed the self-destruct button and my addiction began to spiral out of control again. I was surrounded by my family who adored me, yet I felt so incredibly lonely when I was drinking. How I hated the self-pity that always appeared alongside this awful cycle of addiction, but there was nothing I could do as the illness consumed me once more.

*The addiction had never left, I just wasn't drinking.*

The morning after a big bender, I'd make my way gingerly downstairs to join Jonathan and the children in the kitchen. I'd search their faces for clues as to my behaviour the night before. Often their faces gave nothing away and I'd sigh with relief. Other times, they simply walked out of the kitchen, leaving me alone and loathing myself with a passion. I could never remember what I'd said or done, who I'd drunkenly texted. Often, I drew a complete blank and the only way the gaps could be filled was by Jonathan or my children. Soon, I began to isolate, only leaving the house to get more booze.

Whenever my family left the house, I'd dash to the pile of laundry left for days un-ironed on the bed or rifle through the back of my wardrobe, under piles of shoes, anywhere because I couldn't remember where I'd hidden my secret stash. Once I'd found it, I'd pour myself a glass of wine. Sometimes I used a mug or drank straight from the bottle. One morning, I woke to find Jonathan standing over me with a photo on his phone. I looked into the screen to see a picture of a woman lying in the foetal position, a look of twisted agony on her face as she lay comatose.

*That woman was me.*

'Kim, this is what you ended up like last night,' Jonathan cried. 'This has got to stop.'

My relationship with Dad, never far from my mind, began to fester in my head again. While drunk, I would muse on what had happened, repeating scenes of the abuse in my head, at the same time as asking myself if somehow things might have been different. While drunk, I'd imagine Dad had stopped being a paedophile and maybe regretted what he'd done to me. I'd fantasise about him saying sorry to me, begging my forgiveness. I'd imagine he'd read my letter and felt so bad, he couldn't find the words to respond. For some reason, I still believed an apology or acknowledgement of the pain he'd caused would help me to forget my past. If only Dad would apologise then I wouldn't feel so haunted by what happened. After all, if I couldn't seek justice, maybe I could find peace in my own mind by reaching out to him?

After we moved to our barn conversion in the autumn of 2011, I decided to invite Dad over to our new place, much to Jonathan's disgust.

'Why are you doing this to yourself, Kim?' he asked me. 'You don't need this, you just need to focus on beating the demon drink.'

'Stop telling me what I do or don't need,' I said. 'I'm the one who lived through it all, not you!'

I hated seeing Jonathan's confused, angry look on his face whenever Dad was brought up. Knowing how upset this made him made me feel guilty for having my father in our lives at all. Although I rarely cried, I became very emotional.

'Look, my mum is dead! Dad is all I have. Maybe he might start behaving like a dad to me?' I said.

'But you've tried, Kim,' Jonathan pointed out, 'and all he does is hurt you. He's a monster and people like him don't ever change. The sooner you understand that, the sooner you can get on with your life.'

Perhaps deep down, I knew he was right, but the little girl inside of me who always wanted an ordinary father refused to give up.

It was daytime when Dad came over. Harry and Clara went out – they didn't want to be around him and couldn't understand why I was doing this. But I wanted to make a lovely curry and pretend for once as if we could somehow repair the relationship. Looking back, it makes no sense, but the drink and my fantasy that life could be different skewed my judgement.

I bought the ingredients to follow a specially chosen recipe. Laying everything out so it was ready, I felt nervous as the time approached for him to arrive. But I was certain I was doing the right thing. Jonathan seemed even more anxious than me.

'Kim, you don't need to do this to yourself,' he said, pacing the kitchen as I ground up some fresh spices. 'Your dad is a monster, he will never change. He can't be the man you want him to be because he's a child abuser.'

But I shooed him away from the kitchen as I put the finishing touches to the food prep.

'Just let me get on with this,' I said.

Dad arrived, ebullient as ever. He walked in as if he owned

the house, sweeping me into a bear hug before I could stop him.

'How nice is this?' He grinned, looking around the kitchen. He pulled me to him. 'You smell wonderful,' he murmured. Then he stood back and looked at me. 'You're putting on a bit of weight, aren't you? You need to be careful! Older women store fat around their hips and waist. It's harder to get off at your age.'

The familiar sickening feeling lurched in my stomach. I glared at him and disengaged myself from his clutches.

'Dad, we're having curry tonight,' I said firmly, changing the subject.

Jonathan eyed Dad from the other side of the room. He didn't offer his hand to shake, just nodded at his presence. I was glad he didn't catch what my father had said to me.

We all went into the kitchen. Jonathan pretended to sort out a cupboard while I cooked. I knew he didn't want to leave me alone with Dad, not even for a few seconds.

'I hope you're using virgin olive oil to fry those,' said Dad, peering into the frying pan.

He stood next to me as I began frying up the onions and garlic. For the first twenty minutes, he told me all about his new wife, then launched into a tirade about England and how he loathed it here, especially the climate and the way of life, before starting on about politics.

I had learned to switch off, especially when it came to politics – he was very opinionated and it wasn't worth getting into a debate with him. While listening to him ranting on about this and that, I mixed the onions and garlic with the rest of the spices, ignoring him as he briefly stopped talking about something unimportant to tell me to do it another way. Flashbacks of being a child with aching feet and being made to cook Sunday lunch, fearing a whack on the back of my head, flitted though my mind but I carried on as if these thoughts weren't intruding. I poured Dad a whisky and ginger ale, ignoring Jonathan as he watched me pour onefor myself.

*Tonight, I needed a drink more than ever.*

After listening to Dad criticise my cooking a few more times, we finally sat down to eat. Jonathan looked as if the food might choke him as he tried to eat while politely listening to Dad. I'd forgotten how much my father loved to talk about himself – it had been a long time since we'd been without other family members to dilute his conversation.

After several hours, Jonathan excused himself to use the bathroom. I knew he'd rush there and back, not wanting to leave me alone. As soon as he left the room, Dad stood up and came around the back of my chair.

The hairs on the back of my neck rose to the surface. I shrugged my shoulders, anticipating him touching me, which he did briefly on my shoulders. I pushed out the back of my chair to get a top-up of wine. Inside, I felt like screaming – he made me feel so dirty, even by breathing the same air as me.

Instead of asking how his grandchildren were doing, he went into rhapsodies about his new wife.

'She looks after me so well, better than anyone. You kids have always been like a noose around my neck. I look at Lucy and her drinking and think what a state she is,' he spat. 'No wonder, when she's involved with that working-class nobody! Have you seen the state of him?'

I didn't know what to say. If Lucy struggled at all, it would be partly due to her childhood, I was sure.

For the next two hours I struggled to keep up with any polite conversation. But Dad was in a cantankerous mood and seemed to be vying for an argument. Neither Jonathan nor I rose to it, but deflecting it in conversation was exhausting. I could sense my husband was also itching to say goodbye, so between us we managed to cut the visit short when he offered to run Dad to the train station. After they left, I sank onto our sofa, head in my hands.

*Why did you bother, Kim? Why do you keep trying?*

All I wanted was to run upstairs, have a scalding-hot bath and scrub my skin as if I was washing that vile man off me again. Instead I topped up my glass again. By the time Jonathan was back, I had passed out on the sofa.

The next morning, I woke up with a horrendous hangover and felt tearful again. I had to face facts: nothing was going to change between Dad and me. He didn't feel bad about what he'd done as he still wanted me sexually. This surprised me as I thought I'd be too old for him by now. And nothing made me feel worse. I knew I had to give up on wanting it to be any different.

For the next few weeks my drinking escalated until once again I vowed to have a break, following a row with Clara. My daughter hated my drinking more than anything and when she grew tearful and begged me to stop, I knew I had to make an extra effort for her.

Sometimes I felt as if I had two sides to myself. The Kim who was lost in the past and the other Kim who loved a challenge. One such challenge was my determination to be successful in my newly established aesthetic business. I needed to set myself apart from the amount of competition in this popular, fast-growing industry. Although I'd already had some training in this field, I attended more courses, gaining more credentials and certificates, and set up my own business in 2012.

Of course, it was still hard to cut Dad off completely. Susan and Lucy always kept me up to date with the latest. Dad also rang me every now and again. He always talked about himself, telling me about his new young wife and how he was trying to look after himself better these days. The years of drinking and smoking had finally caught up with him so he'd lost weight and cut down. When I saw Susan and she told me, I even sent him an e-cigarette to encourage him. Despite not seeing him, there was part of me that couldn't switch off, wanting to keep trying to have a normal relationship with him.

One afternoon, Dad rang me and it sounded like he was slurring his words.

'Have you been drinking, Dad?' I asked, alarmed.

'No,' he insisted. 'You know I've cut down.'

I believed him so concluded he must be unwell.

'Dad, do you feel okay? Listen, it sounds as if you've had a stroke maybe. Can you get yourself to the doctor?' I persisted.

'No, Kim,' he said. 'We all have to die sometime and doctors are useless on the whole.'

Later, I heard from Susan that he did in fact have a stroke but had been given the all-clear. She told me he was obviously becoming increasingly frail.

'Trying to keep up with a younger woman,' she attempted to joke.

I didn't laugh but wondered if it might be true.

Meanwhile, the training was starting to pay off with regard to my aesthetic business and although slow to start off, now I was beginning to see some regular clients. I still attended courses and wanted to keep myself up to date with the latest treatments and injection techniques, as well as the best products available.

For the first time in years, I felt as if I had my family comfortably at arm's length. It was only Lucy who continued to worry me: she appeared to be trapped in her own cycle of drinking. She'd often call me to say she'd fallen out with her partner. The only time I allowed myself a drink now was when she came over, but because, by then, I considered her to be a far worse drinker, I didn't look so bad if I joined her.

# Chapter 23

Two busy years passed. I worked hard building my business, but once again found myself trapped in the cycle of binge drinking, on and off.

In April 2015, Lucy came over one evening for a catch up. Jonathan didn't approve as he knew that once we got together it would invariably mean we'd be drinking, but he could hardly stop my little sister wanting to visit. It was always a good excuse for me to have a glass or two of my favourite tipple when family was around. As always, I made her some food and poured us some drinks. We often talked into the early hours, with Dad frequently coming up in conversation. Lucy had told me all about how much she feared him when we were growing up. I agreed with her, but always stopped short of telling her exactly what he did to me. After all, I'd tried years ago to reveal the truth to my family and no one had wanted to take it any further.

Lucy began crying. She was annoyed that Dad was

constantly at her house. He'd make sure that Ralph wasn't in when he got there and seemed to always know when he was at work.

'He makes me feel like shit every time I see him!' she sobbed. 'How can I escape him, Kim, like you have?'

'You need to stop inviting him round, Lucy,' I said gently. 'Just cut yourself off and protect yourself a bit more. That's what I did in the end.'

I put my arm around her thin shoulders as she cried.

'Look at me, Kim. Look at what he's done to me!' she continued. 'I'm a wreck because of him!'

'That's why we need him out of our lives,' I agreed.

Dad knew Lucy had a problem with drink, but it seemed he actively encouraged her. Once, a few years back, I was so concerned about her drinking that I booked her in to see a psychiatrist at a hospital close to her home. Lucy allowed me to organise it all, but when I went to pick her up to take her to the appointment, Dad had somehow got wind of this and was waiting outside at the hospital when we arrived. Despite pleading with her to keep the appointment, Lucy looked relieved once she'd seen Dad. I knew how hard it had been for her to agree to go with me to the appointment in the first place and he talked her out of it, acting as though he was more expert than the specialists.

'They haven't a clue, Lucy. You don't want to get mixed up with psychiatrists,' he told her. 'You're not mental.'

The two of them turned around and walked in the direction of Dad's car. Fuming, I drove the long journey back home by myself. Once again, our father was meddling in our lives, in this case preventing Lucy from getting the help she so badly needed.

*Help was so close, yet so far.*


For the next few weeks, I drank whatever I could lay my hands on after Jonathan had gone to work. I didn't need to ring in sick as I had my own business and decided to take the week off. The next seven days involved a one-person party with me drinking from morning till night.

Every evening, Jonathan and the kids would come home from work to find me passed out on the sofa or in bed. Each day, they would scour the house for drink but my hiding places grew harder and harder to find. Both Clara and Jonathan would cry and beg me to stop but nothing worked now, I didn't care anymore.

A few weeks later, after waking up with another horrendous hangover and yet another terrifying memory, I had a moment of clarity. The retraction statement had weighed heavy in my mind, making me worried that I'd never be believed. But Jonathan believed me, he knew Dad had coerced me into making that statement. I knew I couldn't live like this much longer. It couldn't hurt to go to the police, to see what they'd say? Almost without thinking about it in case I talked myself out of it again, on 9 June 2015, I picked up the phone and rang Durham Police.

'I'd like to speak to someone about my dad, please,' I said simply. 'I feel the need to inform someone of what he did to me and could even be doing to other children.'

The words sounded and felt strange as they emerged from my mouth.

*Was I really doing this?*

The police officer listened carefully, asked several questions and then said they would send someone to the house. I hung up and sat in silence, looking at Jonathan, who had listened to every word.

He looked relieved. 'You've done the right thing, Kim,' he said.

'Then why do I feel like I haven't?' I replied, clutching at my neck. Already I sensed a creeping feeling of regret.

That night, I hardly slept. Tossing and turning, all I could think was: *what will my family say*? Then I'd picture my frail dad's face as he faced arrest, or even worse him being led away in handcuffs to be placed in a grey-walled prison cell. None of this felt easy. Seeking justice for what he did to me was the last thing on my mind – I was more worried about what he'd end up going through.

The next day, Jonathan told me how proud he was of me, but all day, I felt uncomfortable. I longed to blot it out so I took another day off and drank some wine while everyone was at work. The police were sending female officers round later that afternoon but repeating the allegations was the last thing I wanted to do.

These were allegations dating as far back as 1976. I had no proof. No physical evidence. No letters or photographs. It was just my word against his.

The two police officers were ordinary constables from Durham Constabulary. I invited them in, they sat down on our sofa and then I told them about events chronologically. I tried to anyway, but there was so much to tell, I barely knew where to begin. I had no idea if they believed me, or what would happen. I tried to minimise what Dad had done because the regret had turned into a creeping sense of guilt.

They listened sympathetically, calmly took some details and then left.

'We'll be in touch for more details later,' one explained.

Once again, I was filled with relief after they had gone but several hours later found myself sneaking around the house, looking for bottles I'd squirrelled away. Now I had spoken out, I began to feel as if I was on a runaway train that wasn't going to stop. That night, I passed out in bed again, drunk.

Several days later, as hard as I tried to put the impending investigation out of my mind, it felt as if my brain might explode. Susan had yet to find out what I'd done. I was dreading my siblings' reactions. I had no idea when any arrest would be made or, worse still, if they could pursue it. What if, as Dad had always said, nobody would believe me? Unable to take any more stress, I quickly dialled the number the police had given me and in no uncertain terms asked for all the allegations to be withdrawn.

'I am not going to make any further statements and would like the file erased, thank you,' I said, firmly.

I didn't tell Jonathan straight away – I waited until I'd had a few drinks and then told him outright and warned him never to mention it again. He looked devastated.

For the umpteenth time, I vowed to stay sober. I threw myself back into my work, started another new course and gained new clients. I had to focus on something else – I didn't want to throw my life away on booze as Mum had done. This time I managed to limit my drinking to the evenings only before bed. I persuaded Jonathan to let me as it was the only way I could sleep. I even managed to persuade him I could control my drinking and asked him to start drinking again to help me, but quickly things unravelled.

The roller coaster of emotions was impossible to step off. One minute I felt in control, certain going to the police might be the right thing with the help of Jonathan's support. The next, I couldn't stop myself drinking, desperate to blot out memories and emotions that seemed to bombard my senses as soon as I stopped being busy with work. Every time I stepped into our house and closed the front door, I reached for a bottle of wine to soothe my frazzled nerves.

Once again, I was on a downward spiral, taking days off work, rearranging or cancelling clients in the process, and passing out every night. Nothing was going to stop me this time, even the children and Jonathan begging me to.

We didn't hear back from the police again, which I didn't expect to.

Months passed. Every weekend, my drinking grew significantly worse. Even though I avoided booze before work, I was having more days off and things were once again escalating. Desperate to give me a break, Jonathan booked a few days away in our caravan in York.

'Let's go away for a change of scene,' he suggested. It was October 2015 and the leaves had begun to turn a beautiful colour. Usually I'd have loved the chance to spend some time away, but this time I was more concerned about being able to drink my favourite Sauvignon Blanc.

*How would I buy it with Jonathan around me and more importantly, where would I hide it in the caravan?*

Running out of my beloved wine, or not being able to hide it from him or drink it in secret, was enough to make me not want to leave the house at all.

Despite my lack of enthusiasm, Jonathan booked the trip anyway. Prior to this, however, because of my deteriorating health due to heavy drinking, my husband decided to report Dad to the police himself – he felt he had nothing to lose as he was convinced that if I continued drinking to the extent I was, I wouldn't be around much longer. He blamed the entire situation with Dad for the way I was drinking.

On 7 October 2015, he reported it at our local police station in Northallerton and they transferred the complaint to West Yorkshire Police as this was where Dad currently lived and where some of the UK crimes were committed. A police officer called Jo Huddleston from West Yorkshire Police then rang me out of the blue to organise a meeting. Reluctantly, I agreed to this and at that point told her we were going to York in the caravan so we could tie it up with the same trip. I then told Jonathan that I had a meeting/interview pencilled in on 30 October 2015.

Despite having discussed going to the police and setting up the meeting in Garforth, Leeds, when the time came for me to attend, I didn't want to go.

'I'm not going, Jonathan,' I told my husband. 'I've changed my mind; I'm too scared of the repercussions. Everyone will blame me and I don't have the strength to get into further arguments with Susan or the others. They'll go berserk.'

Deep down, I was still terrified that I wouldn't be believed, that the people in positions of authority would take Dad's side, just as they always had. He'd win them over with his charm, as he'd always done and as he'd told me menacingly all those years ago when I signed the retraction statement at his solicitor's office, 'Nobody will ever believe you.' Beside myself with worry, I gulped down a large glass of wine openly in front of Jonathan. I was also concerned as an even deeper part of me knew that if I didn't do this now and kept my secret to myself, it would destroy me. Not only me, it was destroying those around me too. My husband and children were distraught and wanted me to be able to put all of this behind me.

*I was a wife and a mother and they wanted me back.*

I sat there shaking, overcome by the enormity of it, almost paralysed with fear at what I was about to do.

'Please come with me,' Jonathan begged, taking me by the hand. 'You can even bring your wine if you have to.'

Submissively, focused on having my wine, I slid into the passenger seat and took a swig. By the time we reached the police station, he had reassured me that right would prevail but I was very tipsy and tear stricken.

'Please, just do this for me, Kim,' Jonathan begged as we pulled up in the car park.

I pulled off my seatbelt and we walked in. There was something sobering about being in a police station so I pulled myself together as we waited. Once we were invited in, they recorded their first proper interview with me. Jonathan went off for a couple of hours while I endured the painful process of my first video interview.

I talked and talked and talked for hours. The events seemed so painfully clear in my mind, despite the drink. I described how Kenya began as a holiday but how quickly Dad changed. How this was the start of a decade of rape and abuse.

It took a couple of hours and several cups of tea were drunk when I would have preferred wine, but I did it. Afterwards, I sat for a moment, feeling a strange sense of relief although I was still dreading the moment when my siblings found out what I had done.

'You did very well, Kim,' one officer said quietly. 'You should be very proud of yourself.'

The officer introduced herself as DC Jo Huddleston, a liaison officer for West Yorkshire Police. From that day on until the end of the trial, she was to be my main – in fact, pretty much only – contact. I liked her caring but straight-talking manner and the look in her eye told me she believed me while she listened without judgement.

'Thank you, Kim,' she said at the end. 'We are going to do all we can with this information.'

I thanked them and we walked back to the car. Jonathan took my hand in his.

'I'm so proud of you,' he said. And for a moment I felt relieved.

Once again, the feeling didn't last. In the car on the way back to the caravan, all the old fears rose to the surface: *What would Susan say? When was Dad going to be arrested? How would he react?* I felt sick.

The next day, 31 October 2015, Jo Huddleston rang to say Dad had been arrested. The realisation then hit: as supported as Jo made me feel, the fear of what would happen next was all-consuming.

'See what you've done now,' I sobbed to Jonathan. 'This is a nightmare!'

My only thoughts were of concern for Dad. *How could I do this to my own father? What sort of person did that make me?* Suddenly, I feared the facts and the incidents all seemed a huge muddle. I even began to worry if the police believed me after all or if I'd remembered things correctly. After all, it was three decades ago and I had no notes and only a few photographs.

Shortly after we were told Dad had been arrested, Jonathan rang Susan to let her know but she'd already been told by Jo Huddleston. I gathered from Jonathan that she was not happy, to say the least.

Unable to cope, I went to bed after that. I felt as if I had betrayed Dad on the highest level.

The next morning, I received more information about the case: Dad had been bailed the previous day; he denied everything. Then I got a direct message on Facebook from Dad's wife, Julie, in the Philippines. She called me 'evil'.

'How can you do this to your poor, sick old father?' she wrote.

Then, on the same day, another message landed from Julie: 'Please, Kim, I am begging you. Please don't accuse your father, he is too old to suffer this situation. Please, Kim, I really care about your father, he can't even sleep at night, thinking about this accusation. I am crying all day and night.'

I stared at her words with a rising sense of horror.

*What had I done?*

Rereading her message over and over, I opened one bottle of wine, then another by 2pm. She was right: what kind of daughter was I? What kind of *person*? I was hurting my family, hurting so many people … I glugged down more wine. I hated my life, I hated myself … all of this, this whole mess, was my fault.

*The past is in the past*, I thought to myself, drinking more wine. *The past is in the past …*

I woke to find Jonathan carrying me from the car to A&E at Darlington Memorial Hospital. He was crying as a doctor stood over me.

'I found her unconscious in bed,' he sobbed. 'Please, *please*, help her! Can you take her to rehab or something?'

I struggled to sit up as a mental health doctor came in to assess me. He asked several questions about my state of mind and how much I was drinking. By now it was four bottles a day, which by the way he said it made me realise it was rather a lot. I admitted I often felt suicidal but never intended to do anything. He asked what triggered my drinking and it was then that I couldn't stop myself from talking. I told him all about Dad, the abuse and my siblings.

'I just want all the pain to go away,' I sobbed.

He put me on a drip and gave me some drugs to make me feel calmer.

'Can I go on a detox then?' I asked.

I'd never suggested this before but realised now perhaps I did need help. Occasionally, throughout the drinking, I'd have lucid moments and think I'd like to get sober.

'Yes,' agreed Jonathan, anxiously. 'Is that possible?'

The doctor shook his head. 'We don't offer that on the NHS. It's something you'd have to pay for privately.'

We stayed while I sobered up and then went home. By now

it was late and I wanted and needed another drink. Jonathan, however, was in bits.

'Can't you see what you're doing to yourself?' he begged. 'This is killing you, Kim!'

I shrugged. 'I'm fine,' I said. 'I've had blood tests today and the results showed my liver is okay still.'

'For now!' he cried. 'But for how long?'

# Chapter 24

Christmas 2015 passed in a miserable fog. Clara and Harry alternated between sympathy, fury and fear when it came to my on-off addiction to alcohol.

Harry had suddenly announced he was moving out. He left in November 2015 and although I haven't asked him, I believe it was to do with my heavy drinking. It must have been fractious at home, seeing Jonathan relentlessly having a go at me for drinking and me arguing back. I was shocked at the sudden move but I also understood the reasoning behind it – if I were him, I wouldn't want to be around me! I'm surprised Clara didn't choose to follow in his footsteps and I'm also surprised and forever grateful that Jonathan didn't up and leave. Instead, he saw something in me worth sticking around for and persevering. I'm grateful to my entire family and my close friend Sue for helping me during this time.

Once again, I decided to try and stop all the pain, so I called the police station to tell them I was withdrawing the charges again. Jo Huddleston gently explained I would need to email to retract everything, so I wrote an email. But then she told me carefully the decision was out of my hands – they felt they had enough evidence to convict Dad anyway. Part of me wonders if she just said that to prevent me from withdrawing my statement as the police still encouraged me to try and get my siblings on board for that extra evidence.

I admitted to Jonathan what I'd done and he was upset but supportive.

'Please, Kim,' he begged, 'let's just stick with this. One day this nightmare will be over, I promise. You are doing the right thing.'

'Then why doesn't it feel like it?' I cried.

Months earlier, Clara had announced her engagement to her long-term boyfriend Dan and despite everything, I was thrilled for her. Dan is a lovely young man and I expected her to be very happy. Despite all of this upset at home, Clara and Harry had been so supportive of me. I knew deep down they wanted the best for me and I couldn't have been prouder of them, especially considering the mess I had become.

Clara set her wedding date for 24 March 2018, just over two years away. There was so much to organise and do, and as the mother of the bride, I longed to be sober and to be there to help. I couldn't wait to go wedding dress shopping and pick out the décor for the reception. Clara had such good taste and it would be something positive to look forward to. She wanted to get married in a beautiful old church in the village of Hurworth, where we lived. We'd walked past it so many times – it's less than half a mile from our house – and always said what an idyllic venue it would be for a wedding.

But as the months rolled by and my drinking escalated, I found myself unable to imagine actually being there on the big day. I desperately wanted to attend, but worried I wouldn't make it due to a hangover or drink, or even, fearing the worst, maybe I wouldn't be there at all. My blood pressure was extremely high despite taking medication for it. I'd often forget my tablets; I looked ill, I was bloated.

Jonathan was having to take more time off work to look after me. He was told by our GP that I now needed 24-hour round-the-clock care. This meant he was unable to go to work so he confided in my friend Sue and begged her to help me. I'd known Sue for many years – we met through her husband as he'd gone to school with Jonathan and they remained good friends. She might have been aware of my alcohol problem but she never openly said anything to me and I don't think she was aware of the abuse I'd endured – I certainly hadn't said anything to her.

One morning, I came downstairs and Jonathan and Sue were in our kitchen talking. It was 7am so I thought it somewhat strange that my friend was visiting at this time. I must have looked a mess – my hair was unbrushed, I was bloated and had put weight on. When I saw her, I turned on my heels, but Jonathan called me back.

'Kim, I've told Sue everything. She's taking over looking after you as I have to go back to work,' he announced hesitantly.

Sue did odd bits of work as an exam invigilator so she was often free when it was not exam time, but that didn't mean she had a great deal of spare time on her hands as she had a lot of other commitments as well as a husband and children who needed caring for. I was speechless and so angry that Jonathan had told my friend all of this and that he'd in effect asked her to babysit me.

*How dare he! I wasn't some toddler who needed looking after.*

The sad reality unbeknown to me at the time was that I really did need looking after.

I felt so embarrassed and ashamed that Sue knew everything and felt it wasn't right that she should give up her time to be with me. She came most days and stayed until 5 or 6pm when Jonathan came home from work. Although I was annoyed at the time, I'll be forever grateful to her.

One afternoon, Sue and I went for a walk through the village and as we wandered the church grounds where Clara's wedding was booked, I became quite emotional but I didn't let her see this. Instead, I became quite matter-of-fact and asked that should I not make it to the wedding at all, she would ensure that the photographer would get some good shots at various locations in the church grounds. Looking back at this conversation now, I must have been quite ill; the alcohol was clearly affecting my thinking as it would have been Clara asking the photographer for various shots and not me. I was aware that my own mortality might prevent me from being there myself, but it was wrong of me to burden my good friend with all of this.

'The photographer needs to make sure he gets some good shots here and over there,' I said, pointing.

It would be so pretty with the river in the background.

'But, Kim, you're going to be there, aren't you?' she said. 'You can tell him yourself.'

I waved her away. 'Yes, hopefully!' I laughed, trying to make a joke out of it.

Later on, worried about the way I'd been talking, Sue rang Jonathan and told him what I'd said. But I denied everything when he tried to confront me and chose instead to drown my sorrows.

'Kim, I'm genuinely worried you think you won't be there for Clara's wedding day,' Jonathan told me when the kids were out. 'What's going on?'

I had nothing to say; I thought he was being over the top. Of course, I wanted to be there for our daughter's wedding, I just didn't know how bad my drinking would be by then.

By February 2016, the long winter was nearly over but I felt I had nothing to look forward to. Fed up of being nagged about my drinking, I grabbed a rucksack, bottle of wine and our Cocker Spaniel Oscar to go for a walk and drink in peace. It was very cold outside, but I didn't care – all I wanted was to be away from Jonathan and the kids monitoring me about drinking.

I first visited the SPAR to buy a couple of bottles of my favourite wine and wondered where I could drink it in private without the possibility of Jonathan taking it away from me. After making my way back towards the house, I decided the best spot to sit and drink in peace was by the river. Across the quiet road from our house were some dense trees and beyond these was the river bank. It wasn't the best stretch of the riverside as it looked dark and forbidding, but it was private and that's all I wanted.

I made my way across the dense copse of trees and sat by the river. I must have dropped off as I woke at what must have been an hour or so later to the sound of text alerts on my phone. When I glanced down, I saw lots of messages from Jonathan. One read: 'Where are you, Kim? I'm so worried.' I took a photo of Oscar sniffing near the river edge and sent it to him. Then I sent a message with it saying, 'I'm fine, don't worry.' The phone kept ringing so I turned it off. Before I did this, I took one of Jonathan's calls.

'Kim? Where are you?' He sounded distressed.

'Oh, just leave me alone!' I slurred, annoyed he was on my case.

'What? Wait, don't hang up, where are you? We've been looking for you!' he cried.

'Oh, stop fussing! I'm fine,' I sighed.

'Kim!' Jonathan shouted so I hung up and then sent him a photo of me by the riverbank. I was tired of everyone needling me about my drinking. I just wanted to sleep. I settled down and dropped off to sleep again in the muddy grass.

Hours later, it was dark. My jeans were wet through and I was covered in mud up to my chest and felt very cold. Oscar was still by my side, licking my hand.

'Oh, shit!' I cursed, sitting up and rubbing my eyes. I'd lost all track of time. Cold and stiff, I struggled to stand up. Confused, I walked back until I came to a fence with barbed wire. Unable to find a gate, I started to climb over it, ripping my jeans and cutting my leg.

'Oh, bloody hell!' I cussed.

Carefully, I lifted Oscar over the fence too – I knew I was drunk, but didn't want him to cut himself on the barbed wire, as I had. Oscar ran off up the road as our house wasn't far. As I followed him, I heard voices calling my name.

'Mum!'

'Kim!'

Clara and Jonathan were both crying and running over.

Jonathan hugged me while Clara looked both angry and very upset.

'We were about to call the local hospitals and the police!' she cried.

Later, I learned that after I had talked to Jonathan, both he and Clara had rushed home from work and spent the next three or four hours walking miles in the fading light, trying to find me. They didn't know what had happened to me and were terrified, thinking the prospect of finding me alive was fading as it was freezing out. But I didn't think about how scary my disappearance must have been for them and so I pushed them off, feeling so confused. All I could understand was they'd been out looking for me and thought something had happened. But it hadn't, so why the fuss?

'Oh, leave me alone!' I cried. 'Stop being so dramatic.'

I staggered inside, angry at them for being angry at me. By now, it was midnight and I passed out on the bed, oblivious to how much upset I'd caused.

The only guilt I felt was about Dad. Every few days, I'd get messages or texts from Susan and Lucy, asking me why I was doing this. Telling me how Dad was struggling, how he might face a prison sentence. It felt as if he was the victim, not me. I felt so ashamed.

I began to wonder if they were right. Perhaps I was the one who should be stronger and just accept what had happened and move on? Was the abuse really that bad if my own siblings didn't think so? Every night and weekend, I'd drown out the voices in my head with drink. I felt so guilty so perhaps they were right – I *was* selfish?

The next day, Jonathan sat me down yet again to beg me to stop drinking. He'd found some hidden bottles and said he feared for my life. He'd booked me a cottage so I could try and sober up.

'I'll come with you to do a ten-day detox,' he offered. 'Please, *please*, agree to this.'

So, I did. Partly for the kids' sake and partly because I was sick of being nagged.

It worked, for ten days. But as soon as I was home, to more texts from Susan, I put on my rucksack to go to the SPAR for more wine.

When I got back, Jonathan was in tears and handed me a letter.

'If you can't listen to me, maybe you can read what I keep trying to tell you,' he said sadly.

*15 April 2016*
*My darling Kim,*

*I love you so much! I just wanted to set down on paper a few thoughts to express properly how much I love you and how helpless I feel in trying to support you through your illness. Understandably, you refuse to talk about it, which means I've got no alternative but to just let nature take its course and watch your light slowly fade away. I think I've finally learned that after so many years of trying you don't really want to give up alcohol. In turn, this means that I've got to sit back and let you drift away. You'll never know how hard that is to say and to accept. I'm a coward and am terrified of the end. I've tried everything – particularly over the last few months – but*

*sadly all to no avail. And it obviously pains the children*
*as well – our collective happiness is so entwined with*
*your happiness. If the worst happens and I lose you, I*
*swear that I will go after your father and will have him*
*imprisoned, whatever it takes. I know that he is the root*
*cause of all of this suffering and I just wish that you'd*
*had the support from siblings to do what you should*
*have done years ago. I sincerely believe that had you gone*
*through with a prosecution that you'd have taken such*
*strength from it that you'd have come out the other side a*
*stronger person.*

*I simply can't bear for you to slip away and die on*
*me as that's what seems to be happening. My heart is*
*breaking ...*

I wanted to screw up that letter and leave it behind, but I carried on reading. Although deep down, I knew it was a final plea for me to stop drinking and gave Jonathan the chance to tell me how much he loved me and how he was worried I'd not be around for much longer, over the years I'd learned to compartmentalise things – it had been my way of coping with years of abuse. I didn't want to be reminded of my past, nor of what I'd become so the easiest thing was to totally disregard what he had to say. But Jonathan went on to tell me that he couldn't bear for me not to be at Clara's wedding and he wished he could do something for me, although he didn't know what that might be.

*Just the thought of Clara's wedding without you by my side*
*is too much for me to think about. I know that Harry too*

*loves you so much (but he just struggles to express it) – he
just craves your loving attention.*

*I wish there was something I could do to comfort you as
you must be going through agony every day. I also know
that you love us as much as we love you, which is a comfort.
I only wish I was braver and not such a coward and that I
could contemplate and face life without you – but I can't as
I'm too deeply in love with you.*

*I love you, my darling – you were the best thing that ever
happened to me and I feel very, very fortunate to have spent
my life with you.*

*Jonathan xxxxxx*

I put the letter down and picked up my wine.

*He's being really over the top*, I thought.

In my fog of despair, I didn't have the capacity to empathise
with Jonathan's upset too. Looking back, he had written a
love letter while fearing the worst. Deep down, I knew my
husband was worried and upset and that letter must have
been so difficult for him to write. I could imagine him sitting,
typing the words into his laptop, blinded by tears, desperately
wanting to get his message across. It was easier for me to
disregard it and although at the time I thought he was being
over the top, I didn't throw the letter away. Instead, I kept it
among some birthday and Christmas cards I'd saved over the
years from Jonathan and the children.

*Today, if I read it, I cry.*

Jonathan refused to give up. One evening, after work, he
admitted he'd been speaking to Susan and believed he'd

persuaded her to talk to the police. He'd arranged for us to meet up in Saltburn to discuss it.

'Isn't this amazing news?' he said, relieved. 'I think this will make things so much easier for you.'

I lived in hope Susan would stand by me too, so I met up with her. But the meeting was tense. She clearly wasn't as enthusiastic as Jonathan hoped and didn't want to talk much about Dad.

Often I'd gone through long spells of abstinence and during one of my more lucid moments, I decided to try and give it another go. I stopped drinking on 30 October 2016 and this spell of sobriety lasted three months.

On 5 December, during this time of abstinence I had a second long video police interview at Elland Road, Leeds. The police wanted specific details of the UK offences. They'd explained to me that Dad couldn't be tried for any incidents in Kenya so they would focus on the rapes and assaults that happened in the UK. The most serious offences, the ones that took place in Kenya, could be used as 'evidence of bad character' so I mentioned the rapes at the bedsit in London, at the house in Guiseley, at the White Swan in Hunmanby and in the hotels in London on our visits back to the UK when we were visiting Mum.

I knew full well these rapes and assaults were the tip of the iceberg, but I was still frightened of getting Dad into too much trouble so I thought if I kept my accounts to a minimum then he might just get a slap on the wrist. All I ever wanted was for him to acknowledge what he'd done to me and tell me that he was sorry – I didn't want him to get into trouble.

Many people reading this may never completely under-stand the madness of it all. Here I was, reporting my dad for raping and assaulting me, but at the same time not wanting to get him into trouble – it didn't make sense. I knew he was frail and I also knew he enjoyed pottering in his garden and growing plants. How could I take all of that away from him? The more I thought about it, the guiltier I felt. I therefore made a conscious effort to list only a few of the many incidents (it was impossible for me to keep count of them all as there had been so many of them).

The police wanted to gather more evidence, including taking a statement from Jonathan and one from my old friend Keg. I'd always stayed in touch with him and he told me he really wished he'd done something years ago. He was only too happy to tell his version of events, which backed up what I'd said, especially regarding the second abortion. Following all of this, the police decided they had sufficient evidence to pass on everything to the Crown Prosecution Service (CPS). It was now a waiting game to see if there was a viable case to lead to a prosecution. I didn't fully understand the process, but Jo Huddleston explained not all cases were taken on due to lack of evidence. In an ideal world, they needed supporting statements from my siblings.

'Well, I'm losing hope that will happen,' I admitted to her.

But the police were hopeful that in this case they might have enough evidence.

Four months later, the news soon emerged that the CPS had said yes to my case being tried at a Crown Court. My father was to attend Leeds Crown Court on 8 June 2017, where he pleaded Not Guilty to the offences outlined between

31 December 1977 and 1 July 1985. There were six charges being brought against Dad. These were the offences I had listed before when the police asked about the rapes in the UK. As mentioned earlier, they were only a minority of the actual rapes and abuse that he'd inflicted upon me when I'd been here in England.

'It's amazing news,' said Jo Huddleston.

'Is it?' I replied.

Part of me was petrified of my siblings finding out. I knew how much they'd hate me. They'd know it was me bringing down the Beaumont name again.

*Poor Dad*, they'd be thinking, *leave him alone to get on with his life. The past is in the past.* Also, they'd be concerned the story would become public and possibly be concerned that people might put two and two together and realise this man was also their father.

This wasn't all going to miraculously go away. I'd have to go to court and stand there in front of Dad and tell on him.

*How could any daughter do that to her own father?*

'I know this is hard, Kim,' said Jo with such sympathy that I felt tears begin to flow again.

At this point, eighteen months had passed since my first interview with the police. Jo then told me it might take another year before the case was heard.

On hearing this, I broke down completely.

'Another year?' I cried. 'How am I supposed to live with this for another year?'

The idea of waiting for so long, not knowing how this would end up, was completely unbearable.

As 2016 turned into 2017, we went on holiday to Florida, where I remained sober the whole time. Then, on the last day, I found myself watching other holiday-makers standing outside, toasting the sunset with a bottle of wine. I gazed longingly at the wine in their glasses, wishing I could toast it too.

*Maybe I could*, I thought to myself.

I'd gone three months without a drink. Perhaps now I was aware of what drink could do in excess, I could try moderating it. Unfortunately, this is an all-too-common thought of an alcoholic in denial. I knew I didn't have that 'off switch'. There's a saying, 'One drink is too many and a thousand not enough' – in my case this is absolutely true. I didn't tell Jonathan how I was feeling as he wouldn't understand and he would almost certainly not let me out of his sight once we returned home. He was just starting to trust me again to go shopping by myself too.

*If I was to try moderating my drinking, I had to do it in secret.*

Although I'd felt better than I'd done in ages, the worry of any impending court case was never far from my mind. It hung over my head like a black cloud and the only relief was found at the bottom of a glass, or so it seemed.

As soon as the plane landed, I was desperate to get home and have a drink again. A day or so later, I decided to put my new plan into practice. Waiting until no one was around, I drove to the SPAR. Going in, I felt extremely guilty and scoured the small shop nervously to ensure there was no one I knew in there – I didn't want a neighbour seeing me and innocently asking Jonathan later if we'd enjoyed our party as I'd been seen buying bottles of booze!

There was only a small selection here, even less in the

chiller. It had to be perfect, had to be chilled, had to be poured into my favourite lead crystal wine glass. I managed to hide my newly moderated alcohol intake from Jonathan and Clara (Harry wasn't living with us by then) for only a few days. Unfortunately, this moderation didn't last and half a bottle of wine soon became one and then two. Before I knew it, I was back up to my three or four bottles a day and drinking from morning until bedtime.

I was shocked at how fast I was back up to so many bottles. So much for moderation! Within a week, I was once again well and truly trapped within the grip of drink. I felt a mix of emotions – utterly sad, ashamed, guilty, anxious, hopeless and angry with myself – all at the same time.

Once, after a morning's drinking, I became so distraught, obsessively brushing my hair and acting in such a bizarre way, that Jonathan took me to see our GP. He begged the doctor for help, but she admitted there was nowhere they could currently send me as local mental health centres weren't available.

'Kim needs 24/7 supervised care, however,' she warned. 'She is at risk of losing her life through drink right now.'

During one of my hour-or-so spells of not yet starting drink for the day, I begged Jonathan to get me some help. I was becoming increasingly tired of the daily chores of buying drink, hiding it, drinking it in secret, hiding the empties, upsetting the family, etc. Doing all of this had become a full-time job and I desperately wanted my life back.

My wonderful husband took on board my cry for help – I'd in effect given him the green light to get me sober and he wanted to act upon it before I had a drink and changed my mind. Later that day, he told me he'd managed to get me booked into rehab for a month and had paid a deposit on the residential rehab establishment in Runcorn (a three-hour drive away).

By the time I was booked in for rehab, I really didn't want to go. However, on Monday, 20 February 2017 (just twenty-six days after I had started drinking again), Jonathan drove me there anyway, even as I was downing a bottle of wine in the car. When we arrived, I could hardly stand.

I lasted six hours before discharging myself. I hated the place. I was expected to share a room with a stranger and the doctor wanted to assess me over FaceTime. I'd been left to lie in my bed and not had a thorough assessment. I had severe shakes as the DTs were starting to kick in and I'd not been given any medication to help with them. Being a nurse myself, the whole place seemed highly unprofessional. Since I wasn't sectioned, I told them that they couldn't keep me against my will, so they reluctantly booked me a ticket home (using the money they had taken from me when I arrived) and drove me to the train station.

A devastated Jonathan met me at the station in Darlington, near to our home. He was so angry at the rehab centre for the poor, unprofessional treatment and he'd paid a hefty deposit too. With my permission, he booked me into another place two hours from our home – Linwood House in Barnsley, South Yorkshire – in four days' time. Naturally, I was concerned where we'd find that amount of money – it wasn't cheap and we'd already lost our £2,000 deposit on the other place. But Jonathan reassured me, saying my life was worth more than the money it was costing so any amount would be worth it.

I don't know where he found the money, but he took me to the centre the day before so that I could see the place for myself and meet the staff. It was much better and so I agreed to spend a month there, starting the next day: 24 February 2017.

When I arrived in the morning, I was drunk and when Jonathan opened the door to the car, I vomited all over the tarmac. Although I didn't realise it at the time, I'd wet myself too but I didn't feel any sense of shame at the time – it was always the next morning when the self-loathing began.

I had to endure a full week of 'safe' detoxing before the sessions started. Being in the full throes of alcoholism meant if I gave up suddenly, I could die. Every time I even cut down, I'd get the shakes. I was given medication to help and Librium to take the edge off the anxiety I was feeling.

On the day the workshop started, I shyly joined others who were just like me. We were all there for the same reason: to recover from compulsive, out-of-control behaviours and restore manageability to our lives. Words cannot describe the utter despair and shame that I felt and despite being surrounded by so many people, I felt dreadfully lonely.

*How had my life come to this?*

When we started the workshops, I soon learned that they were based on the Alcoholics Anonymous (AA) programme. Over the years, I'd attended a couple of AA meetings and decided this method of staying sober was not for me. I found it easy to fob Jonathan off when he begged me to give it a try

– 'I'm not into all that religious stuff, mumbo jumbo about higher powers and God, I can't be bothered with all that,' I told him. 'I'm not going there and that's that!' Now suddenly here I was in a rehabilitation centre that focused on the 12 Steps to assist with personal recovery and maintain sobriety. I couldn't believe it, but since I was there, I'd best give it a go.

I'd been sober for a full week. I looked at the first step and read it back to myself. This was quite an easy one as I had to accept that I was powerless over my addiction, which in my case was drinking, and that my life had become unmanageable. Well, how could I argue with that? My life *had* become more than unmanageable. My drinking *had* resulted in my life becoming a complete mess and was the reason I was sitting there right now, surrounded by others like me. I knew I was a mess and this might be my only chance to sort it out, so I took it one day at a time, just as the programme advised us to.

As part of my therapy I had to write a letter about what I felt my problems in life were, then sit in a circle of other addicts to share my story. It was easy enough for me to write down the memories of childhood but very hard to read them out. But I could tell my story to the others in a very matter-of-fact way, telling them all about Dad and what he'd done as if it was a story about someone I didn't know very well. People sat in shocked silence, unable to comprehend what I'd just said.

Afterwards, I heard others share stories of how desperate their lives had become and what they risked losing if they didn't stop drinking. Some of them had already lost their jobs, houses and relationships. As I listened to them, it occurred to me how all the patients at the rehab were well spoken and well dressed. They came from all sorts of backgrounds. It proved to me you didn't have to be a homeless person on a park bench to be an alcoholic, you can be functioning in other areas of your life or be from any kind of background. Alcohol is an addiction and anyone – not just those suffering the pain of abuse – might be predisposed towards it. When people spoke in these meetings about being sober, it gave me hope that one day I could be too.

Around this time, Susan wrote me a moving letter to say she supported me in my attempt to overcome the alcoholism. She only knew about alcohol dependency as it was part of her role when she worked in sales as she sold medication to help with alcohol dependency. I was so surprised she'd written to me out of the blue like this and her words meant the world. All I'd ever wanted was my siblings' support. It made it less of a burden confronting Dad as I had done. The last thing I wanted was for everyone to hate me and for me to lose my family too. We might not be as close as we once were, and Dad might have destroyed our innocence, but knowing Susan was there for me for the trial meant everything.

The timetable at the rehab centre was very strict. At times I hated it and argued with staff when they tried to stop me from doing things like drinking sparkling water or eating wine gums, but the rules were in place to try and prevent you from finding another crutch instead of booze. In fact, sparkling water could be a trigger for sparkling wine. Also, we were not allowed any mouthwash or perfume in case we drank it.

No matter how bad my drinking might have been, I would never have contemplated drinking my Jo Malone cologne and I argued the toss with staff when they took it away from me! We had to learn how to live a life of discipline again, as well as digging into the reasons behind our addiction. The more I learned about why I'd become an alcoholic, the more determined I was to give myself a fighting chance to recover and get some sanity back in my life. You can never beat it, but I wanted to be in recovery and remain that way.

We were allowed out, but only into the town centre accompanied by staff. Each day was hard to get through, but little by little, I grew stronger.

During my month in rehab, I completed the first three steps of the AA programme. Being open-minded about the programme, I made a decision to follow a new routine every day, waking earlier, making my fellow inmates morning cups of coffee and leaving the steaming mugs outside their doors after a knock and a cheery 'Good morning'. I read more and more literature on addiction to inspire me. It was key that I should fully accept that I was powerless over alcohol and had to rebuild my life on a daily basis.

*This wasn't going to be easy.*

Exactly a month after I was admitted, and a year to the day until Clara's wedding, I was allowed to go home. By sticking to the regime, I looked and felt better than I had in years. We were taught the fight to stay sober wasn't over – it would never be over – but if I carried on doing the 12-Step programme, I had a fighting chance.

The day Jonathan came to pick me up felt like a fresh

start for us all. I could see how proud he was of me and I didn't want to let him or the kids down. More importantly, I didn't want to let *myself* down. I'd started to see the world in a different light: I was sober and although I'd had months of abstinence in the past, this was different. I knew I could never touch a single drop of alcohol again. I also loved my newfound freedom that this spell in rehab had given me. It was as if I was looking at the world with different eyes – I felt more free than I'd felt in years. I had to make this work – I had to be there for Clara's wedding and also to face the man who'd abused me throughout my whole life.

*And I could only do this sober.*

'It's so good to have you back, Kim,' Jonathan said, kissing my cheek.

The day after I emerged from rehab, on the way back from work I stopped outside our local shop. Despite my newfound sobriety, I found myself hovering around the wine section. I picked up a bottle of Sauvignon Blanc and put it in my shopping basket.

I asked myself what I was doing, but wandered around the shop feeling as if I was carrying kryptonite. If any of my family happened to pop in, they'd go mad and see what I was doing as an act of self-sabotage. I knew I'd drink it, if anyone caught me with it. This was madness, but felt like a test of my own resilience.

After a few minutes, I put the basket down and calmly walked out of the shop. It was as if I had tested myself and passed. I had too much to lose to even contemplate drinking again. This was a choice and I had to do it for my family and myself. Afterwards, I told Jonathan what I'd done – I knew he'd be angry but I also knew he'd be proud that I'd had the strength to put the wine back.

The next day was my birthday and Mother's Day too. We all went out to celebrate my homecoming. As we walked towards the restaurant in the village I couldn't believe how Technicolor the world appeared. I noticed the vibrant green of the trees in bud, the daffodils waving gently in the breeze, the sounds of the birds and passing laughter of children walking by. It felt as if I'd emerged from a cloud into a completely different life. Except the only difference was no alcohol was tainting my view.

When we arrived, someone put a bottle of wine on the table in front of me to wish me a happy birthday, but I handed it straight to Clara.

'Here you go, this is for you for organising such a wonderful day,' I told her.

She gave me a huge hug. 'I'm so happy you're back to being you, Mum,' she said.

Back home, I would usually have waited up until everyone went to bed before opening that bottle of wine by myself but this time, I went upstairs with Jonathan for an early night. Lying together, he told me how proud he was.

'Please just keep the faith,' he said. 'Clara's wedding is almost exactly a year away, focus on that.'

I agreed. We both knew what was happening the next year too: Dad's trial. But for now, I needed to focus on rebuilding my life, beating the booze and seeing my darling daughter marry.

My newfound sobriety came just in time. On 11 May 2017, Dad appeared at Leeds District Magistrates Court for his initial plea hearing for sexual offences that took place between 1977 and 1985. He was now on conditional bail.

A month later, on 10 June 2017, I received a further letter from West Yorkshire Police to say that on 8 June Dad had pleaded Not Guilty to the charges and this was a notice to attend Leeds Crown Court on 9 April 2018. The case was expected to last for five days.

Then Jo Huddleston rang me with an update but also more news.

'Are you sitting down?' she asked.

'Oh God, what's happened now?' I replied.

'Your dad has said he thinks you should do a DNA test. He is claiming you are not his daughter.'

I suddenly felt furious. How dare he try and claim this? It was a desperate lie.

'Unfortunately, I know I am his daughter,' I said.

*What should I do?* A part of me was surprised but not that surprised that he'd pull a stunt like this. *What did he have up his sleeve? What was he trying to achieve by demanding this?*

Jo told me that should the test go ahead, it had to be at my expense too!

'No, I'm not doing it,' I told her firmly.

I cannot recall the reasons underlying this but it was eventually decided that it might be a good idea to provide a swab for the DNA test. I didn't have to pay. But I never heard any more about it. I don't think Dad did a DNA test himself – I honestly believe he was trying various tricks to try and make me succumb to drink once more.

*If I was drunk, I wouldn't be able to be a credible witness.*

After putting the phone down, I sat with my head in my

hands. I didn't know what to expect. Dad pleaded Not Guilty when he appeared at the Magistrates Court and I expected the same plea at the Crown Court.

*But I was ready for this. As ready as I could ever be.*

# Chapter 25

By some miracle, I managed to get through the next year. The police liaison officers were a huge support. I wasn't speaking to Lucy at all, but Susan would call me now and again to let me know how Dad was doing. I still held out hope that she would back me up in court but wanted to wait until a date had been firmly fixed before broaching the idea with her.

The trial was to begin in April 2018, just two weeks after the wedding.

'Why does it have to be so close to Clara's big day?' I cried to Jonathan.

'You can do it,' he soothed. 'We are all in this together.'

Clara's wedding lived up to all our expectations. Seeing her radiant smile as she walked down the aisle was everything I'd ever wanted to witness. It was such a busy, happy time. I was there, sober and able to be present for every minute. The person who had told their friend she feared missing her daughter's wedding seemed like someone else.

Susan and Sean also came to the wedding and reception in a nearby hotel. We made polite conversation and Sean confirmed he'd decided not to attend the trial. I didn't want to discuss the elephant in the room on my daughter's precious day, but it didn't surprise me: my brother stayed away from most family affairs. He was easily led, however, and if he had to decide anything, he'd go with what his other sisters wanted.

As I saw Sean and Susan chatting, I wondered if neither of them supported me in this, would we ever be able to once more have a relationship with each other? Again, I stopped myself from musing on my family, I didn't want anything to spoil such a magical day.

The trial date was set for 10 April 2018, just seventeen days away, and now that the wedding was over I needed something else to focus on. During the wait, I continued with the 12-Step programme and threw myself into my business. I was very busy at work, which helped me cope as I had that to focus on, but my thoughts were never far away from what was going to happen with the fast-approaching trial. Although there were many opportunities to have a drink, despite the stress and anxiety I was experiencing, I didn't feel the temptation to have any alcohol. I also knew if I started drinking again, I might let down the court case or worse still, be an unreliable witness. Despite all this, the closer the date for the trial got, the more terrified I became.

My police liaison officer, Jo Huddleston, had remained in touch constantly, keeping me updated and supported. It must have been a hard job because she couldn't tell me what Dad had told the police and of course I was desperate to know.

The thought of going into the witness stand was frightening, but also, I worried about the effect it was going to have on Dad and the rest of my family. *Would everyone blame me? Would he have a heart attack and die?* The worst-case scenarios whirled around my head whenever I stopped for a moment to think about it. The main one being: *what if nobody believes me?*

Luckily, with Jonathan's support, I managed to stay alcohol-free and my mind was too occupied with work and the impending trial to uncork that bottle again. Some evenings there was nothing more I wanted than to drown out the constant thoughts in my head, but I knew I couldn't let my family down – I had to stay strong to get through the up-and-coming weeks.

Around this time, Susan rang me.

'Kim, we need to speak about the trial. Dad's not very well. He's really upset. He thinks he's going to prison, but look, he's told me everything and says he's sorry. You need to talk to him,' she told me.

I couldn't believe it: *Dad was sorry?* Susan sounded like she pitied him too. Of course, he wasn't sorry, he was only sorry things had got this far! He never once thought I would go ahead and prosecute him. However, I desperately wanted to believe it and for a second, I felt elated, but the thought also crossed my mind that he'd had decades to apologise, so why now? When I asked my sister why he hadn't told me this himself, she said his solicitor had instructed him not to communicate with me so he couldn't. I still had no idea if

Susan was going to make a statement on my behalf supporting me. She said she was going to, but hadn't done so yet. I hoped she might do it at the last minute but time was running out.

A tightness gripped my throat as I remembered the letter I'd sent Dad in 2007. Back then, I would have done anything to have had this apology but he didn't even acknowledge my letter, let alone say sorry.

'Well, he hasn't said sorry to me,' I eventually replied. 'He's had the opportunity, Susan, but that's long gone.'

Sean suggested setting up a family WhatsApp group. He said it was to talk about the trial, so I agreed to this. Jonathan warned against going ahead with this call – he was adamant I was being set up and convinced this would only be a two-way conversation. He was correct because on the Friday, five days before I was due to be cross-examined, it was only Susan when the call came through and Lucy had not been invited to join the group. Susan spent at least half an hour haranguing me and, in effect, lobbying me not to give evidence against Dad. She was also annoyed at having to talk to one of her sons about his grandad (in the event, Susan and Sean met up in London to tell the son). She was clearly furious with me.

'I have to tell my son his grandad is a paedophile because of this court case,' she said, which seemed to infer to me that it was all my fault.

'I'm really sorry, but I had to tell Clara and Harry that years ago,' I replied. 'The kids need to be warned.'

Part of me believed my siblings were trying to push me to my limits. *Perhaps*, I wondered, *they even want to make me turn to drink again so the trial collapses.*

Despite all the upset, Susan said she wanted to support

me again. She didn't agree with what I was doing, she told me, but she wanted to be there for me. She asked when I was standing to give evidence and I told her that it wasn't until the Wednesday and as I wasn't needed until then, I would not be attending the day before. I also approached Sean to ask what he was going to do. He simply said he couldn't make a statement against Dad and that he would not be attending the court during the trial at all, so that was that.

As the day of the trial in early April loomed, Jo Huddleston explained to me what my role would be. The trial was beginning on the Tuesday, but I was to appear as a witness on Wednesday only. I had to be cross-examined. The jury and court already had my statement, they'd seen the videos and I was there purely to be cross-examined.

'Will I do it by video link or behind a screen?' I asked Jo.

'Only if you request it,' she explained.

I thought for a second but then I said no. I wanted to stand there and tell everyone straight about what happened. Why should I hide? I'd got myself sober, something I'd been trying to do for years, so I wanted to face the man who had done this to me without anything between us.

Jo explained I should come to court on the Tuesday to have a look around an empty courtroom so I felt comfortable with the layout and would know where to go and what to expect. It would also help me decide once and for all whether I'd like a video link, a curtain drawn so Dad couldn't see me or whether I would prefer to stand openly in full view of the court. She offered to show me around, saying it would be good to familiarise myself with the witness box, where everyone would be sitting, and to show me how the screening worked, should I have wanted it. It was short notice but still very much appreciated.

Jo went on to say that on the actual day I was to be cross-examined, I would not be allowed to speak to anyone and would have to enter via a back door, to avoid anyone trying to mess with my statement. Jonathan was also to be cross-examined on his statement, but we were not even allowed to speak to each other about it. So, Jo set up the visit to the court and I was shown around on 10 April, the day after I was shown my video statements, which were about three hours long in total.

Two days before the trial, Jo had been asked if I wanted to refresh my memory by watching myself give video evidence to the police since it was a long time ago. She thought it would be a good idea and came over to the house on 9 April (two days prior to me being cross-examined and a day before I went to look round the court). I felt nervous, worried about how I might come across and I was shocked at how ill I looked, especially in the first video statement. But as I watched myself speak, fluently telling the police exactly what had happened, I was relieved. I could guess what I was going to say before I said it. A rising sense of determination filled me: there was nothing to fear from cross-examination.

*The police believed me; the CPS believed in the evidence. After all, I was telling the truth.*

Susan wasn't expecting to see me on 10 April, the day I came to view the empty courtroom. In our last WhatsApp conversation, she'd asked when I was giving my statement and I'd told her it was on the Wednesday, the day after I was being shown around.

Now I knew what to expect, I just had to remain strong and get through it. I did this with the amazing support of my husband, children and close friends. Also, I took comfort in knowing that I was telling the truth. I was absolutely terrified about what Dad's barrister might throw at me in court, but I knew whatever he said, my answers would be just as it all happened. I couldn't trip myself up because it was all true. In the lead-up to the trial and throughout, I adopted the AA philosophy of 'one day at a time'.

On the Tuesday, I arrived at the courthouse where I was meeting the police officers for the tour. I didn't know what to expect but dressed smartly, trying to ignore the rising sense of anxiety I had. Part of me still couldn't believe this was happening. Another part wanted to shout 'Stop!' at everything and everyone. I still feared Dad would become unwell and it would be all my fault. If I was being honest with myself, I still feared what he thought about me too. *Did he hate me for this? Did I deserve it?* I tried to breathe deeply and close off my stream of thoughts as I entered the foyer of Leeds Crown Court.

Busy lawyers holding folders walked briskly among members of the public, all waiting for their own moment of the day. As I looked for Jo Huddleston, she rushed over from a nearby corridor. The expression on her face immediately told me something was wrong.

'Kim, your sister Susan is here with your dad,' she whispered.

'*What*?' I said.

'I just thought I'd forewarn you as we have to walk that way past them,' she said with concern. She understood exactly how this would make me feel.

As I followed the officer into a corridor, where Susan sat closely next to Dad on plastic chairs, I tried not to look at him but noticed how frail he'd become. He was due to turn eighty that year and he'd stopped dyeing his hair a darker shade, which he tended to do for visits to the Philippines to see his young wife, Julie. With his mop of grey, he looked much older than his years and it occurred to me that perhaps he'd been instructed to do this by his barrister. Despite myself, I noticed a smirk on his face – the usual look he gave whenever he saw me.

Susan leaped up when she saw me as if she'd seen a ghost. She clearly wasn't expecting me as I'd told her I was going to be there on the Wednesday.

'Kim!' she cried. She tried to throw her arms around me but I pushed her away. 'It's not what it looks like,' she whispered. 'I had to give Dad a lift, I'm not here for him, you know.'

At this, I welled up as I could see, over her shoulder, my dad's face. His smirk was growing ever-wider. He didn't say anything – he didn't need to. I managed somehow to hold it together until I was out of their view and had entered the courtroom I was being shown.

Jo and another police officer ushered me quickly away to continue our tour, but I could hardly see because of the tears streaming down my face. The hurt and betrayal by Susan was so immense, I felt a pain in my chest. The officer offered me a tissue as Jo explained which entrance I needed to use and where I needed to stand in the courtroom. But I was completely in shock and struggled to take in any information as I thought of Susan sitting next to Dad just yards away. I just couldn't believe my sister was supporting him like this.

Whatever she'd said, I couldn't believe she had decided to stand by him like this when she knew what he'd done to me. I felt so betrayed, I was inconsolable.

As I was putting a hand on my chest to try and calm myself, I heard someone say, 'She doesn't look strong enough to do this.' As far as humanely possible, I had come to terms with what my dad had done, but for my own sister to heap this on me, no. I knew I'd never recover from it. While I could sympathise with her not being strong enough to support me, I couldn't fathom why she'd want to support him.

*Especially as I'd have walked to the ends of the earth for her.*

Ten minutes later, I was outside, trying to calm myself down, with Jo assuring me it would be okay. They understood all too well the shock of seeing Susan there with Dad but I could tell they were anxious I recovered in time to continue as a witness. By now I also knew Dad had his case sorted, but I didn't know what he was going to throw at me or what lies he planned on telling. I imagined there would be an unexpected 'twist' in all of this, but of course, I couldn't find out until the actual day in court.

In the car on the way home with Jonathan and his brother Andrew, my phone lit up with messages from Susan. She tried to claim she had simply driven Dad to the courtroom, that she wasn't helping him, that 'someone had to bring him to court'. However, I knew the court would pick people up in a car if they didn't have transport. I didn't respond to her.

*What was there left to say?*

The next morning, I woke early. I had barely slept but felt strangely full of energy as the nerves took hold. I knew it was too late to back out now, I had to do this. I didn't really want to, but also knew it was far too late to pull out.

As I looked in the mirror to put on some make-up, I stared back at my reflection, thinking of that little girl in 1976 who thought she was going on holiday to Kenya with her dad. I wrapped my arms around my body, closed my eyes and imagined giving her a hug.

*Who could have ever imagined forty-two years later I would be taking that father to court?*

I was petrified about what this day would bring. What his defending lawyer would come up with when I took the stand. How my articulate, intelligent father would try and hoodwink the jury. The whole idea of standing there vulnerable in a courtroom made me want to run away screaming. As my thoughts grew more hysterical, I heard Harry and Clara call me from downstairs.

'We're ready and waiting, Mum,' they said.

Quickly, I brushed the shoulders of my suit to remove any stray hairs and went downstairs. Harry and Clara were smartly dressed and smiling. They both pulled me into a hug when they saw me.

'We are so proud of you, Mum,' said Clara.

As I looked at my husband and my two kids, I welled up.

'I'm so lucky to have all of you by my side,' I cried.

'Come on,' said Jonathan. 'You know we always will be.'

As I walked into the courtroom, I held my head up high to try and control my trembling limbs. I was so frightened, I wanted to be sick. If someone had offered to stop it all, I would have done anything to do that.

From the corner of my eye I could see Susan in the public

gallery and Dad sitting in the dock on a bench elsewhere in court. There was a hushed silence as I stepped into the witness stand. Just before the cross-examination started, words suddenly filled my head that seemingly came from nowhere: *You know what, Kim, you're just telling the truth*, I thought to myself. *There's nothing they can throw at you because you're the honest one.* I stood a little straighter and cleared my throat. I didn't need to go through all of the detail as the two barristers, judge and jury had all seen the video footage. Instead the prosecution barrister – Mr Michael Morley – asked questions and then Dad's barrister – Mr Allan Armbrister – cross-examined me afterwards.

The defending barrister, Mr Armbrister, asked many questions, which I answered as calmly and clearly and quickly as possible.

One line of Dad's defence was that I, as a child, had seduced him. An allegation so repulsive, I struggled to retain my composure.

*This must be the twist I thought was coming.*

To my horror, I heard my father had initially denied the allegations and then a week after his arrest admitted 'consensual sex'.

At one point, Dad's barrister began a question by saying: 'So when your father and you engaged in consensual sex from aged sixteen –'

'You mean, when he raped me from the age of eleven,' I interrupted.

Dad's barrister even touted the idea I had returned to the hotel one time because I *wanted* to have sex with my own father.

'*No!*' I sobbed, breaking down. 'I did not *ever* want to have sex! All I ever wanted was my dad to be a normal dad.'

He went on to try and convince the jury that the reason Jonathan didn't like Dad was because he was jealous of our relationship.

As someone passed me a tissue, I could hear the sound of Susan sobbing too. Then finally, I was free to go. As soon as I had given my evidence, I left the court building with my friend Sue. The trial continued and with hindsight, I wish that I'd remained to watch my husband's cross-examination which followed mine but I was uncertain of the protocol and it had even been suggested to us that it doesn't look good to the wider court for a victim to be seen to want to sit through the entire proceedings.

Jonathan was in the stand for about an hour. Apparently, he broke down a couple of times during the cross-examination, once when describing how he had made the report to the police almost three years earlier out of desperation because he felt it was a last gamble for my salvation. There was, I'm told by all those who attended in my support that day, what we all felt was a mildly comical element during my husband's cross-examination when the defence barrister, Mr Armbrister, grilled him on his role in driving me to Dad's solicitor's office in Guiseley, back in the late 1980s. When asked why he had done this and then asked, 'Do you do everything Kim tells you to do?', he simply replied, 'Yes, don't all sensible men do this?' Presumably in an attempt to discredit Jonathan's evidence, the defence barrister pressed his point. I suppose the inference was that because my husband knew what I (and he, through me) was being coerced into doing – going to a legal practice to make an untruth declaration – that he must somehow be of a dishonest disposition.

I'm told at one point the defence barrister, after pausing for dramatic effect, glanced at Jonathan and told him, 'It's not looking good for you, is it, Mr Chown?' Friends tell me it was like a parody of a trial where it is portrayed that the defence is always trying to tie the prosecution witness in knots. On the other hand, we felt that if this was their best attempt at defending the case, then they must be quite desperate.

After Jonathan gave his statement, the court was adjourned.

Jonathan broke my train of thought by suggesting we go for lunch at a nearby café. As we returned to the court afterwards, someone shouted my name:

'*Kim*! Give me a hug! Oh God, don't cut me off!'

It was Susan, looking distraught. She ran across the road to join us but I recoiled from her open arms. I didn't want to get into a row, not now. Not after what she'd done by standing by Dad. Jonathan warned her off as he ushered me away.

'Now is not the time, Susan,' he said.

'Don't turn my sister against me!' she cried as we ducked inside.

*I didn't look back, there was nothing left to say.*

The following afternoon, Keg was also due to appear on a video link but when this was postponed due to a mix-up with the court and then jury sickness and being down to just nine jurors, it was postponed again. Eventually his statement was read out in the courtroom instead due to technical issues. I sat, feeling deeply moved, as I heard the words of my old friend spoken aloud in the room. He talked about how we met, how he discovered my father was abusing me and how he had helped me all those years ago to have that abortion. Tears welled in my eyes as I thought how he'd saved my life in many ways. While Keg was speaking, I glanced over at my father and saw him shaking his head, as if in disbelief.

*If I'd ended up having that baby, I might never have escaped.*

'My regret is that I did not tell anyone about what I witnessed and that was my biggest mistake (as I see it in hindsight now). I did want to tell my father and thought seriously on several occasions of confiding in him. I never summed up the courage to do so,' Keg's statement said. He also confided in me later that his father had died never knowing the truth and how he feels terrible about this.

I stared at my hands in my lap. Poor Keg, he had been caught up in something no one should ever have to deal with. I vowed to tell him he had nothing whatsoever to regret when I next spoke to him.

My sister Susan and Dad sat together until Dad's cross-examination as he was free to do and sit as he chose outside of the courtroom itself – innocent until proven guilty, as they say. One day, on my way back to court in-between sessions, I spotted my father standing outside the court building. He was near the entrance and leaning against the wall, having a cigarette. As I walked past, he watched me carefully. I tried not to catch his eye.

Before Dad's cross-examination, in another part of trial protocol that was new to me, the entire transcript of his original police interview was read out verbatim. This included all the 'ums' and 'ahs' where applicable. The prosecution barrister – Mr Michael Morley – read out the questions from the police and Jo Huddleston read out the replies my father had given.

It was like a mini-drama being played out in front of me. In that first interview, my own father vehemently denied ever having touched me in an inappropriate manner. Mr Morley and Jo went on to read out his second interview, which took place a few weeks later and in which he changed his story. This time he was claiming (and how convenient!) that very shortly after I'd turned sixteen years of age, I'd seduced him. When asked by Mr Morley why he didn't stop me, Dad said, 'Would you get out of bed if a beautiful naked woman was in beside you?'

*I trust this sounds as ridiculous now as it did when it was first read out in court!*

One of the main thrusts of the prosecution case in discrediting him was that he had concocted a new story and had therefore lied in his original police interview. He declared that he had changed his story because he was embarrassed but now admitted it all happened but that I had initiated it. He also stated that some of the accounts in which I'd said that he raped me couldn't have taken place because he was too busy and didn't have the time!

For the next week, I sat in the courtroom watching Dad put his side of the story across. He was facing six separate charges. Rape of a minor between 1977 and 1979 at a London hotel. Rape of a minor at the White Swan in Hunmanby. Rape of a woman at a London bedsit (two separate charges due to detail given). Rape of a woman at Coppice Wood Crescent, Guiseley, in 1985 (also two separate charges). As I've said earlier, none of the abuse that happened in Kenya could be tried under UK law. These were charges I knew he was going to lie about and I watched as he did so.

*Again, and again and again.*

During his cross-examination, Dad spoke as if he had plums in his mouth, admitting he had 'consensual' sex when I was sixteen. I was disgusted: what father would try and explain away sex with his daughter as 'consensual'? Confusingly, at the very same time as feeling angry, I couldn't help but feel extremely sorry for him. Dad looked like a tired, frail old man as he sat to give evidence. He appeared hunched and his usually strident voice was hoarse and weak. But he still looked down on everyone: he turned his back on the prosecution barrister while being cross-examined and was immediately instructed to turn around, whereupon he muttered something under his breath and turned to face the judge instead. He obviously resented Mr Morley asking him questions; he also denied ever having met Keg.

Despite his denials, I feared what would happen next: *If he should be found guilty, could he survive for long in prison? What would it do to him?*

'Will it be a slap-on-the-wrist length of sentence?' I asked the prosecution barrister, Mr Morley. I imagined he might get a few weeks' or even months' suspended sentence maybe. He looked at me incredulously.

'Er, Mrs Chown, I don't think you quite understand. This is one of the worst cases of child abuse I have ever come across.

I am sure the judge might be considering the maximum sentence. Your father could be looking at a long spell,' he told me.

I was dumbstruck. My father was already seventy-nine. That meant he might never get out of prison alive. I felt so guilty at hearing Dad might go to jail. I was hoping he'd get a fright, possibly a suspended sentence, but not a lengthy spell in prison. *What have I done?*

'*No!*' I replied. 'What he did was that bad?'

'Yes, Mrs Chown, it really was that bad,' he replied, with a grave expression on his face.

A creeping sense of confusion washed over me. *How was it I was the one feeling guilty about this?* I mentioned this to Jonathan and realised something: because the abuse was something I had survived, I'd reasoned perhaps it hadn't been *that* bad. Maybe it sounded worse than it really was? I hadn't made any of it up, but I'd lived with it for so long I'd had to minimise what happened in my head, yet in a court of law it had been judged as being extreme. There was a lot to unpick here, but now was not the time to do it.

'You must think I'm mad,' I said to the barrister.

'Not at all,' he replied firmly. 'You're a survivor.'

Immediately after this session in court, we left.

As time went on, nothing was straightforward either, or so it seemed. We had to endure delays due to jurors leaving or going off sick. At one point we were faced with the possibility of a re-trial as only nine jurors were left (a jury is normally made up of twelve people). Later on, I discovered this was possibly due to the details of the abuse. I was beside myself when I heard this – the thought of having to go through a repeat of this trial was horrendous.

We'd often travel one and a half hours to attend, only to be told the trial was being postponed again for various reasons. This meant a three-hour round journey for nothing, and it happened numerous times.

Lucy, her partner Ralph and some of her children also turned up mid-trial, followed by Sean on the last days. Not to help testify, but to sit in support of Dad too. At times they became very intimidating and I recall some of them even made aggressive remarks. A photo made its way to my phone, showing Dad sitting outside the courtroom with Susan and Lucy. When Susan sent me messages saying she was only collecting Dad to take him to the courtroom, I'd open up that photo of the three of them sat cosily together.

*That photo, wherever it came from, spoke a thousand words.*

Lucy was also apparently overheard telling Dad's barrister, Mr Allan Armbrister, on meeting him, 'I'm here for my dad, Mr Beaumont.' To quell my anxiety, Jo Huddleston kindly managed to find me an empty room to sit in in-between the courtroom sessions.

*Determined as I was to get through this, at times it felt like it would never end.*

# Chapter 26

The trial lasted two weeks. Seeing my three siblings all together, chatting away, supporting each other, felt like a punch in the guts again, but I held my head high.

*What choice did I have?*

On 24 April 2018 we had to prepare to wait for the verdict. Exhausted after experiencing every emotion imaginable, I desperately wanted this nightmare to be over. Of course, the thought of Dad being found Not Guilty was a possibility that hung over us all, but at the same time, I felt conflicted as I couldn't help but want him to be released. Surely by now he realised he'd done wrong? He'd sat there and heard all the evidence, knowing full well I'd told the truth. Would this be punishment enough?

The only thing that kept me going was the knowledge that I had told the truth and nothing but the truth. It wasn't in my control now what happened next.

When the jury were sent for deliberation, we were told the

judge had directed he'd accept a majority of jurors' verdicts if nothing unanimous was reached by noon.

On this particular day, it happened to be the start of a workshop I had signed up for in Morley, Leeds – a good half-hour's drive away. I didn't know what to do, but as an act of self-preservation – and because it seemed unlikely the jury would reach a decision that day – I decided to go. I was eager to focus on other things in my life. For several days we had turned up in court only to be kept waiting or to learn that the trial had been adjourned so I assumed this could happen again. Keeping busy with my growing business helped keep me sane and away from booze, so instead of waiting for news, I decided to attend the course. I left the court at 11am. Jonathan stayed and said he'd let me know if there was any news afterwards.

*Unfortunately for me, the only day I wasn't there was when the jury reached their verdict!*

The course I was doing was in aesthetics, where we were learning a new, injectable treatment (Profhilo) to help lax skin. It was a great distraction to what was happening in a courtroom just a few miles away. I turned the ringer of my phone to silent and focused on the theory lesson we were having. Then I spotted a message from Jonathan:

'Ring me straight away,' he'd written.

I excused myself and went outside to call him.

'Guilty, guilty, guilty!' he cried.

Dad had been found guilty of all charges aside from the first charge (rape of a minor between 1977 and 1979 at a London hotel). At noon, the jury had come back and advised that they had verdicts on three of the six counts so Dad was found guilty at about 12.15pm on Counts 2, 5 and 6 (these were unanimous). They were advised to go back and reconsider on a 9–1 outcome (the judge had said he'd accept majority verdicts). It was not long before they returned with 9–1 verdicts on Counts 3 and 4.

Jonathan sounded jubilant, but I just felt sick; inside I was numb. Once again, the little girl somewhere inside of me felt bad – I'd got my dad into big trouble and it was all my fault. But of course, the adult side of me knew this wasn't true. I took a deep breath as an enormous swathe of emotions coursed through me: utter relief, happiness, sadness and confusion.

'I'll come and pick you up,' said Jonathan.

'I need to finish the day's course first,' I replied firmly.

*I had to carry on – Dad had disrupted enough of my life already.*

When I went back into the room, I struggled to focus but reminded myself this is what happens when you abuse children. It's a crime and the justice system had found him guilty. I let myself breathe a huge sigh of relief while a nagging sense of pity nibbled away at the edges of my mind.

Hours later, Jonathan came to pick me up and took me home.

'You did it!' he said, hugging me.

All the way back, I sat in silence. I couldn't bring it upon myself to be happy. In effect, I'd just signed away the remainder of my father's life – at least that's how it seemed to me. He was definitely going to prison and it was unlikely he'd ever get out as he was not a young man. Justice had been done but nothing was going to bring back my childhood or stop the memories from haunting me.

Dad's sentencing was adjourned until 30 April so I could be there in person. The judge agreed I should have the chance to attend to read my victim statement and be there for the sentencing. Bizarrely, when we turned up, Dad wasn't there as the prison service had forgotten to pick him up and bring him in! Susan never showed. It was another delay (Dad's sentencing eventually took place on 1 May).

We arrived again the next day and I had made a victim impact statement for the judge to be read aloud by the prosecution barrister. Again, I simply told the truth. How Dad's abuse had affected the way I viewed myself, my life and how alcohol felt like the only answer at times.

We filed back into the courtroom, where I watched the judge's inscrutable face as he heard my victim impact statement. This time, none of my siblings were there.

> Despite having such a wonderful family of my own
> and happy memories of the years I have had with my
> husband, seeing our children growing up, there has still
> been a cloud hanging over me. A cloud full of emotional
> baggage, shame, guilt, confusion, anger, bitterness,
> despair and sadness. I would have flashbacks to the
> terminations he put me – his little girl – through. I
> would make myself ill by increasingly drinking to numb
> the pain. He has shown no remorse. I was nothing
> more than a sex object for him – a thing he could vent
> his frustrations, anger, sexual desires – no matter how
> extreme – upon. I was not a person, not his daughter. In
> his eyes, I was put on this planet purely for his use.

Despite having all of my private life laid bare, by far the worst moment in court happened when my father's barrister – Mr Allan Armbrister – gave his summing-up statement. He told the judge how all three of Dad's other children had been there to support him and this should be a mitigating factor he considered when sentencing. Those words took my breath away. As I watched his lips move, I felt such a pain again in my heart.

Even if my siblings couldn't face accusing Dad of anything themselves, they had stuck together for his sake, knowing full well what he'd done to me. They hadn't stood by me after all. This decision, by Susan, Sean and Lucy, felt like the ultimate kick in the teeth. I had respected their decisions to stay away from the court case but to knowingly stand by our dad like this was too much for me to forgive.

*They didn't care about me or what the truth was.*

As his barrister read out those words, I thought about our years together as kids. The abuse we'd suffered. The neglect. Susan's promise to support me. It was as if history had been rewritten.

We had to file out again, in order to wait, then return to our seats to hear my father's prison sentence passed.

I didn't look at Dad as His Honour Judge Bayliss QC, calling him by his full name of Francis Bernard Beaumont, handed him a prison sentence of twenty years. All I did was wonder what was going through his head: *Was he scared? Was he angry?*

As the judge read out the summing-up, he described what my father had put me through as a 'campaign of rape'. He told Dad: 'You are an intelligent man and you knew perfectly well what you were doing. It was calculated by you to degrade her, to make your own daughter compliant to you and make your own daughter submit to your sexual demands.'

I looked at Dad, but his face betrayed nothing. Not even a twinge of recognition for what he'd done.

'Take him down,' said the judge.

Towards the end, His Honour Judge Bayliss QC had made a comment addressing both myself and Jonathan. He said he wanted to acknowledge what dignified witnesses we had been during our time on the stand and while sitting in the public gallery. This was so unexpected and those few words mean a huge amount to me. I had no way of knowing how I'd come across in court and certainly didn't even consider whether he'd noticed us sitting in the public gallery.

I turned briefly to watch as Dad limped off down the stairs, flanked by prison guards.

*That's probably the last time I'll ever see him again*, I thought numbly.

Outside in the foyer, Jonathan, our legal team and the police officers were all smiling, but I didn't join in – everything was so surreal. I felt numb and strangely guilty, even if deep down, I knew I'd done the right thing. After all these years, was this really over? It didn't seem possible.

Jonathan took my hand firmly in his and together we walked outside into the sunny, busy street, where life was carrying on as normal. Yet somehow the world felt as if it had shifted a little on its axis. I couldn't say I was jubilant, but I was relieved. I didn't feel vindicated, but I sensed a new freedom. I breathed in deeply, wondering if Dad was in a prison van right now. Wondering where he would be spending the night. I told myself to stop wondering about him as he'd never be a part of our lives again.

A few days earlier, Jo Huddleston had introduced me to a reporter from the *Yorkshire Evening Post*, who wanted to speak to me about the court case. As a rape victim I had the right to remain anonymous, so this meant the local papers would only report Dad's name and not mine. Instantly, I decided to allow my identity to be revealed. After all, I had nothing to be ashamed of – I wanted people to know the truth about what kind of man Bernard Beaumont really was. It was important that the name Bernard Beaumont be used and not Francis Beaumont as Dad was only known by the former.

The reporter had been sitting in on the trial and was therefore already aware of what it was all about so I didn't need to say a great deal during the interview. On the day of the sentencing – 1 May 2018 – I gave an interview to the *Yorkshire Post*. The next day, my story made headlines:

DEPRAVED LECTURER RAPED DAUGHTER
FROM THE AGE OF 11 AND THREATENED TO
DISSOLVE HER IN ACID

I was shocked by the sensationalism, even more shocked to see my story had made it into the national press, where pictures had been lifted from my Facebook account. I asked them to take it down – after this experience I didn't want to speak out again but everyone knew who Dad was now and what he'd done. Here, I feel it is important to stress that I wasn't fully aware what was meant by anonymity. I was not prepared for the influx of attention from reporters and journalists. They found all means possible to contact me too.

Later, I heard Lucy had accused me of trying to make money out of telling my story, but I didn't get a penny. For me, this was never about money, it was about survival, seeking justice not only for myself but for other survivors. By telling my truth, I hoped that others would find the courage to do the same. If I had not gone through with the trial, I can honestly say that I don't think I'd be here today.

I went back to work straight away, wanting to put it all behind me, especially the experience with the newspapers. But as result of my story being published, something unexpected and remarkable happened. Overnight, I began to get letters, emails and messages from people all over the country. People told me how brave I'd been. How resilient. How depraved and what a monster my father was.

Weirdly, when I read the letters referring to what I'd gone through, I thought to myself, *Poor woman, having to go through all of that.* For the first time I realised I'd disassociated myself from the trauma, which is a common coping mechanism for those who have been abused.

One moving letter was from a woman in her nineties who told me she had also been abused in childhood but had never found justice. Thanks to my story, she said she felt she could finally make peace with what happened to her. After reading about my trial, she knew it didn't matter how much time elapsed, a crime was still a crime.

Other comments included:

'*Having to relive such horrific treatment, in a public court, against your own father, you're an amazing and brave woman.*'

'*That frail old man had no compassion for that frail young girl he abused… don't feel any guilt, feel empowered. He was still lying in court, he deserves all he got.*'

'*Wow! She's one brave, courageous lady, and her family were so supportive for her to give her the strength to do it. Hope others will come forward as I am sure they will.*'

I was blown away. *Could they really be talking about me?* I'd never thought of myself as brave or amazing before. Most moving of all were the stories other people shared with me about their own historic sex abuse cases, for example:

'*I am currently involved in a court case for historic sexual abuse, with my father and his brother – they abused me, my auntie and a cousin. We have subsequently become estranged from our family, as they are sticking by the accused!! It's the same dreadful situation you have already suffered and are suffering …*'

I was gobsmacked. Not only by offers of friendship and support, but strangers reaching out to share their personal stories too. For so long I had felt isolated, alone and full of shame but these letters proved I no longer needed to be.

'*I am sorry you have endured such a betrayal… it is
a difficult burden to carry. I know how isolating these
matters can make you feel… your story really resonated
with me and I felt compelled to offer you words of
support and send you and your family kindness.*'

As I sat down to read those letters with my children and
devoted husband Jonathan by my side, I broke down and cried
for the first time since the trial. This time not with hurt or
pain but something else: gratitude. I had always been unsure
if I was doing the right thing in putting my own dad in prison,
but these letters proved to me I was. By speaking out and
finding justice over forty years later, I'd given hope to many
other sexual abuse survivors. Justice, however, cannot change
what happened to me: Dad still stole my childhood and has
split our family. At the time of writing, I've never heard from
my siblings since the trial.

It doesn't matter how long ago something happened,
telling the truth is what counts. And surviving and staying
sane too, something people in those letters congratulated me
on managing to do. For so many decades, Dad told me, 'Who
will believe you?' but in the end everyone did. They not only
believed me, but believed he deserved to be punished. Best of
all, I learned finally to believe in myself.

# Epilogue

$S$adly, the end of a trial doesn't mean the end of all of the trauma. Often a survivor of sexual abuse, or any abuse for that matter, can find themselves ostracised by family or friends following their fight to seek justice. My story is no different. At the time of writing, I have had no contact with my three siblings since the trial.

Having read other accounts of abuse and speaking from my own experience, it seems that it is quite a common theme that a family is split down the middle with supporters of the perpetrator closing ranks tightly around the family unit and the family being in some kind of denial of anything ever having happened. All too often the bonds of family which most of us rely on and take for granted in giving us a sense of security and belonging can be the very undoing of those same families in times of crisis such as these.

Despite all the good work that goes on by various agencies in reaching out to potential victims, it would seem that sexual abuse of children is as prominent as ever and largely goes on behind closed doors, never to be reported. There are no easy answers because, understandably, no one wants undue interference in their family home and no doubt in the unlikely event that a knock on the door does happen following a discreet report from a concerned neighbour or friend, the perpetrator will use their abundant charm and persuasive powers – characteristics that many abusers possess – to allay and deflect the concerns of any cursory investigation.

I have had well-meaning people say to me in the time since the trial that I can move on with my life now that it is all behind me. The sad reality is that it can *never* be right behind me, but with the passage of time the pain is gradually easing and the frequency of flashbacks reduces.

The mixed emotions I endure which sometimes manifest themselves as guilt in what I had done in having my father prosecuted and imprisoned were partly assuaged in early 2020 when somebody well known to my father contacted me out of the blue to tell me that he had done similar to them as he had done to me. Like myself, they too had tried to move on with their lives but couldn't do so satisfactorily with this huge cloud hanging over them. They even went so far as to make detailed reports to the police but ultimately due to the aforementioned family pressure and the closing of ranks, their statement was withdrawn and I fear their suffering will be ongoing. But from my point of view this disclosure flicked a switch and immediately any remnants of the guilt that I have described have been eased. So even though in the end they could not help themselves, they have been able to help me, so from that perspective, I will always be grateful to them.

I feel now is the time to emphasise that prosecuting my

father and directly facing him in court has been the hardest thing I've ever had to do. I know my siblings blame me for putting our dad in prison, but what choice did I have?

The message from my father's wife suggests I'm happy now that I've got him imprisoned – if only she knew this was not the case. I don't expect her to ever understand and I don't blame her for venting her anger towards me as she too is collateral damage from his heinous acts.

Since the trial there is not a day that goes by when I don't think how this awful situation might have been handled differently and I am very conscious that my course of action in eventually prosecuting my father is not the right one for all victims and survivors.

Not everybody is fortunate enough to have enjoyed the patient, loving and enduring support of two grown-up children and a husband to hold their hand every step of the way, or an old friend like Keg, who was prepared to relive those horrors in my support despite having a life of his own. Some victims will be older, meaning when the time was maybe right for them to have considered reporting things, the police and other authorities would likely have been less understanding and furthermore, the protection of abuse victims in court, both from facing the perpetrator and from unduly aggressive cross-examination by the defence, would not have been available in earlier times.

For those that didn't have the strength or opportunity to see their perpetrator brought to justice, perhaps they can glean some comfort from knowing sometimes – even decades later – justice can be done, and hopefully other perpetrators will rest less easily in their beds knowing that.

I do regret not having had the strength to bring this to a head and do something to confront it twenty or thirty years ago, because as well as helping myself, I would have helped to save others and there must be others apart from the individual I referred to previously. Looking back, I struggled to tell anyone about what he was doing because I was not only afraid, but he'd made me feel so humiliated and worthless that I clung to his every word and completely believed him when he said with a smirk, 'Who will believe you? It'll always be your word against mine.' Knowing how much he was hurting me, he'd continue, 'You're not only stupid, you're mental too and if you were to mention our secret to anyone, they'd laugh at you. After all, who would believe a nutcase over a dedicated, hardworking lecturer?'

As a survivor, I want to scream and kick myself, all the while thinking, *He was only saying this to stop me telling on him; it wasn't true.* Unfortunately, he'd told me so many times that I was stupid and maybe a nutcase, I certainly felt as if I was going mad, if I wasn't already mad (the modern terminology is 'gaslighting').

I can recall my father saying I needed him and that he certainly didn't need me; that he was doing me a favour in putting me up, providing my clothing and educating me – 'I never wanted you in the first place!' he sneered. 'Nor did your mother so I had no choice really. Having you kids here is holding me back from so many things in my life. My relationships have suffered too. No woman wants a relationship with someone who has children, especially children like you! You won't survive in the real world without me!'

The sad reality was that I thought all this was true because over time, he'd made me compliant and fully dependent on him. My life was not my own, it was run by him. I didn't have any money and I couldn't go anywhere as public transport wasn't safe and I was too young to drive. I couldn't even post my own letters, I had to ask him to do that and any letters that might have been posted to me were all sent to his PO Box number for which he had the only key and was therefore able to vet any incoming mail for me, meaning I may or may not receive it. Even when I did manage to escape to England in 1985, he still managed to control me from over 4,000 miles away.

*I was his prisoner.*

After this whole nightmare was out in the open, the reaction I received from my siblings made me think that I was making a big deal about nothing and because my father had coerced me into doing the retraction at his solicitor's office in the 1980s, he often menacingly reminded me that no one would ever believe me now. On reflection, I know I wouldn't be here telling this dreadful story if I hadn't done what I did, though.

Some say writing a book can be cathartic, especially when sharing past traumas. For me, it has taken its toll, both physically and emotionally, as I've had to delve deep into my past and relive many of the horrors I'd somehow managed to expunge from my memory, some of which I have blanked for decades. I've suffered flashbacks along the way. It has not been at all easy for me and some of the things I've revealed within these pages are not for the faint-hearted. There are things not even my husband had been aware of and not everything I've endured at my father's hands has been disclosed simply because there are insufficient pages to put them all down.

Bearing in mind that I am a very private person who likes to keep herself to herself, I thought it essential to try and express what motivated me to want to so publicly disclose some of the very personal happenings in my story. I certainly did not want to experience some strange form of personal gratification in describing my descent into alcoholism nor some of the humiliating acts visited upon me by my father. It was more about trying to transport the reader into the mind of that vulnerable child and later, the insecure adult I grew up to be – and other victims, I'm sure, will be able to relate closely to this – so that they can hopefully gain some kind of understanding of what victims feel, both during the years of abuse and in the years afterwards in trying to rationalise and understand it all.

I can remember being in Kenya, more often than not sleep-deprived, and feeling constant low-level feelings of fear, humiliation and uncertainty about what would happen next, and just how that messes with a young person's head. Sometimes he might go a day – or if I was lucky, even two days – without touching me inappropriately, at which point I would naïvely start to hope and pray the nightmare was perhaps over forever, only for it to start all over again and for the horrific cycle to repeat itself, time and time again. No matter how many times the cycle repeated itself, I couldn't help but get my hopes up, only for them to be constantly and cruelly dashed. I never knew when, where or for how long each episode of abuse would last. I was trapped and effectively imprisoned with no one to turn to, or so it seemed. I totally believed his threats about what would happen to me if I ever disclosed the abuse to anybody. My mind was in a constant whirl, my levels of anxiety were high at all times.

At the time I didn't realise it but I was completely cheated of my childhood and formative teenage years. The cheeky young girl that went out to Kenya who liked to look pretty and girlish soon changed into an introverted shadow of her former self who did everything she could to look dowdy in a feeble attempt to avoid attracting her father's inappropriate attention. The limits of my hopes and ambitions were that eventually the nightmare would stop – that was all that I wanted out of life.

Since the trial, my thought processes and therefore my questions have changed from 'Who will believe me? It's my word against his. Do I have the strength to prosecute? How will he survive if he gets found guilty? Can I live with myself for taking away the last years of an elderly man's freedom?' to 'What did I do to make him do this to me?'

One of my siblings informed my husband that I'd encouraged the abuse as I used to sit on his knee. Does this therefore imply that every eleven- or twelve-year-old who sits on his or her father's knee is asking to be abused? I believe my father chose me because I reminded him of my mother – he always said I looked like her and reminded him of her. Also, he may have thought he'd selected a child who appeared more vulnerable than her siblings and would therefore be easier to groom and keep his secret to the grave.

*How wrong was he.*

I'll never know the real reason why he abused me. Was he perhaps abused himself? Was he born a paedophile and ultimately, was it therefore his fault? Maybe there was some deficiency in his physiology which manifests itself perversely in being sexually interested in children. But I would still argue that if that were the case then he must have known it was wrong and could have sought help, or ultimately, he might have apologised to me – he had ample opportunities but has never shown one ounce of remorse. In the end, it is that lack of remorse that proved to me the gratification that he enjoyed in controlling me as his own personal sex object and using me in any way he chose.

This very lack of remorse went so far as leading him to appeal after the trial. Around the end of March 2019, I learned out of the blue that my dad had appealed his convictions and sentence and that his appeal would be heard a few weeks later on 9 April 2019 at the Court of Appeal in London. DC Jo Huddleston had been on annual leave and returned to find a letter about the appeal on her desk. The letter had been there some time and the appeal was now only two weeks away, although Jo phoned me as soon as she was back at her desk. At the time I was on my way home from King's Cross on a train, having attended a course in Milan over the weekend.

Despite being sober and completely level-headed, this was a very distressing time for me with the uncertainty that he could potentially have his convictions overturned even on a technicality.

On 9 April 2019, in the Court of Appeal, Criminal Division, my father had a renewed application for permission to appeal, permission having already been refused by the single judge. He did not attend. The appeal was heard before three judges on the following grounds:

1. The first ground of appeal, as settled by trial counsel, asserted that the judge had refused to allow him to explore the issue of consent after the complainant said she had not consented.

2. The second ground drafted by counsel was that there was a gap between the giving of evidence and the summing-up, which potentially undermined the safety of the conviction.

This renewed application was denied.

Sue Mitchell, a BBC reporter, had been in contact prior to the renewed appeal. Having come across my story in the *Yorkshire Post*, she was keen to do a few podcasts. One of the podcasts was presented on BBC Radio 4 on a programme called *The Untold*. I called it 'Life on Hold' (my life was literally on hold for a number of weeks) as it was about Dad's appeal following his conviction. It aired on 8 July 2019.

Sue was amazing and, as part of the programme, she attended the Court of Appeal on my behalf. She called me immediately afterwards and in an emotional exchange, I learned the appeal had been quashed.

My fight also continues to stay sober. I haven't touched a drop of alcohol since the day I arrived at Linwood House in February 2017, but it's something I take day by day. Today, I'm able to look back on my mum's descent into alcoholism with a newfound compassion: alcohol took over her life and she was lost to it. She might have let us down as children, but I know in my heart she loved us. Her fate could easily have been mine, but I had a loving, supportive husband and children to help me through – Mum had nobody. She sought solace in the bottle and in the end, it destroyed her life. One reason for remaining sober is for my family – I put them through hell and I never ever want to do that again. And what further inspiration does one need to keep on track than becoming a grandmother, which I did in 2019?

By some measure getting myself sober has been one of the biggest achievements of my entire life. Alcoholism gradually snuck up on me and I was increasingly using it as a crutch to help me to get my head round what happened to me. My sobriety has brought me such clarity of thought. Coming to terms with the horrors of my past with a clear head has enabled me for the first time in my life to properly confront my emotions – emotions that I learned from a very early age to box up and suppress.

The last thing I want is for this book to appear like a witch-hunt against my siblings because it's not. Despite everything, including the lack of contact in recent years – as I've said, at the time of writing not one of them has reached out to me since the trial – I still love each and every one of them and I wouldn't wish any harm on them or their loved ones. It was always my sister Susan that I reached out to – even though she didn't know it, as the eldest sibling, I sought her approval for everything that I did and I suppose that was the reason why I couldn't do anything to confront my past all those years ago because I desperately needed her permission first. I can appreciate now that on reflection my siblings must all be suffering too, but that suffering manifests itself in different ways in all of us because ultimately, we all had different experiences at our father's hands and have all sought to cope with this in our own ways. Because of that, I don't blame them at all and I wish them much joy and happiness in the future.

In this situation we all need to remain focused and remember ultimately there is only one person to blame for the sorry situation that we all find ourselves in and that he is currently safely behind bars serving a long prison sentence.

I understand my father still tries to control my younger sister Lucy to an extent, even from his prison cell. I've heard he calls her frequently, even asking for money to be sent to his young wife in the Philippines. It's unbelievable that he can still exert this level of control, even though he is not physically present. If I cast my mind back far enough though, I can still see how he can get inside your head and I recall that when I first came back from Kenya in the mid-eighties, he was in effect controlling me in a similar manner from thousands of miles away. He is a highly intelligent man and once he has got inside your head, controlling your thoughts and actions, it is very difficult to escape.

Following the outpouring of public support, my desire to help the lives of others grew stronger. While I continue to ponder what shape that help might take, I sincerely hope that in writing this book and having others read it, at least one person can get some kind of inspiration or feeling of strength in wanting to confront their past or at least gain some solace, insight and comfort in knowing that others who have suffered similar fates to them have somehow miraculously managed to come out the other side stronger.

When the time is right for me in terms of my continued healing, and assuming time permits, I would dearly love to get involved in one of the many wonderful organisations out there which seek to help women (mainly) who encounter such difficult situations as I did. One fine example of such a place is Just for Women, the women's centre in Stanley, County Durham, that I have got to know over recent months. They truly are amazing people up there, who so selflessly seek to help others get over whatever particular trauma they may have suffered.

Since I started writing the book, a release for me has been running. I've never been a runner before, but having begun the Couch to 5K when I began writing, I now run on average 5K four times a week. This really helps me to focus and remain positive in moving on with my life. I'd never have thought I'd take up running in my mid-fifties, but it really does help.

I'm conscious this book is my story, but is told from my recollections only. I sometimes wonder what it looked like from others' perspectives – in particular, my husband and my children. While we shared plenty of good times, I wonder how they all coped and what it looked like from their viewpoints, particularly during the darkest hours.

How did my husband restrain himself for all those years, knowing what my father had done to me? How did he and my children cope, watching me suffer and behave so erratically during the more difficult times? I'm sure they would all have very different stories to tell, but we have never talked about these things as we concentrate on our futures together. I do want to ask them all, no matter how hard that might be for everyone – I feel I owe it to them.

Ultimately, I want passionately – despite the difficult subject matter – for the overwhelming message of this book to be one of love, compassion, joy and positivity, and for something good to come out of this nightmare and turn my dream of helping survivors like me into a reality. During all those dark years living with Dad, I scarcely dared imagine even escaping, let alone finding justice and then putting my experiences into a book. It's something that little girl trapped in Kenya would never have thought possible, but I am living proof that in the end, anything is possible.

# Acknowledgements

I am honoured that I have had the opportunity to tell my story. Thank you to Shannon Kyle and everyone at Bonnier Books, particularly Editorial Manager Justine Taylor, for making this possible. I would also like to thank my copy editor Jane Donovan for her patience and for helping me to make the book mine.

I would also like to thank my wonderful family, Jonathan, Clara and Harry. Without the three of you, I dread to think where we'd be now, if here at all. Although you, Clara and Harry, now have your own lives, we are still a very close family. Thank you for making me see what I needed to do and thank you for also making me see that I had too much to lose not to do so.

Jonathan, my dear husband, without you, the trial would never have happened and the outcome would be so different. You believed in me and no matter what obstacles you were up against, you persevered. I could see your hurt, I could see your tears and while in the grasp of my addiction, I chose to ignore this. Now it's my turn to tell you how much you mean to me: I owe you everything. You are such a strong-minded, kind, genuine gentleman. I'm so lucky to have you in my life.

Harry, my eldest and only son, you mean the absolute world to me and I'm so sorry you had to experience immense pain and suffering, seeing me drinking and going through everything as I was. Although you didn't say much, I could tell you were hurting. I know, deep down, that's why you left home when you did and I understand. Despite seeing all of these things, you have become a kind, honest, amazing young man. You've also remained level-headed. I'm so proud of you and what you have become.

Clara, my youngest, my only daughter, you too mean the absolute world to me and I'm so sorry that you also suffered so much pain in seeing me go through such a hard time. It was a hard time for you as well. Maybe you stayed to support your father as we both know he needed it. Your doting husband Daniel once told Jonathan that your happiness was dependent on mine. You must have been very sad, as I know I was! I cry now when I think back to how sad you must have been. Throughout it all, you have demonstrated immense strength and determination. I'm also very proud of you and what you have become.

To my dear friend Keg, thank you for believing in such a mad story, a story you'd normally only hear about on the news. Thank you for not only believing in me but for going above and beyond our friendship in helping me through some dark times in Kenya when we were only teenagers. Thank you also for your statement and supporting me through the trial. I'll be forever grateful to you.

DC Jo Huddleston of West Yorkshire Police, what an amazing woman you are! I'd like to thank you from the bottom of my heart for all that you did for me. You went above and beyond the call of duty, you believed in me when I did not believe in myself. You held my hand throughout and without you, I honestly don't believe the trial would have happened. You were so patient and helped the entire process go as smoothly as it could possibly go. You have an amazing personality; I love your sense of humour. You helped me to start to smile again. I'll never forget what you did for me, what you've made possible now. Thank you.

Heartfelt thanks to the prosecution barrister, Mr Michael Morley, His Honour Judge Bayliss QC and the jury, who ensured justice was done.

Andrew Chown, my brother-in-law, I've known you a long time. I'd like to thank you for supporting not only me but your brother Jonathan over the years and throughout the trial. You selflessly took time off work to be there, to support us when we desperately needed support from loved ones. I'll never forget what you did for us. Thank you.

My dear friend Susan Smith, thank you for selflessly supporting me during my time of need. I'll never forget what you did and I'll always be truly grateful.

My dear cousin, Andrew Beaumont, I'd like to thank you for believing in me. Your support through the years and throughout the trial will always be with me. Thank you for being there and for making me laugh, helping me to forget momentarily all that was happening.

Finally, I'd also like to thank all of our other family and friends who believed in me and took the time to support us, whether it was by being around us at home or surprising Jonathan and I by turning up at the court during the trial. It means more than I can possibly express here on paper – I'm forever grateful.